# Marton
## The story of a Shropshire village

*by*
Doreen Bowen & Felicity Bevan

**Logaston Press**

LOGASTON PRESS
Little Logaston Woonton Almeley
Herefordshire HR3 6QH
logastonpress.co.uk

First published by Logaston Press 2010
Copyright © Doreen Bowen & Felicity Bevan 2010

ISBN 978 1 906663 35 3

Typeset by Logaston Press
and printed in Great Britain by
Cromwell Press Group, Trowbridge

# Marton

## The story of a Shropshire village

# Contents

# Foreword

Strictly speaking the 'Story of Marton' should be about Marton, about the people who have lived within the township boundaries and about events that have happened through the centuries in Marton. But the story strays over the border into Trelystan due to the enticing, irresistible history associated with our neighbouring township. Where tales of saints and heroes beg to be repeated, if only in passing, we give no apologies for this deviation, suffice to say there are unplumbed depths there which deserve their own intimate history.

Most of our quoted references are repeated 'verbatim' in an attempt to capture the patterns of local speech, others are extracts from family histories provided by their descendants. We have been amazed at the amount of detail some individuals can recall from a long gone past. We guess our recordings are only the tip of an iceberg.

# Acknowledgements

Without the support of Marton Women's Institute and a generous grant from the Lottery funded 'Awards for All' this book 'Marton, the Story of a Shropshire Village' would have languished, unpublished, on a shelf. We are grateful to these organisations for both their practical support and their faith in our ability to bring this project to fruition.

When necessary we sought the advice of individuals and professionals whose expertise in numerous fields has been invaluable. Their advice, always proffered willingly was most gratefully received and we recognise their contribution to this book – but hasten to add that any errors in the story are ours alone. Our grateful thanks to the following: Rev. Philip Harratt; Philip Morgan; Sue Johnson, Secretary, Shropshire Federation of Women's Institutes; the late Miss L.F. Chitty, David and Janet Preshous; Helen Haynes; the staff of Shropshire Archives; the staff of Welshpool, Pontesbury and Bishops Castle Libraries; the Heritage Centre in Bishop's Castle; Dr. Ann Welton and The Old Bell Museum in Montgomery; Catherine Wakeling, the Archivist USPG, and Pat Phillips SPCK; the staff of Rowleys Museum Shrewsbury; Clwyd Powys Archaeological Trust; the National Library of Wales, the Shropshire Federation of Young Farmers Clubs; Janet Gore and Margaret Williams for YFC Yearbooks; Betty Kinsey for the Corndon Magazine; Kevin and Kate Nichols for information about Bray's Tenement; Robin and Penny Kenward for documents relating to Pen-y-Bank; the late Betty Mulroy and the late Marion Roberts.

We thank the people of Marton and those from further afield who shared their memories with us – without their words and contributions this would have been a thin book indeed. We are particularly grateful to the following for allowing us to use their oral and written reminiscences:

| | |
|---|---|
| Ruby Bourne | Mari Jones |
| Glenys Broxton | Nesta Lewis |
| Diana Coles | Sybil Lewis |
| Jim Dale | Roy Maddox |
| Audrey Evans | Kelly Mellor |
| Gwen Evans | Dr. S. Nethercott |
| Henry Evans | Joan Paddock |
| Martin Evans | Roy Pritchard |

| | |
|---|---|
| Yvonne Evans | Peggy Pryce |
| Hilda Francis | Sally Pugh |
| John Francis | Elvet Richards |
| Ivor G. Griffiths | Lil Richards |
| Alan Hamer | R. (Dick) Roberts |
| Helen Hatton | Connie Smith |
| Tessa Howard | Patricia Stephenson |
| Edith Humphreys | Muriel Taylor |
| Jean James | Huw Thomas |
| Bob Jenkins | Mona Thomas |
| Glyn Jones | Doreen Trow |

Thank you to Andy and Karen Johnson of Logaston Press for calmly and professionally guiding us through the process of publication.

To our long-suffering families, our thanks for your advice, patience and support.

Finally, we apologise in advance for any names we may have inadvertently omitted.

# Introduction

The minor road, the B4386, that weaves its way through a gently undulating landscape linking the county towns of Shropshire and Montgomeryshire in the green borderlands of England and Wales has always been an important route. It passes through rich arable land drained by the Rivers Rea and Camlad, where cattle and sheep graze and mighty tractors, those latter-day workhorses, till the land.

This is a borderland – a fact we are reminded of occasionally in a place name or signpost – once the scene of battle and skirmish but now a tranquil backwater where English and Welsh live peacefully side by side.

Some 15 miles south from Shrewsbury along this scenic route, and 7 north of Montgomery, lies the village of Marton. It sits on a barely discernable rise at the southern end of the Rea Valley, a country village like countless others. A cluster of dwellings is strung out along the road (see plate 1). Old cottages and 20th-century dwellings, some attractive black and white farmhouses with their historic barns and less picturesque modern sheds, a church and a Congregational chapel, a shop and a couple of pubs make up this little community.

The traveller making his or her way along this road today will see much the same things their predecessors saw 100, 500 or even thousands of years ago. The landscape would be familiar. To the east rise the Shropshire hills; the rugged outcrops known as the Stiperstones dominate the skyline, while to the west is Wales and the Long Mountain's low profile, beyond which lie the River Severn and the Cambrian Mountains. The Rea Valley itself is a flat landscape, the result of glacial scouring which dredged out the valley and the expanse of water now known as Marton Pool – the mere which gave Marton its name, 'Mereton' – literally meaning 'the settlement by the Mere'.

To drive through Marton takes only a matter of moments – there is little to encourage the traveller to stop and explore. It's a working community – those farmhouses are right at the heart of the village. There are no tourist attractions or famous historic sites here. The tourist speeds on his way to Shrewsbury, Montgomery or the 'foodie' delights of Ludlow, although the walker will find many by-ways and paths to explore. Local historian, the late Betty Mulroy remarked that Marton has been described as a 'betwixt and between village, overshadowed by her larger neighbours of Worthen and Chirbury.' She adds that 'in its own way Marton also has a rich historical background and a sturdy independence.'

Montgomeryshire Par...

Woodson...

Upper Leasow
Banky Piece
Big Piece
Wall Piece
Cow Pasture
Little Meadow
Wood Piece
Roughs
Heathway

Barn Field
Long Leasow
High Leasow
Fair Meadow
The W...

Sideland Field
Barley Leasow
Piece by Jones's
Close
Little Meadow
Clover Piece
Cow Pasture

Clover Piece
Field next the House
Little Meadow
The Coppy
Patch
The Felin

Beach

New Inclosures
New Inclosures
New Inclosures
Close
Pound Piece
Mill Hill

New Inclosures
Field on Marton Mountain
Close
Close
Pyecroft
Mill Meadow
Wetting Gooch... Close

New Inclosure
New Inclosure
Inclosure
Close
Closes
Close
The Fenlies
Peartree Leasow

Inclosure Close
Allotment
Close
The Gadirons
Furlongs
Peartree Close

Inclosure
Closes
Close
Peartree Leasow
Furlongs
Marsh

Allotments
Allotment
Close
Rack Furlong
Percy's Marsh
Marsh
The Leys
The Leasow

Highgate
Allotment
Plants
Allotment
Court Meadow
Fitzger's Marsh
James's Marsh
The Leys
Bowdler's Leys
Close

From Pentrenant
Crest Leasow
Piece
Plantation
Allotment
Brick Furlong
Dogtree Furlong
Cot Leasow and Marsh Meadow
Court Leasow
Close Eithen
New Llanmel
The Leys
Close Eithen
The Stocking Close

Rough
Close
Quarry Field
Plantation
Old Yew Tree Meadow
Crabtree Leasow
The Silch
Close Eithen

Close
New Leasow
Close
The Nine Acres
Little Harbor Leasow
Little Or Leasow
The Plecks
New Leasow

Close
Oak Leasow
Big Piece
Slades
Piece with ... in it
Big Horn Leasow
Ox Leasow

Cote Leasow
Banky Leasow
Long Field
Long Plocks
Parks, including Plantation

The Bog
Broomy Leasow
Water Plocks
Folly
From Montgomery

Hassford Brook
From Gunley
From Stockton Township

Worthen

Stockton

*Marton Tithe Apportionment map with field names, 1843*

How true this has proved to be. Ripples from national and international events have been felt in this small Shropshire village; invaders came and went, Parliamentary Acts changed the landscape and wars have claimed lives here as elsewhere, as Marton's War Memorial attests. Marton folk have indeed shown their independent spirit over the centuries. What better example of this can there be than the Rebel School opened and run in defiance of the Local Education Authority. More recently the same grit and determination has seen funds raised for a new village hall. 'Marton folk', as the Reverend Hounsfield noted in the early 20th century 'know how to make things go.'

The following chapters trace Marton's history from very humble beginnings; from a cluster of lakeside huts built on a patch of dry land amidst marshland, to the 21st-century village familiar today. Research in the County Archives, libraries and on the internet has enabled the village's history to be pieced together. Recording the oral reminiscences of older inhabitants – who have often recounted tales told to them by their own parents – has been particularly valuable. Their words have brought Marton's more recent history to life and given colour to what could so easily be a dry historical account. It is therefore more than a story of boundaries and bye-laws, bricks and mortar.

This is the story of Marton and its people; the mere-side fisherman of prehistory, reliant on his catch from the depths of Marton Pool, and the modern young farmer riding high on his tractor bringing grain and silage home to feed man and beast.

Add to the mix some lords and ladies, a deserted village, an acclaimed theologian and the discovery of 24 horses' heads under the floorboards, and Marton's history is not as ordinary as it might at first seem …

# Chapter 1

# In the Beginning

> At Marton Pool the meremen heaped their mound and dug the ditch and let in the protecting waters working in feverish haste for the forests and marshes around were alive with foes.[1]

Was this a likely scenario for Marton's earliest inhabitants some 5,000 years ago? The description refers to the Ghisleys (Geese fields) which is a raised piece of land about one acre in extent on the edge of Marton Pool. Once it must have been an island surrounded by water or marshland rising some 6 feet above the peaty margins of the lakeside. Alder trees, oak, hazel and dense wildwood would have covered the nearby lower slopes of the hillsides in which many dangers lurked, both human and animal (wolves, auroch and wild boar). This strange raised platform of land which is now high and dry overlooking the flat and drained Rea Valley eastwards would have been a safe refuge essential for early man's day to day survival. There are no signs today that there were humans living here in prehistoric times or that humans shaped or raised the banks. But we can assume that our earliest ancestors in this place would have found, in and around the pool, a rich supply of food. Fish, fresh water molluscs and fowl would have been plentiful. Reeds and wood were abundant. Perhaps, once discovered, this island was eagerly taken, adopted and defended for its prime position.

There is a tradition that an early village, Old Marton, lies at the bottom of the pool. 'If you row out on to the middle of the lake on Christmas Eve you will hear the bells ringing below'. This may refer to a long gone folk memory of a time when the island was inhabited. Other stories about the pool linger today.

> In the big freeze [1891?] the story goes that Marton Pool was completely frozen over and someone drove a horse and cart right across the ice and lit a fire in the centre of the pool. (Mr. Jim Dale)

> Mr. Watkins from Wilmington had been turning hay on Sunday morning with the horse so he didn't go to church. When he let the horse go it went for a drink in Marton Pool and drowned. They said it was his punishment for working on a Sunday. (Mrs. Joan Paddock)

1

There are lots of tales about Marton Pool. One is that a man caught a fish in the pool. It got away with hook and line and a man caught it in Woodmoor Pool. They say the pool is very deep and turns up and goes into Woodmoor Pool. A young boy scout on a Sunday School trip from away was playing in the brook that runs along the side of the pool. He just vanished, assumed drowned. He was playing near the edge where it runs into the pool. It goes deep all at once like a pit. One time years ago the pool froze over. (Memoirs of Tom Butler)

There have been two, perhaps three, ancient boats discovered in the vicinity of Marton Pool which have been associated with the prehistoric era and lend weight to the existence of the meremen. The first, a dug out canoe, was found in 1908 when a cut running south and emptying into the north side of the pool was being cleaned out (SJ 2955 0297). The two men working in the ditch on Marton Hall Farm land were Messrs. Gwilt and Richard Evans. They realised that a protruding piece of flat wood lying buried a metre below the surface in black peat had sides to it and reported details of their find back to the landowner, Mr. Edmunds. He recognised it as an ancient boat.[2] It was carefully cleaned off *in situ* before being lifted out onto the grass to dry. It proved to be about 3.5m long, complete at one end but missing a section at the other where it had been hacked off during previous attempts to clear the ditch. The rough stone inside the boat, possibly the mooring stone, was thrown away and lost. Eventually the canoe was taken to Shrewsbury Museum, treated, and subsequently passed to Rowleys Mansion where it was put on display. It has never been dated accurately, but possibly it was used by the meremen to cross the shallow waters between the island and the mainland, or to paddle out into the centre of the pool for better fishing and fowling.

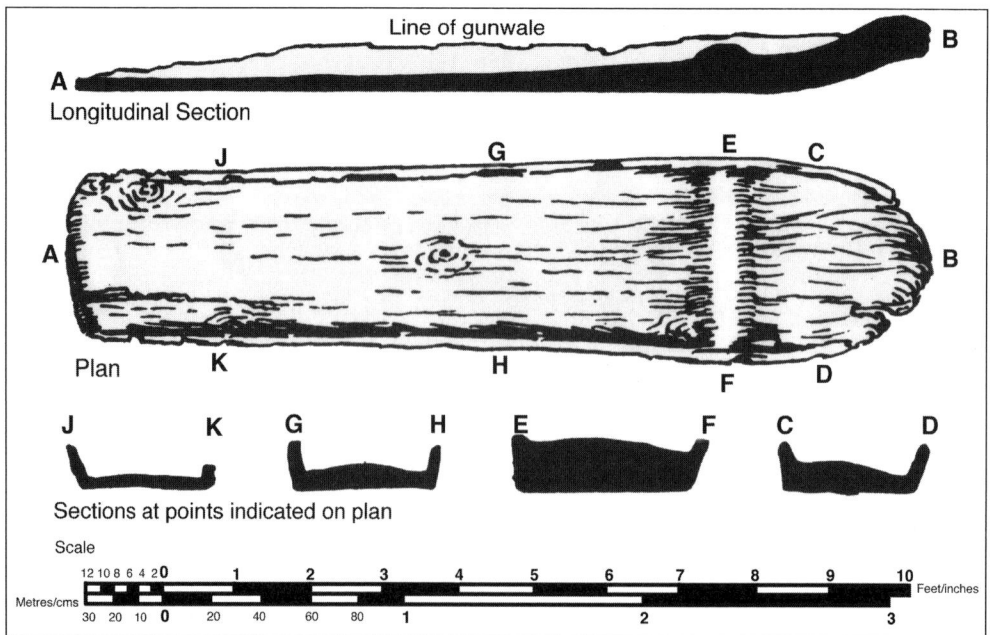

*Plan and elevation of the flat bottomed dug out boat found in a cut at Marton Pool in 1908 (from an original drawing by L. Chitty)*

2

*Reconstruction of a Neolithic settlement at Marton Pool (drawn by P. Kenward)*

The second boat discovered in 1964 was found 6 feet below the surface of the water during an operation to create drinking space for cattle on the lakeside. It was rescued from its watery grave (SJ 294 029) and eventually re-homed in Shrewsbury Museum. In design it is significantly different from the 1908 find being shaped like a rounded oak log, 2.59 metres long with the forward end missing.[3]

Marton Pool almost certainly covered a much larger area in those early times, with inaccessible marshland extending down the valley as far as Worthen if not further. In January 1776, Thomas Farmer and George Roberts measured the pool when it was iced over, establishing an area of 45 acres, 2 rods and 15 perches. The length of the pool was 640 yards and breadth 510 yards.[4] But long gone are the days when the meremen depended entirely on the fish and fowl of the pool for their families' survival. Drainage operations on an extensive scale were undertaken in the reign of King George II and since then invariably man has attempted to wrestle good productive farmland from the valley above and below the pool. In 1851, for example, *Bagshaw's Gazetteer of Shropshire* states that local landowners gained an Act of Parliament to allow them to create a 'canal' to carry surplus water from Marton Pool to the Severn. About 200 acres of land around the pool was covered by water for several months of the year, and since cutting the canal much of this land has been reclaimed and brought into cultivation. By 1891 *Kelly's Directory* gave a measurement of 30 acres, 2 rods and 27 perches, some two-thirds of the size measured just over 100 years previously.

The last boat remnant, that of a flat-bottomed craft, was found during a recent drainage works.

Down by the pool the land is wet and peaty. In some places the peat is thirty feet deep. We have grown potatoes down there but the land is better under grass because it doesn't oxidise. The whole valley has sunk three feet in the past thirty years. You can tell by the boulders which used to be at ground level and are now four feet above the ground.

Two or three years ago we found a boat in the peat. It has a flat bottom with a slight curve on the front. It is similar to the one in Rowleys Mansion. It's made out of oak. There were also some big lengths of oak tree perhaps 25 feet long in the peat. Most of the trees around the pool are alder. The oak grow further away, 300 yards or so where the soil is not so acid. (Mr. Jim Dale, 2007)

'My father built seven punts and one canoe and six boathouses. I helped to build some of them. One punt and a canoe was made for Sir Offley Wakeman. (Memoirs of Tom Butler)

**Uplanders**

While the valley environment was inhospitable and the dense wood covered hill slopes fraught with unseen dangers, above the treeline there were miles of rough heath-land and scrub trees running along the ridge tops. Here on the Long Mountain and Stapeley Hill our prehistoric ancestors left their mark on the landscape in no uncertain terms. Those living at the Trelystan site (SJ 2774 0700) sheltered in conical-shaped huts and cooked on open hearths. Remnants found of their flint tools and clay pots show that they were not made from local materials, indicating that the site was one of perhaps several used during the year according to the season or that the items were gained through trade. Their diet included raspberries, apples and hazel nuts. If these uplanders enjoyed a relatively peaceful existence, and their longterm occupation of the site might indicate this, their burial rites show a progression in custom and thought. Initially the dead were cremated and stored in organic material before then being buried in individual mounds. Later

*Drawing of a funerary urn from Trelystan site. Original now in Powysland Museum, Welshpool (drawn by P. Kenward)*

cremations were placed in ceramic pots and the individual cairns became a communal barrow with the cremations inserted into the top and sides. Twelve individual cremations buried in this manner were uncovered by Clwyd Powys Archaeological Trust during their excavations in 1979, including those of both males and females together with one child.[5]

Along the Stapeley ridge of hills on the other side of the valley an ancient trackway (Yr Henn Fordd) runs past Corndon, eventually connecting to the Kerry Ridgeway. These hills looking down on Marton Pool were the scene of great activity during the Bronze age, *c.*1500 BC. Two stone circles survive from this era: the Hoar Stones (SJ 324 999) which were laid down on the underlying soil before the peat layers developed, and Mitchell's Fold (SJ 304 983). The stones of a third circle, the Whetstones, seem to have been taken up in a field clearance and re-used as a field boundary. Three stones of this circle were still standing in 1838 when the Rev. Hartshorne was exploring Shropshire in search of antiquities. He also described how he saw the remains of a vallum/bank enclosing Mitchell's Fold, as the drawing suggests. In his estimation this circle would have originally consisted of 30 stones with an entrance on the eastern side. The Hoarstone circle had a central stone 4ft high and he observed 32 stones in that circle. His conjecture, that the circles were linked by avenues of stones and banks to form a serpent-like shape reflecting the purpose of their ritual use, is one theory among several.[6] The more common view today is that the stones in the circles are purposefully aligned towards astronomical occurrences such as equinoctial sunrises/sunsets or lunar events. The earliest metal workmanship of these uplanders was in pure copper; later their metallurgical skills enabled them to produce fine examples of daggers and axeheads in bronze.

Nearer to Marton, aerial photographs have revealed a ring ditch of Bronze Age date near Aylesford Bridge, and to the south-west of the bridge was found a Neolithic stone axe of Cumbrian tuff. Tuff is a hard volcanic material often green in colour found in the Langdale region of Cumbria.[7] Some years ago, during yet another drainage operation though this time on Mitchel's Fold Tenement, a bronze axe head was uncovered, while on Corndon Marsh a long slender dagger from this period was also discovered.

*Sketch of Mitchell's Fold Stone Circle on Stapeley Common with henge visible, from Rev. Charles Henry Hartshorne's* Salopia Antiqua, *1841*

5

Trading took place between communities in specialist tools and weapons such as the picrite stone axes of Cwm Mawr, Hyssington. Recently quarried picrite exhibits a startlingly attractive shade of green/blue as observed in recent excavations by Clwyd Powys Archaeological Trust at the Cwm Mawr site. Twenty-four of these distinctive axes have been found as far afield as Bromfield (battleaxe), Frodesley (axe hammer), Norbury (axe hammer), Mathon, Worcestershire (battleaxe), and the Lake District. A large axe hammer which is now in the Ashmolean Museum, Oxford, was ploughed up whilst reclaiming land near the Hoar Stones circle.[8]

The manpower required to build the stone circles and create these tools and weapons demonstrate that communities were organised and under strong leadership. Whether or not the workforce was working on long term projects as a community voluntarily or under duress is debatable. Underpinning this society must have been a secure food base. We can surmise that Marton Pool and its surrounding wetlands would have been one of the accessible sources of food to these uplanders to the extent that their surplus time and energy could be used to create these stone monuments.

# Chapter 2

# Stockton Wood Iron Age Fort

Iron eventually became the dominant metal around 700 BC. It was more widely available than tin and copper, the raw materials for bronze, and it was more durable. The Celts, a warlike and expansionist people from the European continent with knowledge of iron technology, crossed into Britain and moved steadily into the fertile river valleys to settle and farm. Some hill top camps which already existed were expanded with new fortifications, perhaps in defence against these incomers, but there was a rapid growth in the number of new, strongly defended hill forts at this time, with numerous examples in south-west Shropshire. Beacon Ring on the Long Mountain, Castle Ring (Rorrington Hill), the Roundton Ring, Wallop Fort and Stockton Wood Iron Age Fort are all in the neighbourhood of Marton Pool. Some of the smaller earthworks were probably enclosures for cattle or sheep used perhaps on a seasonal basis or as collection points. Those forts with clearly defined defences which show signs of human habitation would have commanded nearby farmsteads and

*The site of the hill fort above Stockton Wood*
*looking east over the Rea Valley towards the Stiperstones.*

settlements where pastoral and agricultural farming existed in basic family units.As the use of the iron technology spread, its application in agriculture speeded up land clearance for both pastoral farming on the uplands, and for growing arable crops on the more fertile soils in the valleys thus facilitating further settlement. If there were small homesteads on the lower slopes overlooking the marshes around Marton Pool their relationship with the hill fort overlooking them can only be speculated. Possibly incoming newcomers created conflict in their attempts to take control of the local natural resources as well as the prime cleared land. Stockton Wood Hill Fort's banks and ditches could have been a communal construction motivated by this threat where people and livestock within a recognised catchment area could shelter. But within the fort there are no signs of permanent settlement from the present evidence, though it is safe to assume that communal meetings took place here, or ceremonial rites were enacted or power struggles were decided. In the last resort, the defensive banks and palisades would have provided a final safe retreat for livestock and people in a threatening society.

In the language of the British Celts of the Iron Age lie the roots of modern day Welsh, Breton and Cornish, but their legacy in local place names in the Marton area is hard to find.[1] The Welsh names that do occur are of relatively recent origin, such as *Cae Melin*, and not from the elusive language of the early Celts. Of that earlier language there is little trace in modern place names or in the field names of the 19th century unless there is some ancient derivation and meaning as yet unidentified in *Watting gooch*. This name is no longer in current use, like many other field names which occur on the 19th-century Field Name Map of Marton.[2] However some words

*Artist's impression of the defensive ramparts and entrance at Stockton Wood hill fort*

have survived the centuries and are still in daily use. The word leasow (OE *laeswe*, pasture) is in common use today at The Cottage Farm in field names such as The Holy Leasow. This appears to be a development of its original name on the Marton Field Name Map of 'the piece with the hole or hollow in it'.

Stockton Wood Iron Age Fort (SJ 26700230) lies along the ridge know as Marton Crest immediately south-west of Highgate farm. Before the conifer plantation rose up to obscure the outlook there would have been uninterrupted views of the Rea Valley, Marton Pool and, in the distance, the Stiperstones. Below the south-eastern defences the Crest falls away into steep rocky and inaccessible slopes currently hidden by the trees. The fort's hinterland stretches across the undulating heights of the Long Mountain towards the north-western edge overlooking the valley of the Severn. It is still just possible to make out the defensive works of Stockton Wood Fort circling the hill top when the sun rises in the early morning or in the evening with the lowering rays of the sunset. But generally the fort is passed by unnoticed by walkers following the footpath through the conifers. A survey of the fort in 1980 produced the following description.

The lines of fortification follow the contours of the hill top using its naturally precipitous sides. There are two lines of defence consisting of built up ramparts forming continuous banks one within another separated by a ditch. Both ramparts are composed largely of small loose flagstones with earth. They turn at the northern end to run along the side of the spur, but have been so reduced by the plough as to be barely traceable. Their course can be followed around the south-western end slopes of the spur, to the edge of the very steep, natural slopes which form the south-east side of the work. The original entrance is above these slopes at the southern end of the twin ramparts on the north-east. The inner rampart is inturned against the entrance, the outer rampart is out-turned. The site is under pasture; there are no visible traces of

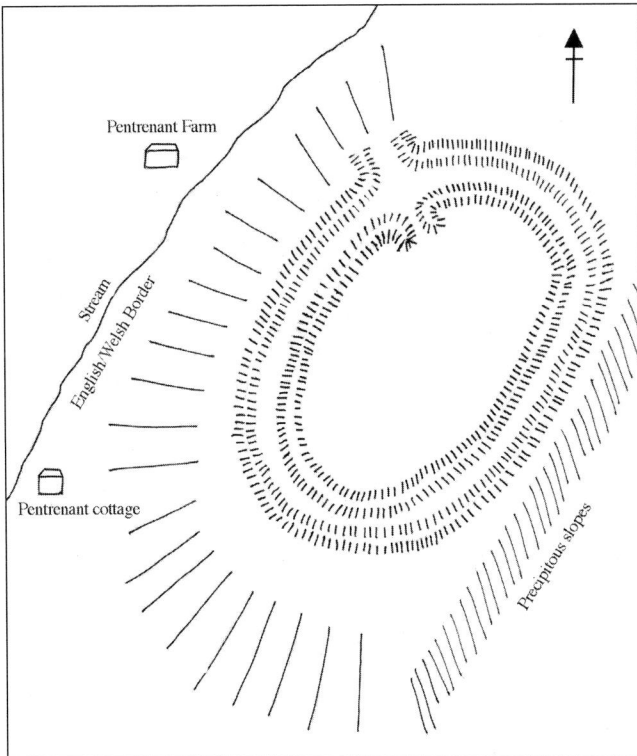

*Sketch plan of Stockton Wood hill fort showing double ramparts and entrance illustrated opposite. The fort's annexe is not shown*

settlement within the fort. On the north-east, the inner rampart measures 12 metres in width, and 0.5 metres in height. Its ditch 12 metres wide and 0.4 metres deep. The outer rampart is 10 metres to 12 metres in width, and 0.3 metres high, and its ditch is 8 metres wide and 0.3 metres deep.

The whole encloses an area of approx. 100 metres by 60 metres, (0.06ha). A wooden palisade may have provided extra security along the rampart summit. There is no evidence of occupation on the site.[3] In comparison the Roundton Fort has an interior of 1,000 square metres, Titterstone Clee something like 25 hectares.[4]

A later survey of the enclosure is different in several respects. The interior measurement is given as approximately 0.55ha. An annexe is noted on the south-west side whilst the main entrance to the bivallate enclosure cannot be located with any certainty. One suggestion is that the entrance may be in the junction of the cross ridge banks and the escarpment on the south-east. Its construction is put between 800 BC and 42 BC, within the Iron Age period.[5]

At the base of the hill the stream, which in part forms the current boundary between England and Wales, could have provided water for animals and families sheltering within the fort. Today, on the English side of the stream in a secluded woody dell is Pentrenant Cottage, once the home of the Richards family, and a stone's throw away, on the Welsh side, is Pentrenant farm.

> I was born at the cottage at Pentrenant. Some of the walls fell out over the years ... Jones had it, then he sold it to these folks from Birmingham and they've done it up. The one wall is stone. They've done a good job of it. There was a baking oven there on the left-hand side by the fireplace with a little door. One day we went visiting, they took me into the room I was born in. Dad worked at Llettygynfach, his home before he was married. He walked back to work there every day for £1 a week. (Mr. Elvet Richards, 2008)

# Chapter 3

# A Roman Road through Marton

The Romans invaded Britain in 43 AD and began their slow but steady conquest of the country subduing the native British Celtic tribes and pushing back the resistant hard core to the highlands of Wales. Part of the attraction of the outlying island of Britain to the Roman Empire was its easily accessible minerals such as the lead which, in this locality, they were able to extract using open trenches and shallow levels on the hillside at the Roman Gravels. A pig of lead was found at Linley stamped with the name of Hadrian, Emperor 117-138 AD.[1]

In their pursuit of conquest, control and peace with all its benefits, the Roman armies marched from Wroxeter via Meole Brace and Stoney Stretton to Forden Gaer, where they constructed a fort close to the ancient and important fording place of Rhydwhyman. Beyond the river a Roman stronghold was established at Caersws, thus consolidating the dominance of their hold over the Severn valley.

From Westbury their route to Wales is known to have followed an existing ridgeway path over the Long Mountain, but a second route along lower ground from the fort at Forden and crossing the Camlad has also been traced. This route runs past Gunley Hall, traversing the Marton ridge then continuing in a direct line to bypass the pool and so towards Brockton and along the higher ground through Monday town and Westbury towards Stoney Stretton.

Both roads may have been used according to the season and local conditions. But for the duration of the Roman occupation these routes were essential to the military domination of this area connecting Wroxeter to the Roman forts and settlements at Forden and Caersws and constructed by an army with all the engineering expertise of an established Empire.

The Roman road from Forden Gaer headed north-east towards the Camlad. (A modern minor road intersects it at GR 209992.) Continuing north-east, the Roman road crossed the Camlad by a bridge, passing south of The Woodlands towards Rhyd-y-groes. At Gunley Hall the agger cuts straight across the bend in the modern road directly in front of the house and continues in the field on the north side of the modern road where it is still visible today.

The making of a Roman road and its agger is explained by Hugh Davies in his book *Roman Roads in Britain*:

> A Roman road typically had two side ditches between which was a raised embankment called an agger bearing a surface metalled with gravel stone or ironworks slag. The ditches might be 80 feet apart, the agger 40 feet wide and 3 feet high and the metalling 20 feet wide. Not all main roads had ditches and agger and the dimensions varied widely even between different parts of the same road for reasons not known. In difficult terrain there were causeways and cuttings.

In 1964 there was a line of four large oak trees running down the centre of the agger in the field to the north of the road by Gunley Hall, parallel with the modern road. These have since been felled, although their stumps remain. Replacing them are six now well grown London plane trees, planted in a line several yards away from the agger but again parallel with the road.

The B4386 then rejoins the course of the Roman road and continues following it towards Marton. In 1964 Professor Putnam from Bournemouth University suggested that the Roman road went to the north-west of the village along an old hedge line so avoiding the wet lands around Marton Pool.[2] However an alternative theory that the road followed the current B4386 to the road bend by Marton Hall Farm then continued directly across the landscape crossing the Lowerfield Brook either by means of a ford or culvert/bridge and rejoining the B4386 in the region of the roadside stile holds equal validity.

*The route of the causeway as a double trackway merging into a footpath crossing Causeway meadow as shown on the Enclosure map of 1815. (Private collection)*

*The remains of the Roman agger at Stockton visible as a raised bank running from the bottom left to the centre of the photograph (and as indicated by the arrows)*

It seems likely that the bend in the road at Gunley Hall was put in to improve the front aspect of the house by removing traffic on the road to an acceptable distance at a time when such powers were in the hands of the local landowner. This would have involved two options, either levelling the agger and carting it away or removing it to the new boundary near the road to reinforce the new line. The latter explanation may be nearest the facts as there is now a distinct low bank running on the inside of the roadside hedge which is not the line of the original agger.

The old causeway marked on the Enclosure Map which cut across the fields in a direct line behind the village hall in Marton is followed very closely by the present-day footpath marked on the OS Pathfinder series 1980, 1:25000. Recently the line of the path has been changed slightly to accommodate the proposed new village hall. But there are still a few uneven lengths of ground in the fields encompassing the north-east end of the route which a trained eye might interpret as the remains of the agger.

On the Enclosure Map of 1815 the causeway is marked by a double line running across the centre of an open field, then as a single continuous line towards the north-east where it joins the Shrewsbury/Montgomery road. On the accompanying schedule the small *field i12*, which is adjacent to the causeway and owned by Thomas Roberts with Edward Jones, is called 'part of Causeway meadow'. By far the larger part of

Causeway meadow was the property of Lawton Parry and Mary Lee, two of the lords and ladies of Marton Manor. However, though the map indicates that some vestiges of a causeway existed in 1815 it was no longer used as a road but was classified as a footway, i.e. 'From Marton by the Causeway meadow towards Shrewsbury' (see illustration on page 12).'[3]

If the land under the causeway was well drained in the days of its construction, then a direct line past Marton Pool was the obvious route. But as it seems more likely that it was marshland, the engineers would have laid out a timber subframe bolstered with brushwood to provide a platform on which to build the top layer to overcome the difficulties of traversing the wet land. In later centuries this direct route fell out of use and was replaced by the current double bend road at an unknown date. But the continuation of the Roman road at Stoney Stretton which is described in the VCH[4] as a 'stony causeway', seems to indicate that a more durable section of the road was constructed here.

# Chapter 4

# Marton, Name and Identity

The collapse of the Roman Empire under increasing pressure from barbarian forces advancing on their home territories left Britain undefended. In 410AD Rome could no longer aid Britain, and withdrew her troops to the continent leaving the country wide open to ferocious attacks from the Anglo Saxons. British tribes were soon forced to share land with the newcomers or to retreat to the west. There was no adequate united answer to the onslaught. Civilised Romano-British society fragmented into family groups and their immediate neighbours, distrustful and defensive – a true retreat into the 'Dark Ages'. It was several centuries before the Saxon Alfred, his son and grandson attempted to deal with the next tide of ruthless invasions from abroad and restore some respect for law, education and the Church to a large part of England.

England in the 8th to 10th centuries was divided into several kingdoms, the most powerful of which were Northumbria, Wessex, Kent and Mercia, with earls of uncertain loyalty to each king. However it was under these Saxon dynasties that the Shire administrative regions developed with their Hundred divisions, each one with a Hundred court and each Hundred marked out into townships. The settlement of Marton lay on the edge of outer Mercia in the Whittery (later Chirbury) Hundred in Shropshire.

Whatever peoples lived in the area surrounding Marton Pool through the preceding centuries, the name Marton itself finally emerged around 750 AD sometime after the Anglo-Saxon invasions and subsequent settlement. The settlement owes its existence firstly to its location, on a low ridge in this rich valley by the pool, and secondly to the Anglo Saxons who named it.[1]

The Anglo-Saxon language was descriptive and vigorous, largely displacing the existing common British speech. Of that earlier language there is little trace in modern place names or in the field names of the 19th century. But the Marton Field Name Map of 1843 has many words derived from Anglo-Saxon, or Old English as it is commonly called. The word Marton itself is a composite of 'mar' from 'mere' which could indicate any pool from a large lake such as Windermere to a small pond, (in Anglo-Saxon charters boundaries were often designated by water features using the word 'mere'), and 'ton' from 'tun', a settlement or later an administrative area. Other examples of Old English words found in field names in Marton are:

*baec*    A valley with a small stream (Marton Beach), also 'batch' as in Pulverbatch
*furlong*  Furlong
*hraca*   Rack, a rough path. (Rack Furlong, Field Name Map)
*hrycg*   Ridge, a word associated with open-field farming (The Ten Ridges and the Six Ridges, Enclosure Map 1812)
*laeswe*  Leasow. (The Wood Leasow, Stockton Leasow Enclosure Map
*pirige*   Pear (Peartree Leasow, The Perry or Perries, Peartree House, Enclosure Map and Field Name Map)
*sic*      Sitch, a small stream
*slaed*   A patch of wet ground in a ploughed field left as greensward (The Slades, Field Name Map)[2]

## Pears and Cider presses

*Drawing of a small branch from the last pear tree along The Perries. Pear trees were common boundary features in Anglo-Saxon charters*

So many name associations with pear trees and perry suggest that it was once a common fruit in the district, notably centuries ago when field names and boundary markers were laid down.[3]

Pear is the tenth commonest tree in Anglo Saxon Charters. Most pear trees were in remote places and were evidently not orchard trees. These are the earliest written evidence for what is now one of our rarest trees, so rare that few Floras recognise it as native. Pear charcoal is widely recorded from the Neolithic onwards. (Oliver Rackham, *The History of the Countryside*)

Along the boundary hedge between the Manor arable land and The Perries, one ancient pear tree clings to life in the shade of a horse chestnut. By any standards this pear tree is large but it usually bears only a very small amount of fruit. A sample was sent to Brogdale Fruit Identification service with the following results:

> We cannot really offer any help with this pear. It is too small to be a domestic variety. It bears a general resemblance to Jargonelle, an August variety, but even this would be much larger than your sample. We do not think it is a perry pear either. It is more likely to be a seedling pear – a tree that has sprung up from a discarded pip and over the years grown into this large tree. (Brogdale, 2008)

> Dad brought two pear trees on the bus from town to replace old pear trees in the orchard. (Bob Jenkins)

> I remember those 'chokey' pear trees. The pears were little green ones but they wouldn't keep. (Alan Hamer)

We hoped, rather optimistically, that one or two of the older residents in Marton might recall some perry-making activity in the village in years gone by, but instead we had a few recollections of local cider production. There are other pear trees in the neighbourhood but, as far as we know, they are either remnants of old orchards or fairly modern plantings. Our impression is that home brewed beer was a more popular production in the locality but two instances of cider making came to light:

> My father made a cider mill and press that used to be taken around the farms in the area making cider. It was sold for a penny a gallon. He also made a rack saw bench that we used to saw oak coffin boards, also a lathe for turning a block of wood into stock for a wagon wheel. (Tom Butler)

> As far as I know my brother Walter Owen, Penbadern, Cefn y coed, Llandyssil went down to Marton and did a spot of cider-making. Could it have been for the pub or around? I can remember the Mill, a 5hp engine on wheels, and press (The Urchin). The Urchin is farmer talk. It was very much like a pulper. It was moved from place to place with two horses. (Eddie Owen, Cwmdale, 2007)

## The Saxon Manor of Marton
Located as it was in the Whittery Hundred, Marton Manor and its lord were obliged to pay tax to the Hundred, a tax based on a unit called a 'hide' which was, loosely, the amount of land needed to support a free family and its dependants or an area of land which could be tilled by one plough in a year, i.e. 60 to 120 old acres approximately equivalent to 15 to 30 modern acres. Behind the Manor House in Marton lay the village arable land which was farmed for centuries using a system developed by the Anglo-Saxons. Each villager was allotted a number of strips (sellions) of both good and poor land. They were also required to work on the lord's sellions. The sellions were grouped into 'flatts', 22yds wide by 220yds long, i.e. a furlong. Ploughing was done with a team of eight oxen in a way which created ridge and furrow furlong lengths. In 1815 this arable land was called the Ten Ridges, the Six Ridges and the

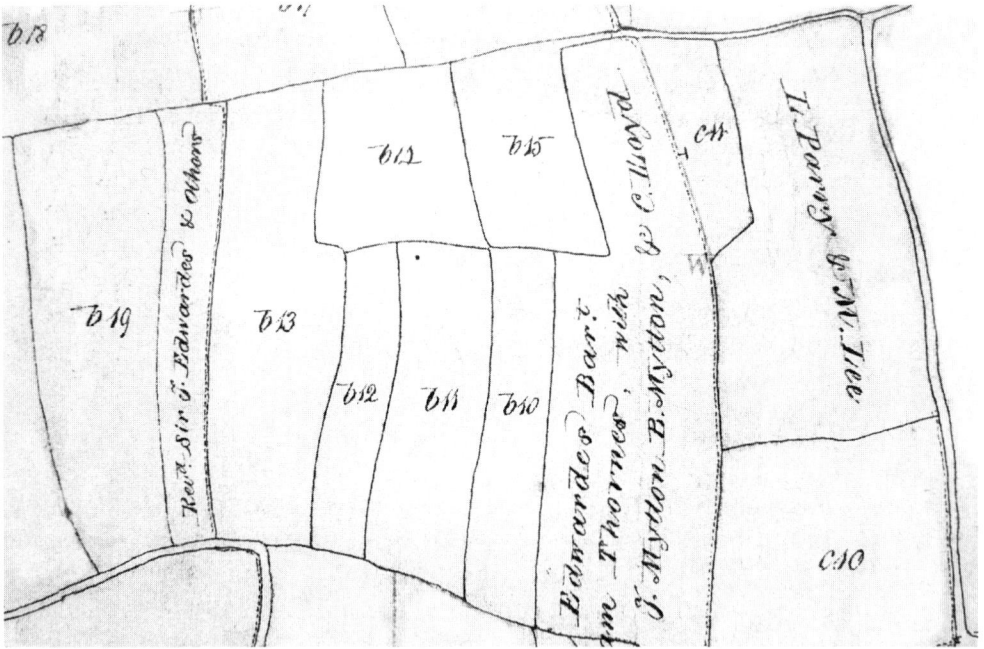

*Medieval Furlong strips behind the Manor House on the Enclosure map of 1815.*
*Named as b12 The six ridges, b11 The ten ridges, b10 The ridges, b14 Little furlong,*
*b15 Little furlong*

Ridges, still recording how it was once farmed in strips.[4] By 1843 they had merged to become two fields called Furlong. On the north-east side of the township other medieval names occur, particularly 'flatt lower field' and the two 'ridge' fields.[5] The remnants of a ridge and furrow pattern in the landscape can still be seen in this area.

At the time of the Domesday assessment Marton was in the possession of St. Chad's Collegiate Church in Shrewsbury. The church had 16 secular canons and extensive rural estates around the town. Its tenant in Marton was Alward, a free man who held several manors in the Whittery Hundred at the time of the Norman Conquest, including Munton (identity uncertain), Ackley, Rhiston and Churchstoke. St. Chad's Church's only

*March, lopping trees*

*June, sheep shearing*

connection with Marton may have been economic, with an occasional travelling priest administering the sacraments. Under Alward the other village inhabitants noted in the Domesday record are three villagers, and one smallholder with 3½ ploughs. The lord had half a plough, owning fewer ploughs in proportion to the size of his estate and less than his villagers on whom he depended to do his work. The three riders also mentioned seemed to be men who rode with messages or provided escort duty for their lord but were also obliged to work on their own lands and pay dues. They were of higher status than the villagers and may also have had some function relating to the defence of the border. These 'radmen' almost always occur in the Welsh border areas covered by Domesday.[6]

It seems likely that Marton was 'farmed' at this time, Alward's dues not being paid to a resident lord but to one living at a distance, as in St. Chad's in Shrewsbury; possibly Marton's tributes and provisions were replaced by a fixed money payment to support the life of the canons. Over and above this payment Alward would have expected to make a profit from the produce of those working the land.

*July, mowing hay*

*August, reaping corn*          *October, sowing seed*

*Opposite, above and overleaf: The villagers' work changed with the seasons*

*November, preparing food for winter*

## A Welsh victory

The kingdom of Mercia under a dynasty of successful kings, among them Athelred, Athelbald and Offa, maintained its supremacy for several generations perhaps reaching its zenith under Offa. His famous legacy, the dyke named after him, marches along the western slopes of the Long Mountain and passes approximately one and a half miles to the west of that ancient Welsh fortress, Beacon Ring, placing it in the Mercian kingdom, before returning to the lower ground at Buttington. The Welsh had occupied part of Mercian territory at an opportune moment before the reign of Offa. Welsh records tell of their victories in Mercia in the early part of the 8th century under Eliseg, Prince of Powys. Offa had conducted campaigns in Wales in 778 and 784 and again in 796. It was an uneasy relationship between Mercia and Powys notwithstanding the periods of peace and co-operation and there was a need to define the border and guard it. This mammoth earthwork with its ditch and escarpment towards Wales speaks of division and order; the desire for peace and stability and a hand sufficiently powerful to attain this vision.

Aethelflaed, daughter of Alfred, who ruled Mercia after the death of her husband in 911, had constructed ten defensive 'burhs' to strengthen her hold in the volatile border regions. Chirbury and Westbury are thought to be two such 'burhs'. But in spite of this provision, when the Welsh prince Gruffydd ap Llywellyn emerged as a particularly strong leader in 1039 he was able to lead an expedition into the area to challenge the Mercian supporters of the regent Harold Harefoot. The absent King Harthacnute who had the weight of Wessex on his side, was in Denmark at this time of uncertainty, betrayal, claim and counter-claim to the throne of England. Gruffydd saw his opportunity and led his warriors to a crushing victory over the Mercians at

Rhyd-y-Groes in 1039. It appears the Mercians were ambushed in marshland along the Camlad by the Welsh who knew the area well and took advantage of available cover to surprise their enemies. It was a fierce fight and according to the *Anglo-Saxon Chronicle* of 1039 many 'very good men' were left dead in the marshes. Among them was Edwin, brother of Earl Leofric, lord of the Mercians.[7] This victory would have extended the Welsh domination past the Marton Pool watershed down the Rea Valley and beyond. Those who lived on the land in Marton may have had no alternative but to accept new masters, and, subsequently, suffer an influx of Welsh migrants looking for economic opportunities. The number of Welsh field names on the Field Name Map provide the evidence that Welsh was part of vernacular speech at some time in Marton's history. Some of the Welsh field names occur around the mill: *Cae melin* (Mill Field), *Close y Gwalia* (Small field of Wales), *The Felin* (Mill), *Close Eithen* (Gorse) and probably *Gelly Furlong* (*Gellyg,* Pear), *Geyfor/Givers/Gewfors* (*Geifr,* Goat).[8] No evidence has come to light which shows when the mill was functioning as such. It is not mentioned in the Domesday Survey and by the 19th century censuses the mill had slipped into disuse and become a cottage or was unoccupied.

However the Welshness of Marton cannot be tied in with particular events. It may be linked to intermittent forays into this disputed border country conducted over several centuries by Welsh princes who took every opportunity to improve their lot,

*Part of the Tithe Map showing field names with Welsh origins,*
*notably The Felin (top centre) and Close y Gwalia alias Cae melin (bottom centre)*

or indeed, by those princes seriously determined to establish Welsh autonomy and independence whoever the enemy on the border happened to be. It could equally have been the result of a process of natural migration to and fro in response to economic opportunities.

There is little evidence to assess the Welshness of Marton in the years following the Norman conquest apart from the Welsh field names which have survived. In 1272 Grifffin ap Madoc gets a mention as a tenant in Marton. The Hearth Tax roll of 1672 names Thomas Bray, Thomas Bowdler, John David, William Foulke, Widdowe Lloyd, Thomas Evans, Roger Bowler, John Smith, John Matthews, Richard Gough, Phillip Coape, Thomas Hughes, Edward Corfield, David Wine, Edward Fowke, William David and Richard Lloyd as payees of the 2 shillings due on each hearth or fireplace in their homes. The list proves little to support an argument for a strong Welsh presence at the time. In the latter half of the 19th century the censuses show that Welsh speakers in Marton were born in Wales, usually in Montgomeryshire, Pembrokeshire, or Cardiganshire. Various reasons brought them to Marton. Often they were work related such as a vacant farm tenancy or an opportunity to work in service or on the land and, occasionally perhaps, marriage to a local girl. In 1891 the Rev. William Bowen, the Welsh speaking Congregational church minister from Pontypool, lived at Providence house, his wife a local girl born in Chirbury. In that same census year four residents in Marton spoke Welsh only, eleven spoke both languages. In the following census in 1901, twelve residents could speak Welsh and English. The facts suggest that there was movement over the Welsh border into England at the turn of the century but that Welsh was not a common language used by the local Marton people at this time.

Returning to those early years in the borderlands there is a strange coincidence in this maelstrom of frontier conflicts which involves Edelstan the Renowned, otherwise Elystan Glodrudd, who was the founder of one of the royal tribes of Wales, and Gruffydd ap Llewelyn. Edelstan was born in 933 in Hereford Castle, a godson to King Aethelstan of England. (Some Welsh princes of the 10th century bore English style names after King Aethelstan – hence Edelstan/Aethelstan – and often attended Anglo-Saxon courts.) Edelstan married the great-granddaughter of Hywel Dda and became Earl of Hereford and lord of the country above Offa's Dyke between the Wye and the Severn. It is thought that he died in a battle at Cefn Digoll (Beacon Ring) fighting against the Welsh who were possibly led by Llywellyn ap Seisyll, Prince of Powys (999-1023), and who were incensed by this anglophile countryman. It is recorded that Edelstan, 'dyed and was buried at Chapel Trest Elistan in Caursland' in 1010.[9]

Gruffydd ap Llywellyn is also said to have been killed by his own countrymen. After losing a major battle against Earl Harold in 1063 he was betrayed by his men, slaughtered and his head handed over to the Earl. The border lands which Gruffydd had occupied were reunited to England and the united Wales which he had created fell apart leaving a vision in its wake for Llywellyn ap Iowerth and Owain Glyndwr to revive in later centuries.[10]

# Chapter 5

# Trelystan … Christianity survives

The Christian faith, which had become a feature of Romano-British life, retreated before the pagan Anglo Saxons into the north and west of Britain. In 597 Pope Gregory famously noted the angelic appearance of British slaves, '*Non Angli sed angeli*' ('Not Angles but angels'), and dispatched Augustine to convert the heathen British Saxons. But in Northumberland Christianity had survived and a monastery at Lindisfarne was founded in 635. St. Chad was educated there and in Ireland and became renowned for his simple living, his missionary work and his modesty. Eventually he became Bishop of Mercia with a see which covered a vast area of 17 modern counties.[1]

In Wales a strong Celtic Christian monasticism developed through which individuals, famous for their faith and humility, had a pervasive influence on all strata of society, many of them becoming Welsh saints. On the hills above Marton a small church is said to have been founded by St. Beuno (d.*c*.640) near Badnage Wood (*Banhenig/Badnich*) in the vicinity of his parents' home. He was the only son of an elderly couple who led 'virtuous lives' and who, according to Welsh manuscripts, were instructed by an angel in a vision to conceive a child. When this child, Beuno, was old enough he was sent away to be educated, returning home on the death of his father to establish a Christian foundation in his home country.[2] The church of St. Mary's in Trelystan could be a continuation of this early Christian tradition although the township eventually took its name from Edelstan the Renowned who was buried here in 1010.

**Churchyard yews**
Trees, springs and rivers had long been associated with religious belief in pre-Christian Britain. Following the spread of the new faith these natural features continued to be a focus for miracles and rites. It was said that all the trees on St. Beuno's land were sacred, a tradition that continued until at least the mid 16th century. Of all the Welsh saints Beuno is most associated with the miracle of a 'staff taking root and growing into a tree', an incident which is often recounted in the lives of Welsh saints. One legend has it that St. Beuno planted an acorn at the site of his father's burial and the tree that sprang from it exhibited miraculous powers over the centuries.

In the churchyard of St. Mary's there are several ancient yews possibly as old as the church's foundation. Yews are very slow growing, often at half the rate of many other European trees. They are also long lived and have been known to survive in excess of 2,000 years. Significantly, they were protected in Welsh law, as in the laws of Hywel Dda, King of Dyfed in 927, when the punishment for destroying a 'saint's yew' was the payment of 60 sheep in compensation. The longevity of yew trees, their mystery and frequent location on ancient sites both Christian and pre-Christian have been subject to much speculation in modern times. In the 20th century the problem of dating old yew trees with a degree of scientific accuracy and without actually cutting them down, has been solved by a calculation which links the measurement of the girth with an established known tree life. The largest yew tree trunk in St. Mary's churchyard sprouts numerous small branches which greatly hampered the accuracy of a measurement taken in 2007. Without removing the obstructing lower branches, a circumference of roughly 9 metres was measured, but a more accurate measurement allowing for these obstructions might be 7 metres. An even more conservative estimate of 6 metres' girth would give the tree an age of over 1,000 years and its establishment at least coterminous with the death and burial of Elystan (Edelstan) in Chapel Trest Elistan (Trelystan).[3] The main church door is on the south-west-facing aspect overlooking the black-and-white recently modernised Lower House Farm, and on this side of the church and to the west are the ancient yews. Significantly there are none on the north side. This aspect has traditionally been known as the dark side, the abode of the devil, and rarely have any burials taken place here in past centuries.

Although in present day terms Trelystan seems but a short step away from Marton, indeed within walking distance, the facts that it is in Wales and that it is in an upland area have historically been dividing factors. The border between England and Wales crosses the road where Dykesford Gate once marked the boundary and this has set the two adjacent townships apart both politically and ecclesiastically. After St. Chad's lost its possession of Marton Manor, Marton became part of the powerful lordship of Montgomery. When the community of Augustinian canons at Snead (between Bishop's Castle and Churchstoke) moved to Chirbury to escape Welsh raids and established a priory there, Marton came under its sphere of influence. For many centuries the landowners in Marton, Stockton and the other surrounding townships therefore paid their tithes to

*A sketch of Trelystan Church
prior to its restoration in 1856*

Chirbury, to the priory in the first instance, and after its dissolution, to the church.[4] All births, deaths and marriages of Marton residents were registered in the Chirbury church registers and those who attended church were obliged to travel the three miles to Chirbury until the 19th century when, firstly, a Congregational church was built in Marton and followed by the present Anglican church of St. Mark's.

### Trelystan church

In the 1947 snow I remember walking to church along Lower House ground. They cancelled some services surely. They had a service every Sunday at 11 o'clock first Sunday in the month, then 3 o'clock. The vicar walked up from Leighton. They had cast iron stoves with chimneys up through the roof. Two of them there was. They had a caretaker in those days. He lived one time at one of the Stubbs cottages. He used to walk through the woods by the Malthouse. It wouldn't be very far. He used to light these stoves in the morning and it would be warm by the afternoon for he'd put a good bit of coal on it. They delivered it where the kitchen is now. They had a good Sunday school, Miss Moss was the teacher. (Mr. Elvet Richards, 2007)

### Red letter days

The Church Fête at Trelystan used to be held around the farms, at Black Park, at Cwm Duggan sometimes. Ever heard of 'em having a camp meeting? They had them at the top chapel, the Methodist chapel. It was a house, then they turned it into a chapel, now its gone back into a house. They used to have camp meetings in the field on the other side of the road from the chapel. They used to have an old horse-drawn waggon for the preacher to stand up in to preach. Red letter day that was! They pretty well died out by the time we got the age to go. There was a burial ground with the chapel but it was never buried on. Nobody was buried there. (Mr. Elvet Richards, 2007)

# Chapter 6

# An Englishman's Home is his Castle

**The Norman Effect**

When William the Conqueror led his army to victory over the English in 1066 he rewarded his closest supporters with vast tracts of land. Roger, Earl of Shrewsbury, Montgomery and Arundel received extensive lands in the Welsh borders. Many of these manors had been 'wasted' by Welsh forays before 1066, such as Chirbury, Hockleton, Walcot and Ackley, but others, such as Wotherton, Marton, Middleton and Rorrington escaped this devastation. It was in 1086, 20 years after the invasion, that William set his administrators the task of recording the extent and value of his island conquest. In the resulting Domesday Book, Marton Manor appeared still under the control of St. Chad's but had increased in taxable value since 1066. The amount of land under cultivation could be extended and hence its tax dues could be increased proportionately. Before the Domesday assessment Marton paid tax on two hides, or approximately 240 old acres of cultivatable land, but by 1086 there was sufficient potential ploughland for six ploughs, approximately three times that acreage. This seems to indicate that the years since the conquest in Marton had been surprisingly peaceful under the protection of Alward, the Saxon, and the church of St. Chad's 15 miles distant in *Scrobesbyrig* (Shrewsbury). The manor was currently undervalued at 6 shillings and 2 pence when it was actually worth 10 shillings.

> In Whittery Hundred.
> The church itself holds and held Marton. Alward holds from the church, 2 hides which pay tax. In lordship half a plough; 3 villagers, 3 riders and one smallholder with 3 and a half ploughs; a further 2 ploughs would be possible. Woodland for fattening 50 pigs.
> Before 1066 it paid 8 shillings; value now 10 shillings, but it only pays 6 shillings and 2 pence.[1]

Within a few years of the conquest it became clear that intermittent and serious warfare on the border with a succession of powerful Welsh princes was inevitable. The Norman response was to construct motte and bailey castles to defend both their new territories and the access routes from the Welsh border into England. Sometime between 1070 and 1074 Roger de Montgomery built the first castle in this part of the Welsh Marches at Hen Domen to guard the Severn river crossing. The need for a new stone castle at Montgomery overlooking the valley to the north-east and set on a strong defensible site was recognised in 1223 by the young King Henry III and he ordered its construction.[2] During those intervening years or immediately afterwards, a series of small castles of a motte and bailey type were set up in strategic positions along the Marton gap which was one of the major routes into Wales. Each side of the gap was guarded by a substantial stone castle: Caus was constructed on the high ground protecting the northern side and Montgomery on a rocky outcrop at the southern extremity. A line of smaller castles across the valley defended two route ways: the western road which passed through Marton from Shrewsbury via Westbury, Caus, and Bin Weston, and the other on the eastern side from Minsterley via Ladyhouse, Bromlow, Wilmington, Wotherton, Hockleton, and Chirbury. Marton motte and bailey castle is one of these 12 castles identified by Miss L. Chitty in this valley and which appear to share certain characteristics and perhaps a similar purpose.[3]

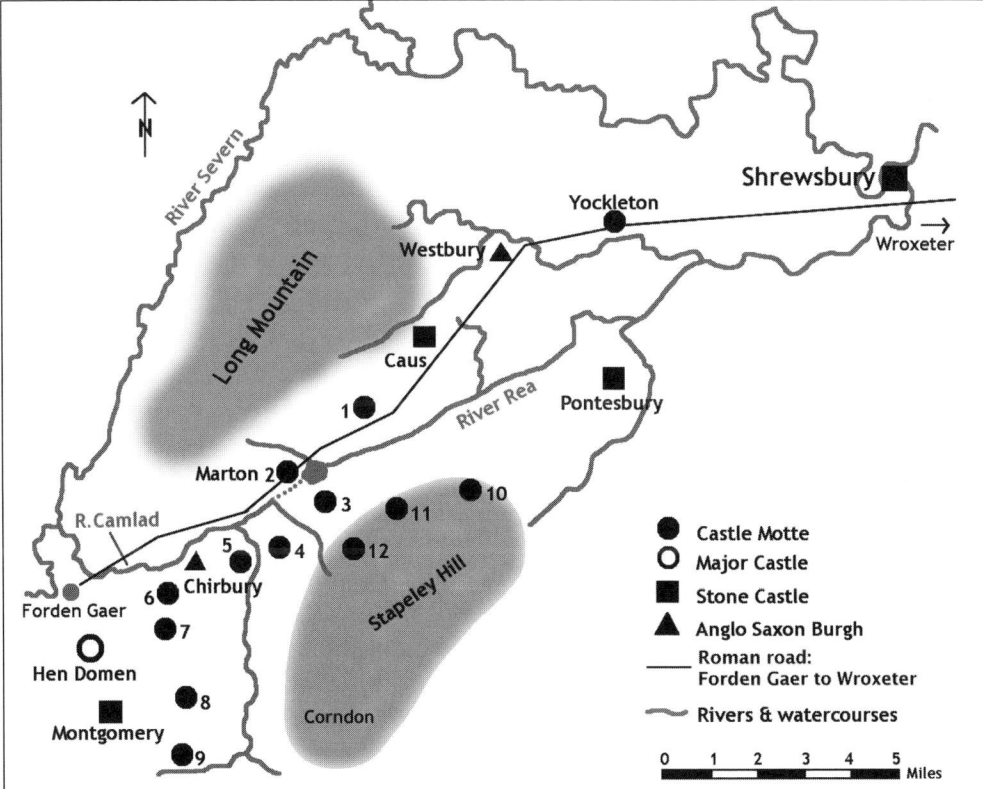

*Castle sites in the Rea-Camlad valley basin and Marton Gap:*
*1 Bin Weston, 2 Marton, 3 Wilmington, 4 Wotherton, 5 Hockleton, 6 Winsbury,*
*7 Dudston, 8 Gwarthlow, 9 Brompton, 10 Lady House, 11 Bromlow, 12 Rorrington,*
*(the last three linked by old road)*

## Marton Motte and Bailey

A survey completed in 1965 gives a description of the castle at Marton before it was destroyed later in that decade:

> Marton stands about a mile south/west of Binweston, at the highest and narrowest point of the Vale. Marton Pool, occupying the watershed between the Rea and the Camlad, confluents of the Severn, is generally accepted as being much reduced from its original size and the position and arrangement of the castle form the clearest indication that this is the case. The site is at the east end of a low ridge on which the village of Marton stands. The motte rises from the surface of the level and miry field which was once the bed of the lake and the bailey occupies the edge of the dry land alongside it, separated from it by a wide shallow ditch. It is conspicuous that the bailey has no bank and very little scarp around those sides which are towards the lake, though its south-western side, towards dry land, has a good ditch, about 6ft. deep, and its western angle, which faces a slope is strongly defended by a bank about 7ft. high at the back. The ditch here has a scarp of about 12ft. and a counterscarp of 7ft. The bank is damaged, but can be traced along the north-western side of the bailey, and running out on to the bed of the lake as a counterscarp bank on the north of the motte. The bailey is fairly large for a castle of this sort, but the motte, though tall – 17ft. above the bed of the lake – has an amazingly small table top. This measures only 20ft. across, and it seems clear that this is the original figure, for there is no sign of erosion or spreading – except at one point where the slope has been damaged by cattle.

One of the common features shared by mottes in this Rea/Camlad Valley is the lack of space on their summits. The diameter of the top of Marton's motte was 20ft,

*Although the site has been levelled for agricultural use, the remains of Marton's motte and ditch are still discernible amongst trees and bushes*

whilst those at Bromlow, Ladyhouse and Wilmington all measure about 25ft at the top. The eight others also have tall mottes with very small tops. Their similarities suggest there was an overall plan behind their construction. This may have been to establish Norman superiority in the area by a visually aggressive 'new build' phenomena, thus emphasising the status of their feudal overlords as well as being practical strongholds in skirmishes with the Welsh. However the military usefulness of the mottes under attack must have been limited by the lack of space on the motte summit, reduced further by the timber palisade which usually surrounded the top.[4] As lookout towers the mottes would have had a regular purpose or as links in a chain of pre-arranged warning signals. Perhaps the main defensive works were the bailey banks and ditches.

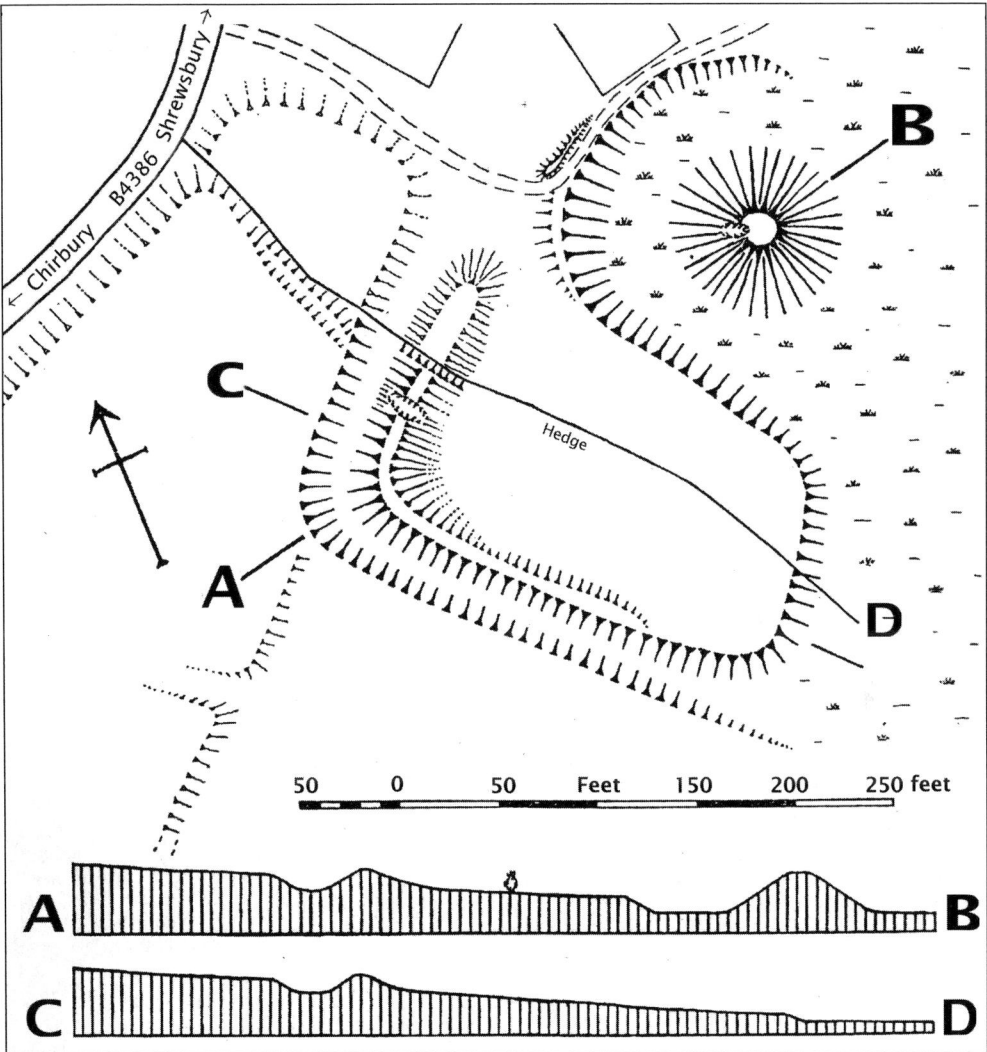

*Plan and elevation of Marton motte and bailey.*
*The eastern aspect of the motte is undefended by earthworks*
*from an original drawing by L. Chitty*

At Marton the extensive bailey, which was defended on two sides by marshes and the lake, probably contained buildings; certainly there were some signs of occupation observed within the site in a survey completed in 1994 by Shropshire County Council's Archaeological Service.[5] As lookout posts Marton and Wilmington were well positioned to view the valley between them, and Marton was particularly well sited to observe any approaches over the Long Mountain as well as along the route to and from Montgomery on the west side.

In 1225 King Henry III issued the following order:

> We command you [Godescal de Maghelins, Bailiff in charge of Montgomery Castle] that on our behalf you straightly charge those who have mottes in the Vale of Montgomery, that without delay they have their mottes defended with good wooden towers for their own safety and defence and that of those parts.

This order makes plain that the mottes were important in the local defence strategy in the ongoing wars with the Welsh and that their holders were obliged to obey commands issued from Montgomery.

Further obligations to Montgomery Castle owed by individual knights in return for their land included military service for up to 40 days a year. In 1255, the lords of Marton, Hockleton and Wotherton each owed ½ a knight's fee and so had to provide castle guard at Montgomery for three weeks of the year, particularly in times of war. As to the identity of the minor feudal lords who built these motte and bailey castles, it seems likely that they were Norman incomers whose loyalty was unquestionable. In some instances these castles in this area were close by a settlement, be it a hamlet or farm of Saxon origin, and the new lord adopted its name, as with Hugo de Woderton (Wotherton) in 1206. The manors which had previously been laid waste had also needed resettlement, and many of these were also taken over by the Normans.[6] Thus

> William de Hokeltun holds half a virgate in the Manor of Chirbury of the gift of Stephen de Bollers, and he holds it included in his service for Hokulton.

Marton, apparently unaffected by Welsh incursions, well endowed and with land and natural resources and strategically placed was taken over anyway, attached to Montgomery and fortified with a motte and bailey castle under Norman control. William Hunald, who held Marton in 1255, was also obliged to send a representative to attend the Hundred court at Chirbury where a jury met to settle disputes and punish law breakers. Yet another duty laid upon the Marton lordship was to provide food for the guards of Montgomery.[7] The details in the relationship between Montgomery Castle and its satellites indicate how essential they were to its defence and maintenance in the wars with Wales.

As methods of warfare changed, the small local motte and bailey became outdated. The settlements near them grew or diminished to a single farm in some instances, as at Hockleton. None of the 12 mottes in the Rea/Camlad Valley were garrisoned in the Civil War, only the major castles of Caus and Montgomery. Leigh

Castle, on a rocky eminence near Worthen, which was garrisoned, is not in this category of twelve.[8]

The road on the eastern side of the gap through Bromlow and Wilmington was still in use during the Civil War (perhaps was even the major route) and is marked on Haywards Map of 1788,[9] but by 1806 the western road through Marton has become the more important highway of the two, as is shown on Charles Smith's Map.[10] This latter road was turnpiked in the late 18th century.

> The original road through to Montgomery was from Brockton across to Lower Wood then to Wilmington, then by Groton and on to Wotherton and eventually to Montgomery. This route avoided the Welsh who held the high ground on the Long Mountain. (Mr. Jim Dale, 2007)

On the Marton Enclosure Map of 1815 the castle site lies on three plots of land. The motte fails to make any appearance at all, but the banks and ditches surrounding the bailey are well marked with a double line and this area forms a separate field called, 'f3 moat close with old dyke'.[11]

It would seem that such castles as Marton made a brief but essential appearance in time serving their particular purpose in the Welsh wars and establishing Norman control over the region and thereafter they became obsolete. In subsequent years many

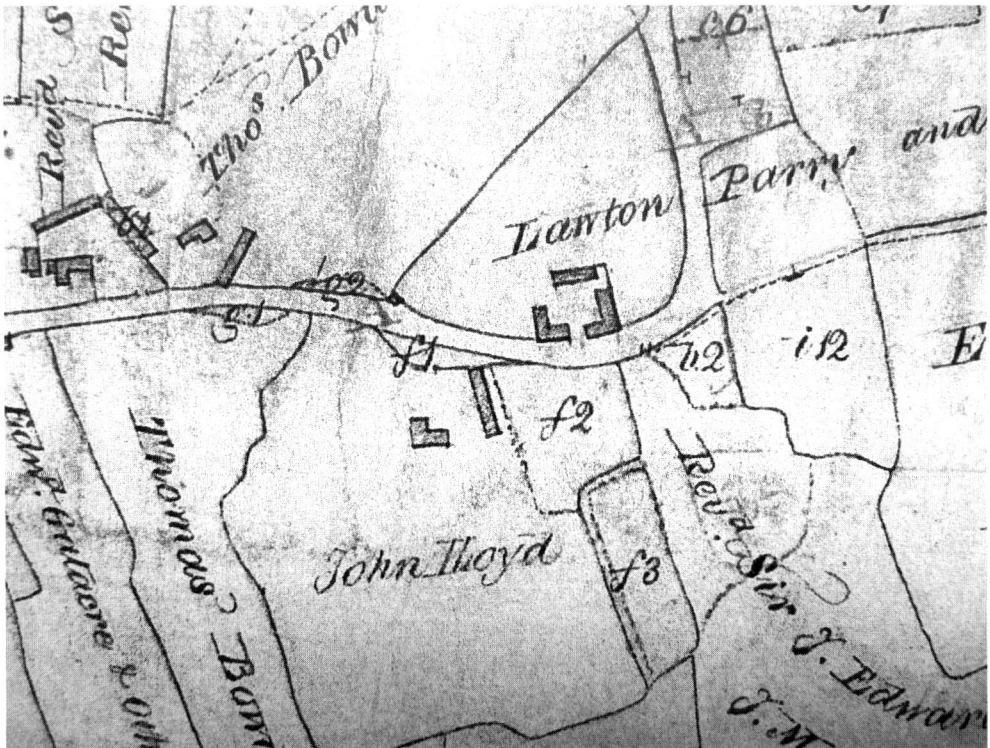

*The Enclosure map marks the defensive ditch surrounding two sides of the bailey:*
*f2 Little close, f3 Moat close with old dyke*

were fortunate to escape destruction. They would not have lent themselves easily to a comfortable conversion to a rural home but it is a testament to their substantial nature and their peculiar features that so many still survive in a recognisable form. The remains of Marton motte today lie obscured by undergrowth and trees. Cattle now feed here in the winter months, sheltering from the weather in the brushwood.

In more recent times this curious landmark gave rise to some interesting explanations:

> It was suggested that the large tumulus or mound on the Marton side of the pool was once surrounded by water and used as a lake dwelling. A further suggestion is that at a later period it was used as a signalling station. (Shrewsbury Chronicle, 1930s)

> I am reminded of a large mound quite high and covered with trees and scrub which stood between the church and the school set back from the road. My father once told me that it might very well have been a pre-Roman site of a fort built when the whole valley would have been marshy. I know that we children called it the Mound or Mount and that I never went near it. (Mr. I.G. Griffiths, 2007)

# Chapter 7

# Marton Juxta Hathewildeford

**A murder takes place**

The boundary of Marton township on the north-east side runs up against Bin Weston township which, in the 13th century, was under the control of that other powerful Norman lordship in the area, the Corbets of Caus Castle near Westbury. A number of disputes over this boundary concerning cattle raids, destruction of houses in Hathewildeford /Halwey / Heathway and a murder on Marton land were taken to the court in Westminster to be resolved.[1] The actual location of the deserted hamlet of Heathway is still uncertain but several possibilities have been put forward in a survey by P.S. Page[2] which are all within Marton township:

1. Marton Beach (OS 284035)
The grid reference for this site is on the side of a very steep-sided stream valley. The sides have been planted densely with conifers as well as shrubs forming a virtually impenetrable barrier. However as far as can be ascertained there are no surviving earthworks.

2. Providence House (OS 284022)
The grid reference is rather vague, but as far as can be ascertained there were no significant earthworks in the area.

3. The Beeches Farm (OS 281036)
Heathway was evidently a thriving settlement and possibly its site under Marton Mountain is now marked on OS maps by an isolated farm called The Beeches. The map also shows an old ford on the Lowerfield Brook below The Beeches. However, there are no traces of a deserted settlement around The Beeches.

4. Marton Beach Farm (OS 283034)
The site of Marton Beach Farm lies at the foot of the slopes by the stream. Here a disused hollow-way of considerable antiquity runs behind the farm from the road

leading to The Beeches which is above the valley, but no house platforms were in evidence at the time of the survey. Perhaps the farm itself marks the site.

The following sites also have some credibility and deserve to be considered:

5. Heathway (OS 286041)
The earliest name for the settlement, *Hathewildeford*, gives clues to its location. The Anglo-Saxons were adept at naming places after features in the neighbourhood and the name identifies a location close to a fording place across a wild stream leading to an open heath. The Field Name Map of 1843 shows a field called Heathway adjacent

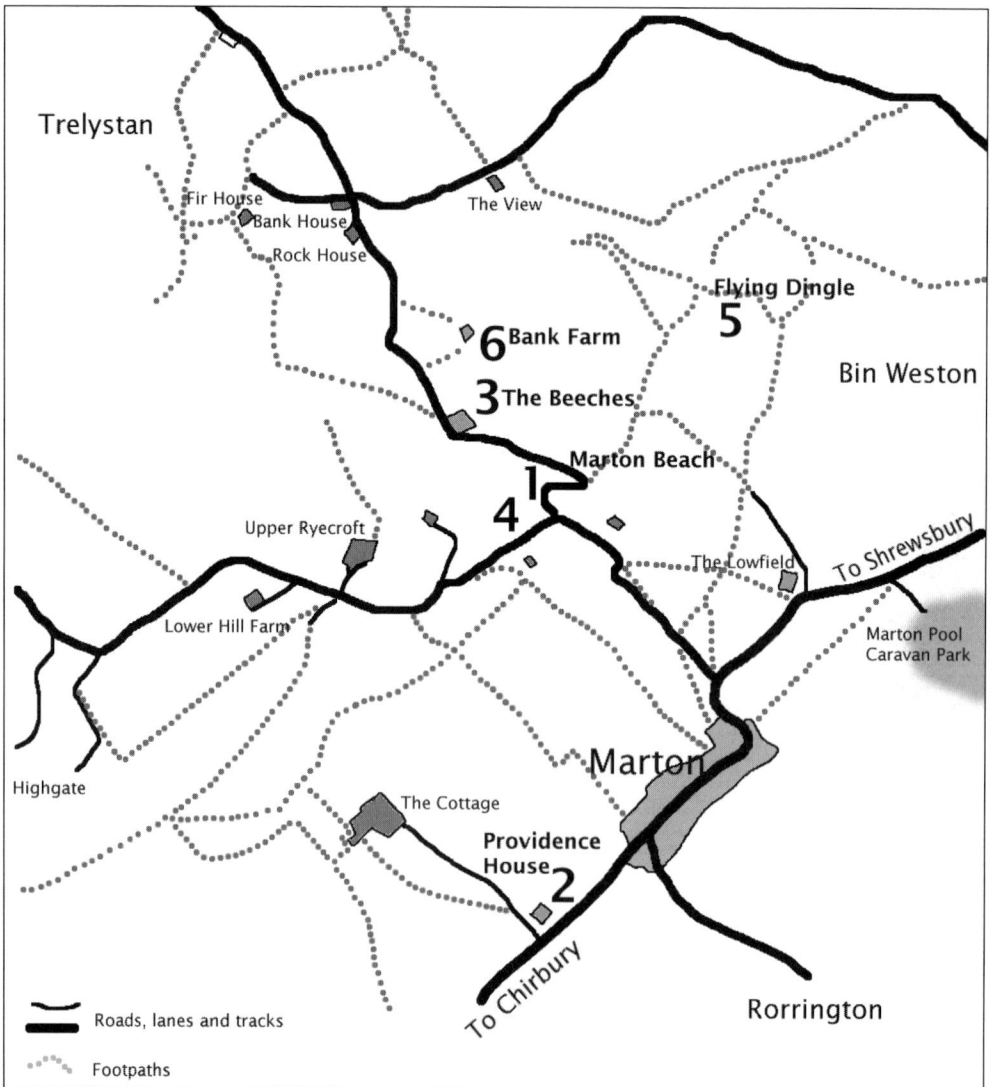

*The actual location of Heathway is uncertain, but several sites have been suggested, the numbers on the map relating to the numbers in the text*

to the Bin Weston township. The north side of this field falls steeply into a ravine and then levels out into a platform. The stream running through this ravine can be crossed here to gain access into Bin Weston although the present footpath crosses the ravine (the Flying Dingle) a little higher up by means of a footbridge.

6. The Hackway (OS 281039)
This is an isolated building, later known as Bank Farm, marked on the Enclosure Map in the north of the township but in 1812 there was apparently no access road.

As for the murder itself, disputes between the Corbets and the Purcels of Marton ran fast and furious during the 13th century. The Corbets were feudal lords who dominated settlements and lands from their demesne in Caus across to the Stiperstones, while the Purcels lived in Marton, a township in the Honour of Montgomery. Both of these lordships were essential to the king in the defence of the Welsh border but with a degree of local autonomy which was difficult to challenge. Their disputes were not something the local sheriff could resolve easily.

In 1266, Richard Purcel, a tenant of William Hunald, was murdered. The Corbets were accused of raiding the fields of Marton and Bin Weston, killing Richard Purcel and stealing 50 head of cattle. Richard's widow, Matilda, demanded justice against the men responsible and King Henry III ordered both parties to appear before him in

*Heathway can be seen a short distance north of Marton.*
*Shrewsbury and Oswestry Old Series (1833-1838) Map 126.*
*(Map extract © Cassini Publishing Ltd. www.cassinimaps.com)*

35

court in Westminster in October 1266. The Corbets sent word to court that they were trapped in Caus Castle by the Welsh and dared not come out. The king adjourned the hearing. Both parties failed to appear in January 1267 when they were called again. Then Matilda failed to show up at the next set date in 1268. Meanwhile the sheriff was ordered not to proceed with any outlawry against the accused or 'trouble their lands'. In 1272, Henry III persuaded by Thomas Corbet, pardoned them all. Their acquittal was on the grounds that the cattle were taken while trespassing on a meadow and garden belonging to Thomas Corbet.[3]

In 1260 Thomas Corbet had prosecuted Roger Frogge and others for insulting him and his men and razing his houses in Heathway. The king ordered the sheriff to arrest the accused and bring them to Westminster, but the court had been informed that they lived in Marton and within the sheriff's influence, to which the sheriff replied that they all lived in the Chirbury Hundred and so out of his jurisdiction. In 1263 damages of 60s. were awarded to Thomas Corbet for the destruction of his two houses in Halwey (Heathway) and the sheriff was ordered to raise that sum by seizing goods belonging to the accused. The sheriff sent word that the order had not reached him in time to execute it and that the delinquents lived within the Liberties of Montgomery. In 1266 the court repeated its order in the knowledge that the defendants had some property outside the Honour of Montgomery which could be taken as recompense.

In 1272 the Corbets of Caus accused three Marton tenants – Loretta, widow of William Hunald, Matilda Purcel, and Griffin ap Madoc – of cutting down the trees in the woods of Bin Weston which belonged to Petronella Corbet.[4]

A field adjoining Bin Weston township is known as the 'battlefield' to this day. At least two local farmers have mentioned this independently. Verbal tradition states that the battle was between Bin Weston and Chirbury/Marton.

> Thomas Corbet died in 1274 aged 92. He was involved in constant litigation which revealed his character…. Quarrelsome, crafty, vindictive, the foe of his own relations and his own vassals. (Eyton)[5]

> It was testified that three serjeants of Thomas Corbet seized two mares outside Chirbury in distraint for a debt owed to some of Thomas' men and drove them to Wythigruk in Welshry. Thomas Corbet comes and says that it is the custom between the land of Wales and [the] Englishry that if anyone from the land of England is indebted to anyone from the land of Wales or vice versa they may take distress from either region until the party has been satisfied. (Roll of the Shropshire Eyre, 1256)[6]

# Chapter 8

# Conflict over the Manor of Marton

Following the death of Roger, Earl of Shrewsbury, Montgomery and Arundel, and the rebellion of his son, Marton became one of the manors in the Honour of Montgomery held by Baldwin de Boulers (or Bollers/Bowdler). When the Bowdler family fell from power, a dispute over the ownership of the Honour of Montgomery arose in 1241 which was resolved by a decision for joint ownership between Vitalis Engaine and William de Cantilupe.[1] Chirbury Hundred Roll of 1255 also gives the overlordship of Marton to the Cantilupe family, one of whom (Thomas) was Bishop of Hereford between 1275 and 1282.[2] Their tenants, the Hunalds, held both Marton and Frodesley Manors. Marton still consisted of two hides at this point, almost 200 years after the Domesday assessment. From the various records of the 13th century dealing with disputes over land it seems that the Hunalds' undertenants, and those who actually lived on the land in Marton, were the Purcel family, together with Howel ap Adam, Robert de Hope, Griffin Seys and Robert Coleman.[3]

By 1316 there had been three joint lords of Marton: John de Hunald, Regis de Mathehurst and Simon de Hunald. By coincidence or design, Joan, daughter and heir of John Hunald, married John, son of Reginald Scriven who was already connected by marriage to the Hunald family, thus bringing the lordship of Marton into the Scriven family.[4] When Thomas Scriven of Frodesley died in 1536, an enquiry was made into the full extent of his estates – an 'inquisition post mortem'. Should the estate prove to lack an heir or the heir was under age, the property passed into the hands of the king, the land then being handed to the care of wardship of a favoured courtier – for a fee. During the inquisition any disputes over the ownership of Thomas Scriven's estates or a part of them would be settled by a jury. One claimant to the property was Thomas' son, also Thomas, a 15-year-old teenager who had to prove his claim to the Manor of Marton against a counter-claim by the Earl of Arundel. Thomas maintained that historically Marton was held by the Scrivens from the king in return for military service at Montgomery Castle. The exact details of the extent of the military service were not known at that time, which seems to indicate that the Scrivens had not been called upon to take part in any such defence within living memory. Time had erased the original feudal link between the Scrivens and the king. Earl William claimed that Marton Manor did not belong to the king at all but belonged to his castle at Clun and owed one fourth part of a knight's fee to his castle. Each party refused to give way to the other's claims so a trial at the Assizes in Shropshire was held where the jury gave their verdict in favour of the Earl of Arundel. At this point the king 'was removed from his possession of the Manor'.[5]

The Scriven name in connection with Marton turns up again less than 40 years later in 1570 when Richard Lloyd of Marrington died. He was a freeholder in Marton and Chirbury, a knight and JP for Montgomeryshire. The inquisition post mortem on his estate declared that the Marton lands and houses were his 'as of the Manor of Thomas Scriven' but the jurors 'knew not by what service', thus repeating the earlier admission of 1536.[6] Oddly there is no reference to the Earl of Arundel's possession of Marton Manor and no dispute over the Lloyds' occupation of the land. For the following several centuries the Lloyd family enjoyed the benefits of property in Chirbury, Marton and Stockton and were able to increase their holdings by occasional purchases.

The feudal system had established the lords and ladies of Marton Manor in control of their property by inherited right given to their ancestors by the king or his representative in return for military service. The land yielded rent when it was let out to tenant farmers in addition to the produce and profits from their own 'in hand' demesne. As lords of the manor their obligations to their tenants included administering justice in routine matters through the Manor Leet and maintaining the customs of the manor. The tenants frequently owed service to the lords and ladies of the manor in return for their tenure. Freeholders were unencumbered in their possession of their property. It was theirs outright and they had the right to pass it on to their heirs or sell it to a person of their choice.

**Turmoil continues**

The storms of war with Wales in the 13th century left a legacy of friction in the border country which from time to time erupted into local violence and raids. The Prior of Chirbury protested to the king that their tithes had been stolen by a raiding party from Strata Marcella, the Cistercian abbey near Welshpool which was a hotbed of Welsh nationalism. In 1393 another incident occurred in which the prior exchanged heated words with Robert Modelton: a sword was drawn, and the prior's sergeant took aim with his bow in his defence. Bloodshed was averted in the nick of time by supporters coming to the prior's rescue.[7]

At some stage during the Welsh wars the Master Forester of Corndon was granted a tax (puture) levied on the king's land in Montgomery to provide him with the financial resources to guard the border and keep the peace (the Forester also acting as local law enforcer). This was afterwards replaced by a local tax called a serjauntespein. However the Master Forester continued exacting the tax without undertaking any of the tasks for which it was paid and c.1324 the people of Marton, Whittery, Priest Weston and others petitioned the king requesting justice. The king ordered an inquiry into the matter and the results to be reported back to him, but records of these have not been preserved.[8]

In the wars with Owain Glyndwr in the early 1400s, Montgomery Castle was one of those ordered to equip itself with 50 men-at-arms and 150 archers to act as a strong point against the Welsh. No doubt the knights and squires of the Vale of Montgomery were called upon to make up these numbers. In 1403, every person of property to the value of 100s. living in the borderlands was ordered to return home and be in constant readiness to resist attack, an order which implies some preparation of defences.[9] It is possible that Marton motte fulfilled a useful role at this time. We cannot assume that it was re-fortified, but it may have been an used once again as a lookout tower or warning post in these dangerous times.

When Glyndwr's rebellion came to an end much of the countryside between Clun and Minsterley was left severely damaged. It was 40 years or more before peace and order were fully re-established. Anti-Welsh legislation quickly enacted in 1401-1402 in response to the initial uprising became even more repressive. No Welshman was allowed to buy land in England or hold a top post above the position of Chief Forester. The Long Mountain uplands to the north-west of Marton continued to be

> *Manor of Marton.*
>
> On an Inquisition taken in the 27th year of Henry 8th, upon the death of Tho' Scriven of Frodesley Esq', the Jury found, that among other estates, he died seized of the Manor of Marton in the County of Salop, and that the said Manor was held of the King by military service, as of his Castle of montgomery, but by what part of a Knight's Fee they could not say, And that Thomas Scriven was his Son and Heir, who was then fifteen years of age; of which Inquisition William Earl of Arundel, made his Complaint to the Court of Chancery, and denied that the said Manor was holden of the King, averring that the said Manor of Merton was holden of him the said Earl, as of his Castle of Clone, by the service of one fourth part of a Knight's Fee, and not of the King, as of his Castle of Montgomery, as the said Verdict alledged. whereupon issue being joined between the parties a trial came on at the ensuing Assizes held for the County of Salop, when the Jury gave their Verdict, That the said Manor of Marton was holden of the said Earl of Arundel as of his Castle of Clonne, by the service of one fourth part of a Knight; Fee, and not of the King, as of his Castle of Montgomery, and Judgement was accordingly given in favour of the said Earl of Arundel, and the King removed from possession of the said Manor.

*Note found in the papers of Rev. Sir John Cholmondeley Edwardes Bart.*
*(SA D365/B/1/5/309/3)*

a lawless area subject to Welsh raiding parties. Even in 1557 a hayward was paid to guard the stock on these hills against outlaws and thieves by the tenants in Winnington because of the regularity of the raids. Over the years, other tenants refused to take on land which was subject to these raids, leaving acres of pasture to deteriorate into rough scrubland. Marton lying as it is in the shadow of the Long Mountain was in a vulnerable position. Its inhabitants would have regarded strangers with suspicion and slept uneasily in their beds during these unsettled years.

# Chapter 9

# Civil War 1642-46

**Reluctant participators**

At the outset of the war Shropshire was largely Royalist. In the remoter areas the gentry in general sided with King Charles I and inevitably exerted a strong influence over their own communities both economically and politically. Those who were tied to the arduous daily rhythm of agricultural life would have wished to avoid any conflict altogether if possible, but if not, it would have been the lesser evil to follow their master's lead rather than risking their livelihoods by following the opposing side. Most were reluctant participators, begrudgingly contributing to the need for supplies and money from their own hard won resources. However the Civil War was essentially a conflict between two ideologies: the King's right to rule and raise taxes without consulting Parliament on the one hand, and the rights of Parliament to be consulted and have the final veto on the other. The conflict was exacerbated by deeply held opposing religious views, Roman Catholic and Puritan. There were men of faith and individual conviction prepared to take a stand for the King and the old order, or for Parliament and the Puritan tenets of faith, and risk losing their property and their lives as a consequence.

It seems unlikely that a small rural hamlet such as Marton, the 'poor cousin' of its larger, richer neighbour Chirbury, would be drawn into this civil war conflict in 1642. But the whole population of England was caught up in the turmoil sometimes in decisive major battles but often in local skirmishes. Shropshire had its full share of castles both large and small which were garrisoned and fought over until the war ended.

Edward, the first Lord Herbert of Chirbury was 60 years old at the outset of the war. He had retired to Montgomery from court life in London hoping he could remain neutral in his seclusion and justified, successfully, his inaction to both sides on the grounds of ill health until he was forced to hand over the control of the castle to the Parliamentary forces in 1644.[1]

The Reverend Edward Lewis, vicar of Chirbury for 48 years from 1629 and a man of exemplary Christian piety, preached two sermons in the church on Sundays.

This was seen as an act of excessive Puritanism and a departure from custom which caused offence to Captain Pelham Corbet, the Royalist officer then in charge of Caus and Leigh castles, who sent a detachment of horse to arrest him during a church service. They rode into the church, raised their pistols and dragged out the Rev Lewis. He was imprisoned in Caus along with John Newton, a Justice of the Peace from Heightly.[2] He was eventually freed and returned to continue his life in Chirbury notably founding a free school for the children of Forden and Chirbury in 1675. The date of his arrest is not known but there were soldiers set on guard in the churchyard at the time to watch out for any Parliamentary troops from Montgomery Castle who might be sent to his assistance.

During the course of 1644 Captain Devilliers was appointed Royalist governor of Caus and Leigh castles. He was a Florentine mercenary experienced in warfare and one of a number of foreign mercenaries employed on both sides in the early stages of the conflict when experience in warfare was invaluable and lacking among the English gentry.[3] His orders to the Hundred constables reveal an inflexible attitude combined with a determination to extract the necessary provisions and money from the local people to maintain his army by force if necessary. He issued the following summons to all the petty constables of Stockton, Walcott and Chirbury in the King's name:

> All men between the age of 16 and 30 were to be ready with what arms they could muster to join the Captain when required. No locals were to supply the rebels but must warn the nearest garrison if they were approached. Any village which rang bells in warning would be set on fire.[4]

In 1834, when parts of Marton Hall were demolished in an improvement scheme, old documents were discovered in the thatch which revealed how Marton and Stockton became involved and their reluctant participation. The parchment roll stated that Captain Devilliers of Caus and Leigh castles in October 1644 required the constable of Stockton 'to send me on Friday morning at six of the clock four men with hand barrows and pitchforks on payne of 2s. for every man that refuseth to come.' Further orders followed, dated 19 November, demanding a week's provision of food to be brought to the garrison at Leigh Hall, the old farmhouse below the castle: 'Viz. One quarter pound of beef, one side of mutton, three strikes of oates, two of rye, fourteen pounds of cheese, seven pounds of butter, one cuple of pultry, in money 5s. which if you refuse you may expect my coming to fech it.'

There was a marked lack of co-operation from the constables and local people in response to the command, and further threats became necessary in an order dated 26 November; 'I forebeare no longer and if any mischeife befall you bye my soldiers going forth [to fetch the contributions] you must blame yourselves for itt and stand to ye perill.'

After the Captain was removed to Caus Castle, David Lloyd of Marton Hall was left in charge of Leigh. He was in a difficult position because he was obliged to maintain a supply of food and men from the Chirbury Hundred to Leigh. However, judging from his letters written between 23 January and 3 March 1645 to the constable at Stockton which conclude with 'Your loving friend, David Lloyd', he was well acquainted with him and regretted the stand he was forced to take. Nonetheless, compelled by Captain Devilliers he urged the constable of the Hundred to send 'one team and five workmen out of ye township and then send them to Lee Hall this day to labour as directed; this fail not at your perill and to bring meate for ye same, and spades and pickaxes'.[5]

By the middle of March 1645 many Royalist garrisons in Shropshire had been withdrawn through lack of men to maintain them and in most cases the castles were left in an unusable state, either demolished or burnt as was Leigh. Caus Castle continued to hold out under Captain Devilliers (perhaps David Lloyd also) with 300 men who resisted a siege in June until a rather civilised surrender was arranged in which Parliamentary forces gained the castle, its arms and ammunition, whilst the officers of the garrison were allowed to walk away with their colours and swords and had safe passage to the King's next garrison.[6] When a garrison surrendered, even if it had resisted at first and inflicted casualties on the attacking troops, the commanding officer usually allowed the defender to march away with arms and baggage.[7] This was not always the case. At Hopton Castle the garrison (for Parliament) repeatedly refused to surrender to the Royalist forces. The final offer of terms contained the threat that no quarter would be given if it was refused, as the castle was by then so damaged and deemed indefensible under the then prevailing rules of war. As it was rejected, the garrison was ultimately slaughtered.[8]

*The Chirbury churchwardens' accounts show the sum of 19s. 6d. being given for the relief of maimed soldiers. By 1663 this sum was to rise to £1 4s. Further down the page 6d. is allotted to keep 'dogges' out of the church*

43

In the aftermath of battle, those ordinary soldiers who were injured and survived basic surgery were frequently left with amputated limbs and quite unable to return to their former working life. Some provision was made for them in their home parish. A rate was collected under an Act of Queen Elizabeth I in 1593 to provide pensions for soldiers injured in the Crown's service.[9] By the end of the Civil War in 1646 this fund was often in the red because of the number of injured men. In Chirbury's churchwardens' accounts for 1647, the yearly handout/pension for an unknown number of maimed soldiers was 19s. 6d. In 1663 the amount paid out to maimed soldiers was £1 4s. By comparison the sexton's wage for that year was £1 10s.[10] The pension was some compensation for the injuries incurred in war and would have provided the old soldiers with a glimmer of hope for the difficult life ahead.

# Chapter 10

# Thomas Bray, 1658-1730

In a sheltered hollow on the side of Marton Mountain is a long low cottage known as Bray's Tenement which has been recently extended and modernised. The outlook from here over Marton ridge to the hills beyond is superb. This smallholding is named after the Bray family whose illustrious son, Thomas Bray, is Marton's famous offspring, born in 1658 to Richard and Mary Bray. Richard (b.1637) was the only son among the six children of Mauritius Bray of Dudston. Richard and Mary Bray had two other children, Richard (b.1659) and Anna (b.1660).[1]

The Chirbury baptisms, marriages and deaths register begins in 1629 so that Thomas' baptism on 2 May 1658 is recorded. There are several Bray families with entries in the first part of the register that is in the early seventeenth century, and

Birthplace of Dr Bray
Founder of S.P.C.K and S.P.G.

Tralgston, Montgomeryshire.
From a photograph procured
by Bishop Montgomery.

*Bray's Tenement, the birthplace of Thomas Bray (1658), in an early 20th-century drawing (courtesy of USPG: Anglicans in World Mission)*

their places of residence are stated as Rorrington, Dudston, Timberth and Marton. It seems the Brays had lived in Chirbury parish for some time and were represented by several families in the different townships. Though Thomas Bray's origins were humble, in the sense that he was not of royal or aristocratic ancestry, the Bray kinfolk were not living in poverty but as respected yeoman farmers on equal terms with their farming neighbours.[2] At the marriage of Gwen Lloyd with the first Thomas Bray the family were already notable and well established.[3] In 1564 Thomas Bray of Marton and others 'witnessed the ancient tithe customs in the parish of Chirbury at the ripe old age of 80 years'. William Bray, son of Gwen and Thomas was a ratepayer for Marton township in 1604 and it was his grandson, Thomas, who was the founder of the Society for the Propagation of the Gospel.[4]

However another branch of the Bray family also headed by a Thomas Bray lived in Marton at this time. Several Bray family documents dated 1688[5] and 1694[6] have survived showing their ownership of Marton property, listing the field names and some acreages, such as lands called 'Heighway, over oxe leasow, lower ox leasow, the three furlongs, a new meadow,' and the 'Gidsley meadow'; in all 80 acres of land, 40 acres of meadow, 80 acres of pasture, 30 acres of wood, 5 acres of moor and common pasture in Marton and Heighway and one messuage. The documents relate to a marriage settlement and to a jointure settlement of property on Elizabeth Bray, wife of this particular Thomas. Their daughters, Hester (b.1658), Mary (b.1661) and Elizabeth eventually inherited equal thirds of half of the estate when their father died, followed by their mother's possessions after her death. Perhaps it was this Thomas who led the Hearth Tax list in 1672 in Marton with five hearths paying 10s. a year. The three daughters made well-connected marriages, Mary to Jonathan Edwardes of Marton, clerk; Elizabeth to John Griffiths of Glanhafren, gent., and Hester to Hugh Davies of Dysserth. In Hester's marriage settlement the following instructions were included: '... Hugh and his wife shall from the date of the marriage, until 1 May next have house room, meat, drink, lodging, washing, wringing and other necessaries befitting their degree at the charge of Thomas Bray.' It would be reasonable to assume that the Brays were an upwardly mobile family in these latter years of the 17th century. In 1688 Thomas Bray is described as a yeoman, and six years later he had moved up the social ladder to become a gentleman.

A formative influence in Dr. Thomas Bray's youth may have been the Reverend Edward Lewis, vicar of Chirbury 1629-1677, founder of a free school in Chirbury and owner of a library of chained books. This was the man who offended Royalist sensitivities by preaching two sermons on Sundays, but as a lifelong vicar of the established church he obviously had no separatist leanings. Dr. Thomas Bray himself regarded dissenters with fervent distaste and in the aftermath of the Commonwealth his talents were fully recognised by the Church of England and employed to their maximum within it.

In 1675 the Reverend Lewis gave lands for the foundation of Chirbury School in trust to be administered by 12 trustees.[7] At the school's foundation Thomas Bray was almost 20 years old, well beyond the age when he might have attended such a school. However he may have been taught privately by the vicar prior to his early formal education which took place at the Free school in Oswestry, (called Free because it was independent and 'free' from any religious affiliation). The Oswestry school was an early foundation dating from 1407, but, centuries later in the 1600s, the school trustees, once all non clerical, became a mixed group of lay and clerical men headed by the Bishop of St. Asaph.[8] Coincidentally, one of the bishops of St. Asaph was another local boy – none other than Edward, son of Richard Jones of Llwynyrhedydd, Forden, a not-so-distant neighbour and of the same era as Thomas Bray. Bishop Edward's father was one of the original trustees of Chirbury school and therefore known to the Rev. Lewis. It's not unlikely that Edward, too, was influenced by the formidable Reverend Lewis. Edward Jones attended Trinity College, Cambridge in 1661 and taught in Kilkenny, Ireland where one of his pupils was Jonathan Swift. He became Bishop of St. Asaph in 1692, but ran a corrupt and oppressive regime until he was deprived of his office in 1701. Though soon reinstated, he died in 1703.[9]

Thomas took his MA degree at All Souls College, Oxford in 1675 as a 'puer pauper' (poor boy), probably paying his way through college by waiting on wealthier students. In 1681 he was ordained and took up the position of Rector of Sheldon near Birmingham 1690-1706. Later he became the incumbent at St. Botulph's, Aldgate, London.

This was all during Restoration England; the monarchy under Charles II had returned to power with popular support, though the king's 'divine right' to rule autocratically was somewhat dented. To an extent Charles' life reflected this age of freedom, an age which produced great literary works but was equally dogged by moral decline and cynicism. But there were men such as Thomas Bray, together with other devout Christians, who were very concerned over the state of the nation. Thomas looked to the Church of England to set a moral standard and found it lacking and demoralised, becoming particularly disturbed by the dearth of devout reverential men in the clergy. He decided to devote his life to rectifying these ills, producing a teaching course based on the catechism and suitable for three different age groups. In practice this led to groups of young people well grounded in Christian principles and equipped to lead the worship in churches. He later expanded on this theme with his book *Catechetical lectures on the preliminary questions and answers of the Church catechism*. This sold 3,000 copies and made a profit of £700.

While he was still holding the post in Sheldon he was appointed Commissioner for Maryland by the Bishop of London, Henry Compton, who was concerned by the lack of ministers of the Church of England in the colonies. At that time there were less than six in the whole of North America. Thomas left his parish in the charge of a curate and moved to London to devise ways of persuading clergymen in England to go to the new colonies and once there to be more effective workers in the missionary field. He believed that those who lived simply among the people they hoped to convert would have more convincing results. In London Dr. Bray gathered together a number of supporters of like mind who were influential in society and in court. His determination and passion to succeed in this venture appeared to inspire others and within three years he had persuaded 29 graduates to go to Maryland, each equipped with a box of 52 books and a number of free handouts. He made a personal visit to the colony in 1700 with the specific purpose of establishing the Church of England on an equal footing in the state with the Quaker and Roman Catholic faiths. Again he was successful, this time in negotiating a recognised status for the Church in state law.

After such an auspicious beginning the question was how could this provision of men and books at home and in the colonies be continued in the long term? The answer was a visionary step forward leading to the formation of firstly, The Society for Promoting Christian Knowledge (SPCK) in 1698, and secondly The Society for the Propagation of the Gospel in Foreign Parts (SPG) in 1701. The former was to assist the spread of Christian knowledge at home, the latter had the same purpose but in foreign lands. The five founding members of the societies were able to muster many wealthy patrons, and in 1696 a library of 1,095 books valued at £350 had been amassed and sent to Annapolis. Thirty other libraries were in hand and plans for another 70 underway. It was a huge undertaking but with a royal charter signed by King William III,[10] the draft composed by Dr. Bray, the future of the work begun by these ardent men was assured.

Thomas Bray's family life remains shrouded in uncertainty. His first marriage to Eleanor (?) ended in 1689 with her death whilst giving birth to their second child. He raised the two children of this marriage alone, until his second marriage in 1698 to Agnes Sayers. Agnes was born in 1677 in St. Martin in the Fields, London, and was his junior by at least 20 years. There were two children from this union: Coditha (b.c.1700) and William (b.c.1702), with perhaps a third.[11] Dr. Bray's interest in the welfare and education of children is evident from his earlier teaching courses aimed at youngsters and families in church, but beyond that he was also involved with setting up charity schools for poor children. No doubt he took an active part in the education of his own family in spite of his heavy work output.

He died on 15 April 1730 in London where he was parish priest of St. Botolph's church. Among his published books is *Bibliotheca Parochialis*, a catalogue of books that he believed clergy should read. In the first volume are 62 pages listing subjects to be covered and 412 pages of book lists, fully annotated in Latin or English. In the same year, 1707, he produced a new edition of the *Course of Catechetical Instruction* urging schoolmasters to use his successful methods. His own education and passion had taken him from the small rural village of Marton to meet the great and the learned of his age as an equal, but more importantly his achievement was to improve the lives of many others in a profound way. In Marton church there is a commemorative plaque to Dr. Bray which marks the occasion of the tercentenary of the SPG in 2001. This organisation has moved on to become the USPG, the United Society for the Propagation of the Gospel which works in partnership with Anglican and United churches in more than 50 countries, offering exchanges of people, resources and training. It is the major mission agency of the Anglican church in England and Wales.[12]

The connection between Marton and Oswestry school has been maintained over the centuries by an annual visit by the Chirbury vicar to lead a church service in the school.

# Chapter 11

# The Lloyd Family of Stockton and Marton

Richard Lloyd of Marrington, Sheriff of Montgomeryshire in 1554, had nine sons and a number of daughters. His eldest son, also Richard (II), a J.P. in Montgomeryshire and sheriff in 1616 seems to have erected the sundial in 1595 now in the garden of the Lodge at Marrington.[1] Among the symbols chiselled in the limestone obelisk are two armorial shields: the Bowdler coat of arms of two choughs, and the Middleton coat of arms of three lions passant set on a bend representing the marriage of heiress Margaret Bowdler to Peter Middleton. The three horses' heads of the Lloyd family coat of arms are carved singly on three faces of the obelisk. Margaret, the heiress of the Middleton family, married David Lloyd, thus bringing the Marrington estate into the Lloyds' possession some years previously.[2]

Richard Lloyd II, who appears to have built the Elizabethan Marrington Hall, in 1595 donated a chalice to the church, erected a sundial, and left another permanent reminder of the Lloyd family on the wall in Chirbury church in the form of a *memento mori*. He had three younger brothers – John, George and Edmund – who were connected with the Chirbury parish, particularly with Marton and Stockton townships. They leave a fascinating historical trail through wills, church documents and letters.[3] It becomes clear that every effort was made to keep the land 'in the family', sometimes through cousins marrying, and when there was no direct descendant, a son or daughter to inherit, the property was passed to a member of the extended Lloyd family.

## Lloyd wills

Many of the Lloyd family wills and inquisitions post mortem found in the Montgomery Collections were transcribed by members of the Powysland Club at a time in the 19th century when Victorian gentlemen took a consuming interest in history and archaeology. The Club had a learned membership consisting of leading figures in society from all over Wales. Many were clergymen with the necessary classical education which enabled them to read early documents and produce an accurate translation. In 1873 the Rev. W. Valentine Lloyd contributed a very detailed account of the Lloyd family documents to the Powys-land Club under the title 'Sheriffs of Montgomeryshire'. Valentine Lloyd was a descendent of the Rev. Peter Lloyd, Vicar of Forden, and had a connection with Marton for a short time from 1857 when he was Vicar of Marton's new Anglican church. His researches covered the sheriffs of Montgomeryshire and their family ancestry, but as several were members of the Lloyd family it is possible as a result to produce a summary of the main facts relating to the Lloyds and Marton.

Briefly, the inheritance was passed down through the generations as follows: Richard I of Marrington (d.1570) split his property between his various sons, leaving land in Marton and Trelystan, including Badenage (Badnage) wood, to George I, and property in Stockton to Edmund I.[4] Edmund I was a churchwarden for Chirbury at the time the church was being renovated (1604-5), at which point the ten commandments were painted on the church walls, the church roof was tiled and a new communion book bought from Ludlow, thereby avoiding the need to travel to Shrewsbury where there was an outbreak of plague.

George I left a will in 1627 written in his own hand.[6] After the death of his wife Elizabeth there were no surviving children, so all their property in Marton and Badenage went to his nephew David Lloyd of Marton Hall, the son of his brother John.

When Edmund I died in 1624[5] he left property in Trelystan, which he had bought, to his son Alexander; George II was left all the property in Stockton; whilst Edmund

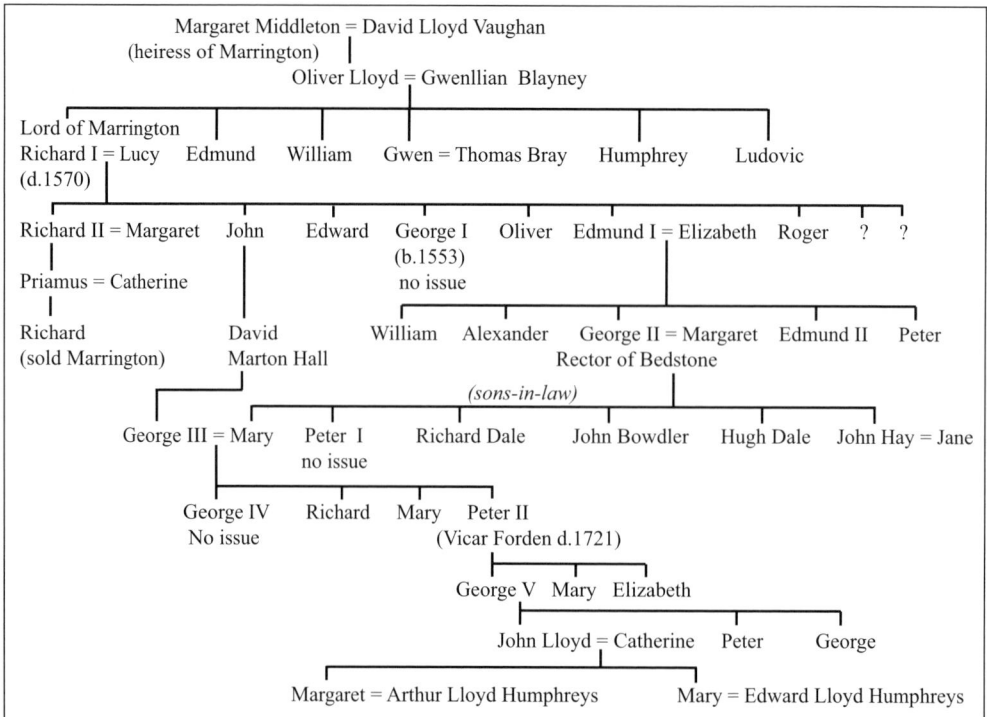

*The Lloyd family tree*

50

*The three horses' heads, the heraldic charge of the Lloyd family are seen here on a memento mori to Richard Lloyd in St Michael's Church, Chirbury. See also the sundial at Marrington (Plate 9)*

II inherited all 'lands and tenements in Marton purchased from Edward Scriven'. In other bequests his granddaughter Jane received 'one heyfer, now in calfe'.

George II became Rector of Bedstone and in his will of 1666[7] he left his lands in Stockton to his son Peter I together with the Scriven property which he had bought from his brother Edmund II, as well as the field called Bent by Marton Pool and his library of books. However Peter I died childless and intestate in 1668[8] and his inheritance passed to his sister Mary Lloyd. She had three other sisters one of whom married John Bowdler, a descendent of Baldwyn de Bollers who had married the niece of Henry I and was Lord of Montgomery. The Bowdler family are named in the 1815 Enclosure Award as freeholders of land in Marton, and a small plot of land near The Sun Inn is still in their possession. It seems likely that it has been in their continuous possession since 1815 and probably for many years before that. The Bowdlers have the distinction of being the only remaining family with this long landowning connection to Marton.

In 1656 Mary had married her second cousin George III, the son of David Lloyd of Marton Hall. When her brother Peter I died, Mary inherited the Stockton estate[9] which was 'well worth £100'. George III and Mary lived in Stockton until their deaths. George III was a churchwarden in Chirbury in 1665 and he was one of the original trustees appointed by the Rev. Edward Lewis at the foundation of the school in Chirbury in 1675.[10] As 'George Lloyd of Stockton in the county of Salop, gent.', he appears as trustee to the marriage settlement of his niece Esther Bray of Marton and Hugh Davies of Dysserth on 9 September 1688. On the death of his mother, George III succeeded to the Marton property.[11]

Their son, the Rev. Peter Lloyd, sworn an hereditary burgess of Welshpool in 1708, is styled on the burgess roll 'son of George Lloyd of Marton'. Peter was educated at Shrewsbury School under the headmastership of Mr. Andrew Taylor. He took his BA degree at St. John's College, Cambridge in 1686 and became Vicar of Forden.[12] His elder brother Richard was also educated at Shrewsbury and Cambridge gaining a BA in 1676 and MA in 1679. Richard went on to become Rector of Croft cum Yarpole in Herefordshire after a short period as Head of Shrewsbury School. His portrait was at one time hanging in Walcot, Chirbury. He was buried at Yarpole in 1723.[13]

**Letters to Stockton**

Three letters survive written by Peter II whilst he attended school in Shrewsbury and as an undergraduate at Cambridge. Two are addressed to his 'Hon'rd Father' living at Stockton in Chirbury parish, and one is an enclosure to his mother.[14]

> These for Mr. George Lloyd living at Stockton in Chirbury parish. Deliver.

> Honoured Father – I hope you received your 4s. and 6d. I sent you by Thomas Ffoulk for ye discharge of Thomas Rogers' bond. I pray tell my mother that my hosen are mightily decayed and that if she cannot easily furnish me I will buy me some which I think is the best way. You were talking about the gun; if you will send it I will see for some ... or bargain.
>
> ... I pray send me word whether my sister hath my common prayer booke or not; and faile not to send to Cosen Thomas Bray [Dr. Bray, Founder of the Society for the Propagation of the Gospel in Foreign Parts] about his coming home, and either send me word or els my brother Richard; and likewise send me a few good quills, for I want some very much, and send the key my mother knows of. October ye 7th [16]82.

> ... Yours dated ye 26th of May I received last night by ye carrier, together with £63 10s. ... I think I shall be more chargeable unto you by comeing down than staying here, for if I come home I must pay half the tuition, chamber-rent and detriments which will amount to allmost as much as if I stay. Camb. June ye 2nd 1686.

The enclosure of the same date read:

> Loving Mother ... I fully desighn'd to see you this summer but I finde now it will be inconvenient both for you as my self, for we performe all publique exercise for our degrees betwixt this time and Michaelmas; however let what will happen, if you desire it I will come ... My cloaths are indifferent, my shirts

and stockings are worne thin, and I must trouble you once more for a supply, which I hope will be ye last time. Thus, wishing us a joyfull meeting, I rest yo'r dutifull sonne.

As mentioned above, Peter II became Vicar of Forden. His Latin Bible was at one time kept at Walcot, Chirbury.[15] His sister Mary II eventually married and also lived at Yarpole. In her will she left her property in Marton to her husband Simon Brown and on his death it reverted back firstly to her brother Richard and then her other brother Peter Lloyd.[16]

On the death of George Lloyd III in the early 18th century, his son George IV inherited half his father's Marton property but was obliged to pay his sister £65, his brother Peter £30, his brother Richard £30 and fulfil various other legacies out of his father's estate. George IV also inherited his mother's Stockton property on her death and the other half of the Marton estate, again with the stipulation that various sums of money be raised for the other siblings.[17]

There are few details surviving about George IV of Marton whilst he was alive and his last will and testament proved in 1727 indicates that he had no children, and may not have married, however he did have a concern for the poor in his local society and the means to assist them. His will set up a charity with an investment of £40, and from the interest 5s. a year was to be used to buy:

> penny bread for the poor of the parish of Chirbury on the next Lord's day after Midsummer, for ever.
> 'cloath coates' to the Poor of the Seven towns on the lower side of the parish of Chirbury. Marton and Stockton to be first served if needed but not by the same persons every year.[18]

As the *Shrewsbury Chronicle* of *c*.1930s reported:

> The picturesque church of St. Mark's was built in 1855 and some of the older inhabitants can tell you how on Christmas Day many years ago loaves of bread were distributed to the worshippers after service.

The surviving members of the original Trustees of Chirbury School passed on their responsibilities to another generation of local gentry in 1738, one of whom was George Lloyd V of Marton, the son of the Rev. Peter Lloyd of Forden and the main beneficiary of his uncle George IV's will.[19] On the death of his uncle, George V moved to Marton. He outlived the other Trustees and as the sole survivor in 1782 he appointed 11 others to replace them including his son and heir, John Lloyd of the Wood, Forden.[20]

The final link in this long chain of inheritance in the Lloyd family is with the two daughters of John and Catherine Lloyd. Margaret married Arthur Lloyd Humphreys, and her sister Mary married his brother Edward Humphreys of Walcot, Chirbury. On the death of their father in 1831 they had possession of estates in Marton and Stockton and in Lower Munlin and Little Hem in Forden parish.[21]

What do these documents spanning 200 years say about the Lloyd family? In the first place they lived very comfortably on their estates in Stockton and Marton; their family ties were strong; they valued education (the best); they laid out time and money to help the poor in their own community (school and charity); in times of war they fulfilled their duties; their loyalty to Church and King was unquestionable. But those untold tragedies of childhood mortality and sudden death which were so much part of life before modern medicine lend a hidden backdrop to their history and an unenviable perspective. But some things never change, such as the hard up student worrying about his finances, his clothes the worse for wear, in college minus the very items essential to his needs, and the inevitable urgent letter home to his mother.

## The Distaff side

We can assume that there were instances where the female beneficiaries received land or property in lieu of payments when circumstances dictated but the details are unclear. What is certain is that the surviving marriage settlements show that the Lloyd daughters and wives were well provided for and independent. There is at least one significant marriage in the Lloyd family, that of Gwen Lloyd (sister of Richard I) with Thomas Bray.[22] One of her descendants, Dr. Thomas Bray was the founder of the Society for the Propagation of the Gospel in Foreign Parts. There is nothing to tell us of a settlement of land made at the time of Gwen's marriage, but in 1688 Esther Bray, niece of George III, married Hugh Davies of Dysserth in Montgomeryshire. The marriage settlement gave Hugh and Esther £15 a year and income from property in Welshpool and Esther was also promised a third share of her father's property in Heighway (Marton) and an interest in the 'jointure' lands on the death of her mother.[23]

Over 100 years later, in 1785, the Davies family of Dysserth crop up again in another marriage settlement which begins with a explanation of events leading to Elizabeth Davies' ownership of a third of Marton Manor. (When Mary, the daughter of Maurice Lloyd, an apothecary in Shrewsbury, married John Davies of Dysserth, her inheritance, shared with her sister Susannah, was a third of the Manor of Marton. John Davies had the means to buy out Susannah and did so. On his death he had accumulated considerable property which his three daughters inherited. The third part of the Manor of Marton went to his daughter Elizabeth). In due course Elizabeth married the Rev. William Thornes of Alberbury. In her marriage settlement the Manor possessions are described as 'a capital messuage and farm' (Marton Manor, tenant David Lloyd), together with three other properties, the tenants being William Maund, John Betton and John Roberts.[24]

A lease in 1791 between the landlords (John Edwards of Ford and the Rev. William Thornes) and the tenant, Peter Lloyd of Marton, details the rent (£71 8s.) and the tenants' obligations:

> The tenant is to pay all taxes except Gaol tax. All hay to be consumed on the premises and all muck spread and the land to be cultivated in a husbandlike

manner. No timber to be felled or cropped except what is allowed for repair of pales, rails, gates and stiles and for fencebot. The tenant is to find at his own cost sufficient straw to said messuage and buildings. He may not sublet without licence except cottages and the parcel of land known as Halfway Piece.[25]

In 1796 Elizabeth Thornes died and her share of the Marton property fell into the hands of her husband, the Rev. William Thornes. There follows a gap of ten years in our knowledge of events and then he employed Mr. J. Meredith of Westbury to conduct a survey of the estate in Marton.[26] This showed that there were three joint owners of the estate: the Rev. W. Thornes, the Rev. Sir John Edwardes, Bart. and Charles Jones. The accompanying map of the estate reveals its very piecemeal nature. There are one or two blocks of land which run together such as the Parks fields at the Chirbury end of the village and Barn Close, Close Velin, and Long Furlong near the Manor house, whilst there are several isolated pockets of land which demonstrate clearly the scattered nature of pre-enclosure estates.

| NAMES | QUALITY | QUANTITY | | |
| --- | --- | --- | --- | --- |
| | | Acs. | Rds. | Pcs. |
| 1. Fold, garden, stackyard | | 1 | 0 | 8 |
| 2. Barn close | pasture | 2 | 2 | 0 |
| 3. Close Velin | pasture | 6 | 3 | 15 |
| 4. Long furlong | arable | 10 | 2 | 4 |
| 5. Marsh meadow | meadow | 3 | 0 | 35 |
| 6. The Parks | arable | 7 | 3 | 9 |
| 7. The Parks | arable/meadow | 10 | 3 | 19 |
| 8. The Parks | rough/arable | 6 | 2 | 4 |
| 9. Little Close | pasture | 0 | 3 | 21 |
| 10. Ox leasow | arable | 7 | 3 | 14 |
| 11. Upper leasow | arable | 3 | 3 | 20 |
| 12. Close lane end | arable | 5 | 1 | 15 |
| 13. Rack furlong | pasture | 14 | 2 | 25 |
| 14. Upper leasow | arable | 5 | 1 | 20 |
| 15. Nether leasow | pasture | 7 | 0 | 17 |
| 16. Upper wood leasow | pasture | 11 | 3 | 18 |
| 17. Wood and wood leasow | pasture | 16 | 1 | 16 |
| 18. Corn stubble | arable | 14 | 2 | 20 |
| 19. Cow pasture | pasture | 15 | 0 | 18 |
| 20. Town meadow | meadow | 2 | 2 | 30 |
| 21. Moor meadow, pool side in | meadow | 10 | 1 | 13 |
| 22. Gullets, pool side in | meadow | 6 | 3 | 15 |
| 23. New meadow | meadow | 3 | 1 | 8 |
| 24. Geese leys | pasture | 11 | 1 | 10 |
| Bank on same, pool side in | | 2 | 1 | 23 |
| Roads | | 2 | 3 | 4 |
| Total | | 186 | 0 | 11 |

*1806 Survey of Rev. W. Thorne's Estate in Marton by J. Meredith, Westbury*

The accompanying letter to the Rev. W. Thornes read:

Rev. Sir,
Above is the survey of your estate at Marton. I hope you will not be very much displeased at finding it to be really more than you expected. I sent a duplicate to W. Niccolls yesterday am.

Your's obligd. And humble servant.
J. Meredith. Westbury.

| N.º | Names | Quality | Quantity |
| --- | --- | --- | --- |
| | | | A. R. P |
| 1 | Fold. Garden & Stack Yard | | 1 . 0 . 7 |
| 2 | Barn Close | Pasture | 2 . 2 . 0 |
| 3 | Close Velen (inclosd) meadow | Dº | 6 . 3 . 15 |
| 4 | Long Furlong | Arable | 10 . 2 . 4 |
| 5 | Marsh. Meadow | Meadow | 3 . 0 . 35 |
| 6 | The Parks | Arable | 7 . 3 . 9 |
| 7 | | Dº & Mead. | 10 . 3 . 19 |
| 8 | Rough in Dº | 6.0.20 Arable | 6 . 2 . 14 |
| 9 | Little Close | Pasture | 0 . 3 . 21 |
| 10 | Ox Leason | Arable | 7 . 3 . 14 |
| 11 | Upper Dº | Dº | 3 . 3 . 20 |
| 12 | Close Lane-end | Dº | 5 . 1 . 15 |
| 13 | Rack Furlong | Pasture | 14 . 2 . 25 |
| 14 | Upper Leason | Arable | 5 . 1 . 20 |
| 15 | Nether Dº | Pasture | 7 . 0 . 17 |
| | | | 94 . 1 . 36 |

*Mr Meredith's neat copperplate hand records the size and usage of the Reverend Thorne's estate in Marton. There are several separate parcels of land described, 1-5 The Manor House and adjacent fields, 6-8 The Parks land and adjacent fields 9-12 separated by roads, 13 –17 make up three isolated parcels of land under Stockton wood*

# Chapter 12

# Lords, Ladies and Freeholders of Marton Manor

At this point in the early 19th century the subdivision of the ownership of the Manor of Marton over the previous generations had, in several instances, led to a state of shared ownership sometimes into as many as five equal parts. The arable land under individual or shared ownership had already been enclosed, fenced or hedged and thus protected from wandering animals. But in Marton the commons and waste land remained unenclosed until 1815. By Act of Parliament it was possible for the landowners to put this process into motion under the control of an appointed commissioner. The common grazing land lay on the flat land running between Marton ridge and the Trelystan boundary and much of the waste occupied Marton Dingle. Apart from the common grazing, which was potentially useful agricultural land, the rest was marginal, wooded and rough. But after the enclosures took place and the fences went up the poorer classes lost the right to graze their animals freely here as had been the tradition for centuries. The land was distributed among the existing landowners, enclosed by them and added to their farms. However, in many instances the cottagers in Marton who lived on the parish boundaries and along the Perries and in Beach Dingle were allowed to rent and enclose a few acres around their homes to provide for their animals.

The complexities of dealing with multi-owners must have added to the difficulties of the Commissioner, Mr. William Jones of Garthmyl, in his task of enclosing the commons and waste in the township of Marton when the enclosure process began in 1812.[1] The lords and ladies of the Manor of Marton at that time were: The Rev. Sir John Edwardes; Rev. William Thornes; Mary Lee; Edward Gatacre and Annabella his wife; John Wynne Eyton and Jane his wife, formerly Jane Lloyd; John Mytton and Bridgett his wife; Catherine Lloyd; Lawton Parry; John Lloyd; and Thomas Bowdler Jones. But it was a freeholder, Richard Pryce of Gunley, who owned land on the north-west of the township who instigated the enclosure of Marton commons and waste. The other freeholders involved were Thomas Roberts (with David Jones, George Roberts and Edward Jones), Edward Humphreys, Pryce Jones, John Bowdler, Samuel Perkins, Thomas Wildblood and Sarah Franks, Lawton Parry and John Lloyd, (the latter two were also lords of the manor).[2]

The solicitor, Mr. John Williams, conducted all the legal procedures on behalf of the lords and ladies and freeholders. His bills directed to both parties were received by Richard Pryce who allocated the individual dues.

Mr. Jones, the commissioner directed some of his bills to individual lords and ladies when they concerned property alterations, building matters or letting.

It is beyond the intent and purpose of this book to trace and explain every line of the Lloyd family and their connection with Marton, but it seems plain from this list and surviving correspondence that there was still a powerful Lloyd influence on the allotment of land during the Marton enclosure process. The detailed family pedigree has been traced by 19th century antiquarians and is published in several parts in the Montgomery Collections. A letter to the *Marton Mirror* in April 2008 stated:

> According to *A Complete Guide to Heraldry* (by Fox-Davies) 'the record number of officially proved and recorded quarterings is at present held by the family of Lloyd of Stockton in Chirbury, County Salop.' The arms of Lloyd of Stockton contains 323 quarters. Many of the quarterings[3] are mere repetition owing to constant intermarriages. (Mrs. Jane Cooper)

# Chapter 13

# Enclosure Award, 1812-18

Much of the accessible and productive farmland in Marton township had already been enclosed by 1815. It was the commissioner's task to establish existing ownership of all the land in Marton by means of maps and a perambulation involving all parties and then to allocate the commons and waste lands to respective claimants with their mutual consent, and also to encourage the exchange of lands where landowners wished to create more compact farms by agreement.

His first step was to advertise a perambulation of the boundaries of Marton and encourage all those interested to attend and bring their own maps on the day.[1] This duly took place, but the maps proved to be a disappointment being both unreliable and inaccurate. As a result, a new and complete survey of the area had to be undertaken with the land strictly measured and recorded in acres, roods and perches. The completed map covered the whole township of Marton, and included footpaths, bridleways, roads, quarries, watering holes, streams and ditches, fields, meadows, commons, waste and encroachments. Waste land seemed to include acres of woodland in the Beaches Dingle, cottages and encroachments at the Perries, marginal land below the Crest and cottages and encroachments on Stockton boundary. Using this new map, drawn up with the assistance of a surveyor, Mr. Jones spent eight days in Marton with the surveyor allotting 320 acres of commons, waste and encroachments, and valuing the 385 acres of freehold land which was to be 'given and received in exchange'. The schedule accompanying the map detailed each landowner's re-jigged estate, the names of the fields, their acreages and tithe value.[2] The next step was to advertise the map and schedule to enable everyone in Marton to double check it and likewise for the wider public through the local newspapers, *The Shrewsbury Chronicle* and the *Salopian Journal*. Anyone with objections then had an opportunity to state them in the expectation that the commissioner would resolve the difficulties.[3] The final legalisation of the Enclosure process took place at the Manor Leet.

The largest portion and best of the land to be enclosed was the common land lying along the flats between Marton Crest and the Trelystan boundary. This land was allotted to Marton Manor (owners Rev. Sir John Edwardes, Bart.; Rev. William

Thornes; John Mytton; his wife, Bridget Mytton; and Catherine Lloyd) and to Marton Hall Farm (owners Lawton Parry and Mary Lee). The regular field divisions introduced at this time are still apparent in the field shapes.

As mentioned above, the waste land had included some woodland in the Beaches Dingle. Mr. Jones advised the lords and ladies of the Manor that some of the trees were worthless and difficult to fell, particularly those on the extreme slopes. His report noted that 'The trees are for the most part very old, damaged, decayed or pollarded … these trees ought to be felled without delay.'[4] Some of the best timber that was accessible was duly felled and used in new building

> **MARTON INCLOSURE.**
>
> THE undersigned, the Commissioner appointed to divide and allot the Commons and Waste Lands within the LORDSHIP of MARTON, in the County of Salop, DO HEREBY GIVE NOTICE, That I shall leave for Inspection at the Cross Inn, in Chirbury, for twenty-one Days from the 19th Instant, a Map of the said Lordship, with a Schedule or Reference distinguishing the several Freeholds and their respective Common Rights, Rights of Way, Water, &c. &c. also Cottages and Incroachments, and the general Lines of the Roads over the Commons, public and private, the principal of which are trigged out.— If any Omission or Inaccuracy shall appear in the said Map and Schedule, it is requested that Notice thereof in Writing be left at the Office of Mr. JOHN WILLIAMES, in Welshpool, the Solicitor to the Inclosure.
>
> I DO ALSO GIVE NOTICE that a MEETING will be held at the Public House in Marton, on THURSDAY, the 10th of September, at Ten in the Forenoon, for the Purpose of hearing and determining any Objection or Dispute which may arise in Respect to the abovementioned, or other Matters relating to this Inclosure; and for submitting certain Proposals to the Proprietors for their Approbation previous to laying out the Allotments.
>
> WM. JONES.
>
> *Garthmil, 10th August, 1812.*

*In 1812, the Commissioner, Mr William Jones, gives notice in the local newspaper, that a map of the Lordship of Marton will be available for inspection prior to the allotment*

projects at either the Manor Farm or Marton Hall Farm and on Marton Mountain. The following extract is from Mr. Jones' bill to the lords and ladies of Marton:

> 1814. July 12th. Examining state of farm buildings taking dimensions of same and determining to pull down part and convert Hay bays into three cowhouses.
>
> 20th. Drawing plans for alterations of said building and contracting workmen for same.[5]

The best of the remaining wood was sold to a Mr. Weaver who took it to Belan Wharf where it was weighed and the bark removed.[6] Between 1780 and 1850 the leather trade reached new heights of production and oak bark was much in demand for use in the tanning industry. Cordwood was less easy to dispose of. There were a few offers well below the asking price, forcing Mr. Jones to hold an open auction, but this too failed to realise a satisfactory bid. Eventually Mr. Henshaw, a Steward from Forden Workhouse agreed to take it.[7]

Meanwhile, contractors were employed in the considerable task of fencing the newly enclosed fields and cottages. There were 170 separate holdings/fields to fence as a result of the enclosure process but having the necessary timber at hand must have made the project economically attractive.[8]

The location of the 200 pollarded trees which were felled and barked under the instructions of Mr. Jones is not certain.[9] There is at the present time one pollarded oak tree in the boundary fence between Manor Farm and the Perries; there may be others elsewhere. It is quite clear from the collection of letters concerning the enclosure that the diplomatic skills of the commissioner were often called upon. For example, the Rev. Sir John Edwardes and Rev. William Thornes; John Mytton and Bridget Mytton; and Catherine Lloyd in three equal shares were allocated 184 acres and 5 perches of land which included The Ten Ridges, The Ridges, The Bents, Part of Lady Meadow, the Big Geifor and Peartree Leasow, together with cottages and encroachments and newly enclosed commons along the flat between Marton Crest and the Trelystan boundary.

In addition there were the land swaps to be considered. On 15 May 1813, William Jones wrote to Rev. Wm. Thornes, Alberbury as follows:

Dear Sir.
Agreeable to your request I send annexed the total acreage of lands exchanged to and from Mrs. Lloyd's farm at Marton. You will find is added 53 acres nearly all comprising the best of all the common.

|  |  | a | r | p |
|---|---|---|---|---|
| Lands exchanged from Mrs. Lloyds farm |  | 124 | 2 | 37 |
| Do. Woodland |  | 4 | 0 | 0 |
|  | Total | 128 | 2 | 37 |
| Added to Mrs. Lloyd's farm, including messuage | | 97 | 3 | 0 |
| Gardens, orchard occupied by Dau. Jacks | | | | |
| Wasteland including 4 cottages | | 85 | 2 | 27 |
| And encroachments. | Total | 183 | 1 | 3 |
| Old Farm | | 183 | 1 | 17 |
| Exch. Away | | 128 | 2 | 37 |
| | Total | 54 | 2 | 20 |
| Exch. obt. | | 183 | 1 | 37 |
| | Total | 238 | 0 | 37[10] |

This example also illustrates the extent of the change that affected landowners as a result of the Enclosure Act. Mrs. Lloyd acquired the ownership of the property where her daughter was tenant, in exchange for handing over 128 acres of land which she owned. It would have been an unequal exchange without the 53 acres of common land which Mrs. Lloyd gained in the Enclosure arrangement, for it seems she was given the best of the common land, probably land with the potential for arable use. The final outcome was a substantial gain in the acreage she owned.

A number of factors held up the Commissioner during the Enclosure Award process. As Mrs. Catherine Lloyd from Llandinam was reluctant to sign the agreement regarding the exchange of lands, this prevented the new tenant, Mr. Phillips, from taking possession of the Manor Farm. Mr. Jones wrote again to Rev. W. Thornes on 8 December 1813:

The fact is I was prepared and would have settled everything weeks ago had not Mrs. Lloyds concurrence been lacking as she has never signed the agreement to exchange. I feel it is somewhat awkward at least if not hazardous to Set and Let and to thereby guarantee the possession of lands which strictly and legally we have no control over and (until Mrs. Lloyd sanctions the measure) cannot be said to belong to anyone except herself.[11]

Mr. Perkins also refused to sign his agreement in the first instance. There was also a dispute between Mr. Roberts and Mr. Bowdler which could only be resolved by the Commissioner checking the original purchase deed of the land. Then there were other parties like Mr. Thomas Roberts who wished to get on with the business of fencing their new lands. The following is an extract from the bill sent to the lords and ladies and Freeholders from John Williams, solicitor, which include's the cost of his clerk's journey to see the commissioner:

Letter and clerks journey to William Jones of Garthmill informing him that I was applied to by Mr. Thomas Roberts to know whether they were at liberty to enclose their allotments of common or not and whether he had marked them all out.[12]                                                                7s 6d

In spite of all these difficulties Mr. Jones carried out the enclosure process successfully, a process that was begun in 1812 and not completed until 1815. Even then, letters between the participants disputing the various charges incurred continued until 1818.

It is particularly noteworthy that Mr. Jones supported the interests of the cottagers who may have had no legal right to their homes and land prior to enclosure other than unspecified obligations to the lords and ladies of the Manor. In the following letter he suggested that they paid rent for their property to the Steward of the Manor, thus legalising their position in modern terms. He also pointed out that this was the best way to deal with so many detached, small homesteads. These were the six cottages along the Perries, cottages and encroachments in the Beach Dingle, three cottages and encroachments on the Trelystan boundary, a cottage in the field opposite the Mill turn and others on the Stockton boundary.

*An item from the solicitor, Mr. John Williams' bill (1812) to the lords and ladies and freeholders of Marton for his expenses for attending the perambulation of Marton Mountain*

COTTAGERS OF MARTON
To the Rev. Thornes, March 21 1814

Dear Sir, The cottagers at Marton being extremely desirous to have a bit of land to rent each according to his ability I trust you will not disapprove of having the allotments made in respect of the Royalty disposed of in this way which I think preferable to dividing those allotments into distinct and equal parts among the Lords of the Manor. In the latter case there would be so many detached parcels from each estate and which owing to various circumstances would not be occupied to much advantage. In the former way individuals might have what will best suit him and the rent being paid into the hands of one individual (The Steward of the Manor for instance) they must be accounted for in equal portions. I shall be obliged by having your sentiments upon this as early as possible for the people are now wanting to fence what may be apportioned to them respectively and the season for quickening will soon be too far advanced.
Yours etc. Wm. Jones.[13]

An item in Mr. Jones' 1817 account with the lords and ladies of Marton shows that he allotted parcels of land to the cottagers, valued their holdings and drew up agreements for the tenants to sign in 1814. But there was some opposition to his suggestion.

A Leet was called, which the Commissioner could not attend. Those present were Colonel Gatacre, Miss Lloyd, Mrs. Lloyd, Mr. Mytton and the solicitor, Mr. Williams, who paid all their expenses and for the jury's dinner and ale at the time, then recouped the money in a later bill. Following this Leet the solicitor was instructed to draw up notices to quit and have them delivered to the cottagers. The unfortunate Bailiff was charged with the duty of serving the notices to each tenant and of instructing them to meet to pay their rents or risk being 'distrained' upon. (Some arrears of rent were due from 1801).

On 13 October 1815 Mr. Williams travelled to Marton to receive the rents but 'none of them attended nor paid their rents'. By this boycott the cottagers demonstrated their refusal to accept the eviction notices in a very effective manner. It was a bold move and likely to incur the anger of the landowners and possibly retribution. But a further entry in Mr. Jones' bill in 1816 is a charge for 'attending at Marton to review all premises and take down proposals for leases to different cottagers as directed by the lords and ladies at the Leet'. In effect the majority of cottagers won the right to stay on in their homes, and had the Commissioner to thank for his support of their interests. The cottagers in 1817 paying rent to the lords and ladies of Marton Manor were Thomas Bowen, Thomas Gittins, Richard Wilcox and Thomas Nicholls, Edward Gardner, John Evans, Edward Davies, Thomas Morris, Elinor and Thomas Morris, John Roberts, John Gardner, Edward Hughes, Edward Tipton, Catherine Bishop, John Wilcox and Edward Gardner.[14]

Whilst words and the spelling of words is a constantly changing factor in the English language, a modern reading of the Enclosure Map and accompanying survey is further complicated in the border region by the existence of Welsh words misspelt by English scribes. It can only be stated that the accuracy of the spelling of Welsh field names depended on the Commissioner or his clerk's mastery of the Welsh language. On the evidence of two field names, Rhossy and Rwbia, which appear to have Welsh derivations, the former from *rhos* (marsh) and the latter from *wybrau* (sky), it's perhaps fair to hazard a guess that neither the clerk nor the commissioner were Welsh speakers. Any unfamiliar Welsh words would have been written down phonetically as they were heard. Thus *gwelltyn* (grass) became *gwestyn,* and *Felin* (mill) became *Velin, Gellyg* (pear) became *Gelly, Geifr* (goat) became *Geyfor.*[15] This interpretation of word anomalies is open to further research and adjustment by anyone with a better understanding of the Welsh language.

The final stage in legalising the Enclosure Award took place at a Court Leet held at The Sun Inn in Marton, of which the landlord was then David Morgan, after several Leets had been postponed or cancelled because some participants were unable to attend. The bailiff, Thomas Gittins, was ordered to summon a jury and with all the interested parties present (or their representatives), the agreement was signed on 30 November 1815 (see plate 12).[16] (The Court Leets generally dealt with minor matters of local justice, and had the power to levy fines and to imprison for some offences. In later years they became the Petty Sessions which were also held at The Sun.)

Thus another layer in the pattern of the Marton landscape was added by the Enclosure Act of 1815. The arable furlong strips behind the Manor House were enclosed before in 1815 and their ownership established. This Act also irrevocably took away the ancient grazing rights of everyone in the village to pasture their animals on the common land, the land being divided between the landowners and fenced. The poorer villagers who had only one or two animals were obliged to fight to retain a few acres around their cottages to pasture their animals permanently, although in some instances they too gained a small new enclosure. These 'cottagers' cleared and fenced plots of previously waste land, and began to pay rent to their landlords. The landowners gained in all respects, some farms being enlarged by the addition of conveniently adjoining waste or common land. The two main farms, Marton Manor and Marton Hall Farm, acquired the best of the common land between them. This previously common, unimproved land could be cultivated and put to good arable use. Land swaps with neighbouring property owners achieved more compact, manageable farms. Those landlords or tenant farmers who had cattle breeding programmes could fence out strays and runts and prevent cross breeding.

During the Enclosure process all the wood and timber assets in the township were evaluated. Much old woodland was cleared, trees were pollarded, fences constructed, hedge boundaries laid and new farm buildings erected. The changes brought about by the Enclosure act set the pattern in the landscape which exists today for anyone to see who cares to look closely.

# Chapter 14

# From Tithes to Rent or Cash replaces Corn

Tithes were originally a payment of one tenth of the land's produce (every tenth cow or one tenth of its milk or the corn produced in a field) to a monastery or later to the Church for the support of the parish incumbent and the parish church. After the dissolution of the monasteries the right to receive tithes was often obtained by laymen. The Church could also buy or sell its entitlement to tithes. Following the dissolution of Chirbury monastery the tithe dues of hay and corn became Crown property and were, in 1571, bestowed by Queen Elizabeth I upon the Governors and Trustees of the Free Grammar School of King Edward VI in Shrewsbury. A small proportion also became due to Edward, Viscount Clive.[1]

By the 19th century landlords and farmers became convinced that the system of tithe payments was an unfair burden on agricultural land, in that the gains made from investment and improved harvests provided unearned increments to the tithe owners. Many countrymen also felt they paid an unfair proportion of the cost of maintaining the parish church, and especially so if they were members of a nonconformist congregation. The government was obliged to deal with the growing unrest and in 1836 produced the Tithe Commutation Act in which the payment of produce was converted into to an annual rent on land to be paid by the landowners. This commutation was facilitated by detailed maps for each parish with an accompanying record of acreages, value, landowners and tenants. The gross rent for Chirbury parish, commuted in 1843 and encompassing all the townships, Marton included, was £1,003 3s. 6d. of which the Governors and Trustees of the School received £1,000 and Edward, Viscount Clive £3 2s. 6d.[2] Marton landowners paid towards this collective obligation.

The detailed documentation that accompanied the process of commutation adds considerably more information to that already provided by the earlier 1841 census. On the schedule each landowner is named, and every tenant and each house, cottage, plot of land, field or close is listed. Alongside every arable field is given the amount of corn it produced. The last column states the amount of rent due and the total for each farm or holding. On the map which accompanies the schedule, the numbered fields and houses match the schedule list. From these sources it is possible to build up a good picture of village life at this period.

At this time, almost half way through the 19th century, most of the land was still in the ownership of the lords and ladies of Marton either individually or collectively. Changes had taken place through death and inheritance but, with a few notable exceptions, the unifying element linking the landowners was still the connection with the Lloyd family. The landowners were William Jones, Richard Jones, David Hamer, Mrs. Catherine Lloyd, Margaret Bowdler, Edward Humphreys, the Rev. Thomas Thornes, Lady Edwardes, David Edwardes, John Lloyd, Arthur Lloyd Humphreys, Martha Wildblood, Samuel Perkins, Richard Pryce, and William Nevett.[3] Only the latter three were probably unrelated to the Lloyds.

## Large farms

None of the above landowners appear on the 1841 census as residents of Marton with the exception of William Nevett.[4] Mr. Nevett lived at Marton Villa (later known as The Cottage Farm) with his wife Mary, three children, three agricultural labourers, and two farm servants.[10] Though his stated occupation was farming he owned other property in Marton: The Smithy (Samuel Roberts), and two houses No.13 (John Jones) and No.28 (John Griffiths). In the census 25-year-old John Griffiths is the landlord at The Sun. Mr. Nevett was also a Trustee of the Independent Chapel in the village and one of the Lords of the Manor, but was unlikely to be connected to the Lloyd family as he was a relative newcomer to the village. In addition he was the owner of the New Inn at the Lowfield, where the tenant was William Lewis and the maltster William Richards, aged 20. Five fields with the Lowfield were under arable cultivation, and three were meadows.

The three main farms in the village, The Manor Farm, Marton Hall Farm and The Steps, were occupied throughout most of the 19th century by tenant farmers

*Manor House, an imposing timber-framed building with an extensive range of historic barns, is now a busy modern farm. The number of panels in a timber-framed building from cill to wallplate usually denotes the status of the house. Built originally in the 1600s with later additions and alterations, the Hall section has four square panels from cill to wallplate (as does the gable end from cill to tie-beam), and three rectangular panels in the cross wing. Also seen is the weather-boarded timber-framed barn set on a rubble plinth. The cart entrance is in the second bay from the left*

who had no security of tenure or guarantee that their son or sons would be given the tenancy in their own declining years. Nonetheless, Mr. Meddins at the Marton Hall Farm and Mr. Phillips at the Manor kept their tenancies for 20 years and were followed by a son and step-son respectively.

The latter years of the century brought a decline in agriculture as a result of cheaper imports of corn from America, the resulting drop in prices of home produced crops affecting both tenants and landowners as each struggled to make a profit from the land. The resulting instability was reflected in a more frequent turnover of tenant farmers as shown in the census. In 1891, The Steps lost most of its farmland and was split into two dwellings, one of which was uninhabited and the other the home of an agricultural labourer.[5]

There were estate sales in 1860[6] and 1862[7], but whilst this resulted in a change of ownership, the landholdings remained largely intact. The system of landlord and tenant continued under a new regime. Marton Lower Farm (Manor Farm) which was the subject of the 1860 sale, was bought by Mrs. Edmunds of Edderton Hall; Marton Hall Farm, the subject of the 1862 sale, was bought by Mr. Edward Humphreys of Walcot. Mrs. Edmunds also acquired the Bytuck and surrounding farmland. The men of 'new wealth', won through personal enterprise or through success in commerce or industry who wished to invest their money in land, were represented by Mr. Naylor from Leighton, who bought land that was sold in the sale of 1862 on the Trelystan boundary adjacent to property he already owned. These individuals were local landowners in their own right and were adding to their existing estates.

*The farmhouse of Marton Hall Farm*

The estate owner selling part of his property in 1862 was John Hamer of Montgomeryshire whose mother Mary (Lloyd) had inherited part of the Glanhafren estate which included property in Marton.[8] This sale was remarkable in one respect in that those local tradesmen who had prospered in business, Mr. Hughes of Ryecroft and the blacksmith Mr. Thomas Gardner, bought the homes and businesses which were their livelihoods and became the first of the tenants to move up the social and economic ladder to become property owners, Mr. Hughes paying £260 for Ryecroft; Mr. Gardner £165 for the Smithy.[9] Those virtues of hard work and thrift valued by the Victorians, combined with modest ambition were thus rewarded in this age of opportunity for some.

Marton Villa farm, the home of Mr. Nevett, was eventually sold in 1879. It was at this point that the Oliver family bought Lot 2, The Parks.[11]

Three other large farms in Marton were under the management of tenant farmers, Mr. Richard Phillips and his wife Grace at the Manor Farm had five agricultural labourers and three farm servants living in (landlords Thomas Thornes, Lady Edwardes and Mrs. Catherine Lloyd); at The Steps, Thomas and Elizabeth Jones' household included one farm servant and three agricultural labourers (landlord Richard Jones); at the Hall Farm, Mr. John Meddins and Jane, his wife had three sons of working age living at home together with four agricultural labourers and two farm servants (landlord David Hamer).[12]

The land in the north-west of the township was divided between two farms, Bank Farm and The Beeches Farm, the former under the tenancy of Francis Bevan

*The Steps. Probably built in the 1600s on a rubble plinth, modern pebble-dash covers a brick and timber structure with later alterations and additions*

(landlord Richard Pryce) and the latter in the ownership of and farmed 'in hand' by Samuel Perkins according to the 1843 Tithe details, yet neither Francis Bevan nor Samuel Perkins appear on the 1841 census for Marton. The site of Bank Farm in 1812 is marked on the Enclosure Map as The Hackway. The next certain appearance of Beeches Farm is in the 1881 census when it is farmed by John Clarke Davies and his family. Two-year-old Samuel Perkins Davies was his son.

Edward Humphreys, a landowner and non-resident, also farmed an area of land 'in hand', this being mainly patches of woodland near the Stockton boundary together with The Perries cottage and land below the Perries, along with some plots in the village. He also owned Highgate, where the tenants were John and Mary Ford with their seven children. John Ford was a mason by trade. Mr. Humphreys held other property near the Stockton boundary which was farmed by Matthew Williams (again not in the 1841 Marton census), and several cottages with their 'closes' – or small fields – also adjoining the Stockton boundary.

> William and Mary Ann Roberts farmed The Bank farm (1891) with the help of their nephews and nieces as labourers or servants. One of them, Molly, was 12 years old when she left her home in Wednesbury to work on her uncle's farm. Her cousin, Samuel Mills, was born in Middlesborough but went to Wednesbury to work as a clerk, staying with his cousins. Although he did not work on the farm in Marton with his cousins he must have visited because on 9 March 1918 he married Elizabeth Roberts from Gunley Hall, Forden. He died in action on 18 April 1918. (Diana Coles née Price, 2009)

*The Beeches was probably built in the late 1600s but has many later additions and alterations. It is constructed of limestone and shale slabs*

When we lived at the Bank Farm there was no water in the house and no electric. We had to carry water from the bottom of the field. They took the combine up Eddy's field to get to the top land but it was better soil there. (Alan Hamer, 2007)

When we bought The Beeches in 1968 there was an old pipe organ built into the house, from the ground floor to the attic. We took it apart and numbered all the sections and sold it to a chap from Oswestry who did it up. I think he was a music teacher at Oswestry school.

There was a Lister Blackstone engine here with twin fly wheels and a piston the size of a bucket. It was in the barn and drove the shafting for pulping and grinding etc. Someone from Shawbury bought it to restore.

There was a horse carriage in the end of the house, it was four-wheeled, four-seated and pulled by two horses in line. That went to a carriage company at Wellington to renovate.

In the end room of the house were two pianos, we still have one of them. There was also a harp, but I don't remember any of the family being musical. (Martin and Audrey Evans, 2007)


## Three Settlements in 1843 (since deserted)

### A. Beach Dingle

Many rural parishes had lines or clusters of settlement in earlier years which for varying reasons failed to survive into the 21st century, and Marton is no exception. The thriving Beach settlement (see plate 15) in 1841 has left little trace today other than a hint of a wall here and there or a few large stones oddly placed. The houses in Beach Dingle were built on the level land near the Lowerfield brook ford. Thomas Gittens had a cottage with several small enclosures along the banks of the Dingle, and two other enclosures between the Beach Dingle and Ryecroft with a separate field which was part of the orchard meadow along the Shrewsbury road. He was one of the three 80-year-old men (and one woman) on the 1841 census living in Marton, was of independent means and lived alone. His nearest neighbours were James and Mary Gittens who had six children of varying ages from 12 years to four months. Other occupants of Beach Dingle were Thomas and Sarah Evans with their children, and lodging with them were Thomas and Edward Gardner. All three of the men were agricultural labourers but Thomas Evans also had a few steep acres in the Dingle with a small close opposite the White House (now in ruins) at the end of Pen-y-Bank drive. The White House, which was part of the Marton Hall estate until 1919, was in 1841 occupied by 80-year-old William Jones and his elderly wife Elizabeth and dependants. The property included nine acres with a house and a 'quillet' of land adjoining Marton Pool. (A quillet is a tiny piece of land in an open field marked by boundary stones, often allotted to cottagers.[13]) In the census, William gave his occupation as an agricultural labourer. In 1843 John Evans had a house, garden and two enclosures in Beach Dingle and one close lying on Ryecroft bank producing arable crops; Thomas Bowen had a house, garden and seven plots of pasture and rough grazing there in 1843, but not apparently at the time of the census of 1841; Ann Wilcox also had a cottage and an enclosure under arable crops in 1843 but not in 1841; whilst Sarah, Mary and Elizabeth Wilcox (no occupation) lived in Beach Dingle in 1841.[14]

All these residents were tenants of the joint lords and ladies of Marton. At what point this settlement in the Dingle began is difficult to say, but four houses or cottages in this valley are shown clearly on the 1812 Enclosure Map. The houses must have been liable to flooding, particularly those nearest the brook. At times the ford would have been impassable, and these two factors combined may have led to families eventually deserting their homes.

| House | 1841 census | 1843 Tithe apportionment details |
|---|---|---|
| 1 | Thomas Evans, Sarah Evans and family, Thomas Gardner, Edward Gardner | Thomas Evans |
| 2 | Sarah Wilcox, Mary and Elizabeth Wilcox | Thomas Bowen |
| 3 | Thomas Holloway, Ann Holloway | Thomas Gittins |
| 4 | Thomas Gittins | John Evans |
| 5 | James and Mary Gittins and family | Ann Wilcox |

*Details of occupants of houses in Beach Dingle*

## B. The Perries

One of the other deserted settlement areas is along the track through the Perries (see plate 16) where there were six cottages shown on the Tithe Map of 1843, of which only one has survived to the present day. The area, along the lower slopes of Marton Mountain, was always unsuitable for agriculture. But a determined cottager could clear the land, grow vegetables and fruit on the south-facing slopes and trust the streams flowing down the hillside for drinking water.

Perry Cottage (see plate 17), currently uninhabited and the first dwelling on the route which is now a public footpath but was once a carriageway for two-wheeled vehicles, was the home of Mary, Pryce and Jane Morris in 1841. Mary was of independent means and Pryce was an agricultural labourer. The next dwelling known as Givers or Geyfors Cottage was the home of Thomas and Priscilla Roberts. He too was an agricultural labourer and rented two 'closes' adjacent to his home.

> Thomas and Priscilla Roberts went from Minsterley to live in Marton in approximately 1810. Thomas was a labourer. They lived at Geyfors Cottage. They had a son Samuel. (Mrs. Sybil Lewis [née Evans from Santley], 2007)

It seems probable that Givers Cottage was the same property as The Den that appears on later censuses.

## A Mining Aside

The Den was the home of Richard Williams, his wife and family in 1861. He was an agricultural labourer at this time but turned to mining at Wotherton when the opportunity came. He was one of a number of local men who chose to exchange the drudgery of farm work with its poor pay and long hours for the better wages down the mines and risk the known dangers – rope ladders snapping, volatile explosives and rock falls. (His youngest daughter Harriet married Nicholas Wood and emigrated to Canada with her husband and small child in 1889. Her second child John grew up in Toronto, enlisted in the Second World War and was killed in Sicily in 1943.)[15] In its early years the barytes industry at Wotherton needed men with mining knowledge, skills and experience to trace the outcrops and set up machinery to begin the extracting process. Those with such skills from the mining industries in Wales and Cornwall were perhaps head-hunted by the mine managers and encouraged to migrate to the promising ore fields in Shropshire. Alternatively, those miners with expertise in the industry possibly followed the boom trail into Shropshire, stayed while the industry prospered and then moved on.

In the early 19th century the Maginnis family were owners and part owners of the Wotherton mine. The census of 1871 records that John Maginnis, a spar manufacturer, his wife Margaret and four children lived at Pool Quay, near Welshpool. He was born in Monaghan, Ireland. The family lived in some style with a governess, a cook and a housemaid. Ten years later Margaret Maginnis appears on the census as a widow.

On the Marton census in 1871 Elizabeth Tay, farmer, hailed from Cornwall as did her two sons Stephen and John, and both were barytes miners. William Tay was a mining clerk born in Carmarthen and John Rowe, their lodger, was a mining agent also born in Cornwall. Over the next 30 years there were six barytes miners living in Marton township: William Jones, Jacob Maddox, Pryce Jones, Edward Gittens, George Blockley and Richard Williams.[16] These were local men taking up this new line of work as the opportunity arose.

Wotherton number 2 mine under the ownership of the Wotherton Barytes and Lead Mining Co. achieved a maximum production of 6,100 tons in 1901 and an average production of 3,000 tons during the period 1873-1911. There were an average of 30 employees at Wotherton increasing to 60 in 1909 when the mine was following a good run of spar.[17] Employment in the local mines was rewarded with better pay if the vein was rich, and sometimes the miners were able to influence their working life through the power of their numbers and united opposition to employers' demands.[18] It was an attractive alternative to many when compared with the prospect of a lifetime of toil on the land. Between 1851 and 1911 agricultural workers left the land at the rate of 100,000 every decade.[19] But those who stayed in agriculture did so only if their home was a decent cottage at a fair rent with a good sized garden and possibly an allotment. The hope was that one day the cottage could be turned into a smallholding and a degree of independence achieved, providing the motivation for permanence and hard work.

I recall Mrs. Nethercott telling me that she could remember seeing the lights of the miners' helmets as they were going to work in the morning at Wotherton mines. This was in the 1890s. After the shift they walked home again about three or four o'clock in the afternoon to do their own work on their smallholdings. [Mrs. Nethercott was brought up at Wotherton Hall.] (Mr. Jim Dale, 2007)

## More of the Perries

Next along in sequence was a house, with four closes adjacent, its tenant on the tithe details being Thomas Clayton. In this area also lived Jacob Maddox, his wife Mary and a son also called Jacob. He appears to be the tenant of a close and a section of Weir Meadow. In 1861 the Maddox family occupied a house, buildings and garden with two closes above the road and two below.

As the track turns uphill, a cottage stood below the road with 11 small closes situated above and below the roadway, where William and Mary Jacks lived in 1841. In the boundary hedge between the site of the cottage and Peartree Leasow is the one surviving old peartree of those which gave the area its name. Six of the small fields were arable, three pasture, one meadow and one simply 'a close'.

Finally, where the slope becomes even more precipitous and a stream flows down from the mountain, were the two cottages where Mary, Ann and Thomas Blockley lived and John and Sarah Gittens. Mary was aged 85 and 40-year-old Ann was a seamstress. Both John and Thomas were agricultural labourers.

To the north of these last homes was one other holding, accessible from the Trelystan road via the footpath past Bray's Tenement. This latter property consisting of five arable closes, five of pasture and a rough, was occupied in 1841 by 80-year-old William Bray, a shoemaker, and his wife Mary, but it was owned by Martha Wildblood. After the census of 1841 there are no Marton residents by the name of Bray on any subsequent census. A little further on was a cottage and closes, one arable, two of pasture, which was the home of Peter and Mary Corbet and their family.

With the exceptions noted above, all the tenants of the houses and small fields in this area paid rent to Thomas Thornes, Lady Edwardes and Mrs. Catherine Lloyd.[20]

## C. Stockton Wood

One of the 11 private carriage or 'occupation' roads in Marton township in 1815 passed Bray's Tenement and continued along the lower slopes of Marton Crest, running parallel with the Crest to reach three small cottages close to the Stockton boundary before continuing into present day Gunley wood (see plate 14). John Wilcox, Sarah Gardner and Catherine Davies were tenants in this remote and inaccessible part of the township in 1843. Each of the holdings had at least one close set aside for arable crops. On the census, Catherine was a laundress and Sarah was the wife of Samuel Gardner, a 35-year-old agricultural labourer. The signs of human habitation are evident in the cottage ruins and the small fields that still surround it.

On the lower slopes of this west side of the township was another cluster of cottages and their pertaining small closes. Here was Ben's Nursery which was once the home of Mr. Elvet Richards' family. In 1841 Benjamin and Elizabeth Broxton lived here tending a productive garden and three small closes laid down to arable use. Benjamin and Thomas were both agricultural labourers.

> My Dad lived along the Crest, Ben's Nursery they called it … a little holding, but I think it's gone now. There was a very good orchard there, see. This Ben's Nursery wasn't far from Brays Tenement. They had a lot of apples at Ben's Nursery. My Grandad worked at Stockton. There was an old building in the fields up above Stockton somewhere and there were cattle in them. My Dad had to go down to get swedes and mangles out of a clamp and pulp them for the cattle before he went to school. He would be 6-10 years old. He lived at The Steps once. There were Watkins at Marton Hall and at Stockton and Rhyd-y-Groes. He worked for Watkins of Stockton. He used to build the ricks at Stockton in harvest time on the roadside. You build all the walls up, the shoves [a colloquial form for sheaves] should be slanting out right to the peak to make a proper job of it to keep the water out. (Elvet Richards, 2007)

This pattern of employment and land use was also followed by Lewis Davies and John Clayton who were both living in the immediate neighbourhood with their families. Three meadows along the Aylesford Brook were included in John Clayton's holding.

Curiously, Thomas Parker and his wife who were living in this area in 1841 and again in 1851, are not mentioned in the Tithe Apportionment details, but in the process of time these three holdings became one now known as Parkers Tenement and accessed by a private lane from the Montgomery/ Shrewsbury road. A small, derelict stone dwelling to the east of Parkers Tenement now known as Birch Cottage, is the only standing and unaltered example of the many small cottages which populated the marginal areas of Marton in the 19th century. This was a larger holding in 1843 farmed by Alexander Jones, whose landlady was Mary Pugh. The original track to Birch Cottage, that also gave access to the fields alongside, was another private carriage or 'occupation' road which left the Montgomery/ Shrewsbury road by St. Luke's cottages and continued in an almost direct line to Birch Cottage. An off-shoot of this road went to The Cottage Farm.[21]

**Pen-y-Bank**
Pen-y-Bank house has its own continuous and distinct history, beginning in 1792 when John Lewis sold an area of land near Beach Dingle to Robert Sockett, yeoman, from the parish of Oswestry. One of the witnesses to this deed of sale was John Pryse, schoolmaster of Marton. Around 1807, Robert Sockett sold the property, upon which he had lately constructed a dwelling house, to Thomas Roberts Esq. from Wilmington. At the time of the sale Benjamin Sockett was living in the house. In 1818 Thomas Roberts had enlarged the holding to six parcels of land as well as the house. Some of the additional acreage he had acquired through the division and enclosure of Marton Mountain. The property was sold at this point to John Evans, wheelwright, for £182

10s. and it continued in the Evans family until 1860 when it was sold to Mr. Thomas Jones of The View. In 1841 John Evans, aged 50 and a wheelwright, and his wife Abigail were living there.[22]

## Ryecroft

The term Ryecroft on the Tithe Map seems to cover the area to the north-east of the Trelystan road where the steep ascent levels out, and after the appropriately named Ryecroft bank field on the right. The original stone cottage on the roadside, which stood on the site of the new house which was built in the latter half of the 20th century by Mr. Steven Roberts, included closes and was owned and occupied by Elizabeth Jones in 1841, aged 50, a lady of independent means. Two sons living with her were agricultural labourers and her daughter, aged 20 was a dressmaker. The next house (Upper Ryecroft) with four closes (one arable) and on the right-hand side with its own access road, was occupied by Edward and Sarah Hughes and their family, the landlord being David Hamer. Edward was a mason and 55 years old.

*The Hughes family of Ryecroft*
*Back row, left to right: Jessie, Sophia, Harry, May*
*Front row: Martha (wife), Anne, William (b.1850), Ernest, Frederick,*
*William, whose parents were James and Jane Hughes of Ryecroft, went to live at*
*Jubilee House (Marton) on his marriage to Martha*

Ryecroft holding was the Hughes' family home for many generations as far back as the 1600s according to the Trelystan church records. It was a 16-acre holding with turn out on the common. The Hughes family were masons by trade and Edward Hughes and his sons are mentioned on numerous occasions in the Trelystan church accounts in the early 1800s as doing repairs to the church and stable there. James Hughes married Jane Harper from Llanllwchiarn after a seven-year courtship. In 1841, Jane was working at The Hall farm in Marton and they were married in 1848 at St. Chad's in Shrewsbury. James built the timber hut at Trelystan in 1859-60 which served as the school. Two other properties built by the Hughes family were both in Montgomery – Tre-Llydiart, a substantial house, and the Baptist chapel which no longer exists. The family firm had other sidelines such as a monumental business and the smallholding. This smallholding made them self sufficient; they had produce from garden, orchard and livestock. When James died he had the gravestone which he had carved placed over his grave in Marton churchyard. Due to re-planning this has since been removed. (Mrs. Mari Jones, 2007)

Seiffen or Lower Ryecroft, with its surrounding small fields overlooking Pen-y-Bank, was occupied by Matthew Edwards, aged 45, wheelwright, his wife Eleanor and their family, their landlord being Arthur Lloyd Humphreys. John, aged 15, was a wheelwright's apprentice. Lower Ryecroft was originally a stone cottage with 19 acres of land. In 1843, six of the eleven closes were set with arable crops, two were roughs, two pasture and there was one meadow. This smallholding was the home of the Pritchard family in the 20th century.[23]

> We had 14 cows which had to be milked by hand. I had to milk three of them before going to school every morning. (Roy Pritchard, 2009)

**The Bytuck, Lower Hill Farm and border encroachments**
The land on the right-hand side of the road towards Trelystan and beyond Ryecroft and as far as the Welsh border was, in 1843, included in the tenancy of the Hall farm. It was newly enclosed land and farmed as one with the home farm. A house/cottage, The Bytuck, was erected sometime between 1814 and 1843 in a central position on the land to enable a farmworker to live 'on the job'. The house stood until recent years and is still remembered by the older residents in the village, but it is not named on the census as the Bytuck until 1861. Two other cottages were tucked in on the Marton side of the Welsh boundary within their own small field enclosures or closes and two more unidentified homes existed by the roadside at the point right on the border. One of the roadside houses is likely to have been Dykesford Gate mentioned in a later census. None of these houses have survived into the 21st century.

The only property on the left-hand side of the road north of Bray's Tenement other than Highgate, which is set in the middle of newly enclosed farmland in an area called the Seven Wells, is Lower Hill Farm. The surrounding land as far as Highgate was part of the Manor Farm estate in 1843 and farmed with the home farm.[24] Following the allotment of this land to the Manor in the Enclosure process it was probably thought necessary to build a house and farm buildings here for the same reasons as those which gave rise to the Bytuck.

# Chapter 15

# Just another Farming Village in Shropshire

In 1841 Marton was a Shropshire farming community very similar to many others in the county. It had the advantage of lying on a main route between Shrewsbury and Montgomery, and two inns, The Sun and The Lowerfield, provided hospitality for travellers. Both were small farms of under 30 acres as well as hostelries. But the 1840s can not have been the busiest of periods, for Mr. Griffiths at The Sun employed only one living-in servant and William Richards at The Lowerfield, who was also a maltster, had one farm servant living on the premises.[1]

| Year | Population |
|------|------------|
| 1841 | 287 |
| 1851 | 273 |
| 1861 | 279 |
| 1871 | 268 |
| 1881 | 218 |
| 1891 | 208 |
| 1901 | 160[2] |

*Population statistics for Marton Township 1841-1901*

The total population of Marton at this time was 287 – a peak not repeated again in the remaining decades of the century. Indeed there was a declining population over the next few decades, becoming more marked in the last three decades. The township was in the registration district of Montgomeryshire in the census of 1841 and 1851, but in England. In 1861 it was included in the Montgomeryshire statistics, but in Wales. Thereafter it was included under the Chirbury returns in the Forden district in England.

The community was essentially and unquestionably heavily involved in agriculture. The central years of the 19th century mark the culmination of earlier technical improvements in agriculture, particularly the four course rotation of crops: wheat, turnips, barley, grass or clover. Previously winter rations for stock consisted of hay and straw in amounts only sufficient for over wintering a few stock, the higher yielding root crops allowing more animals to be taken through the winter season. Prior to this it was the custom to slaughter the majority of the beasts in the autumn. New farm implements, such as ploughs and drills were available, and improving breeds of cattle became a matter of interest for farmers.[3]

## Montgomeryshire Smoky-faced cattle

By the mid 19th century over half the cattle in England were Shorthorn though the local strain known as the Montgomeryshire Smoky-faced breed, a good dual purpose animal, survived until the last quarter of the century. At Wilmington, Thomas Roberts advertised a bull of this breed in 1804 whilst in 1876, 12 bullocks were offered for sale at Bishop's Castle by Mr. Pugh of The Beech, Linley. The final dispersal sale of the Beech herd of Montgomeryshire Smoky-faced cattle occurred in 1885 under the hammer of Messrs. Morris and Marshall of Chirbury. It was a notable occasion with buyers from all over Shropshire attending and enjoying luncheon set out for them on the premises before the sale began. The chairman of the proceedings, Mr. Robert J. More Esq. stated that 'He could prove by most positive testimony that the family of Everall, now represented by Mr. Pugh, had, as the catalogue stated, been on the Beech Farm for more than 400 years … and that there was no reason to suppose that any other herd of cattle had been kept by them in that time. The first Herefords were known to be mottled, and, to his mind, there was a great corroboration of the descent of Herefords from Smoky-faced cattle … as even in the present breeds there occasionally appeared a smoky-faced spot'. Mr. Morris of the auctioneers added that 'This was the last pure-bred herd of this notable breed, the best all-round breed for producing milk and beef in exposed conditions and on poor pastures,' and he advised potential buyers not to neglect the opportunity of buying some of the hardiest and best cattle he knew of. Suckler cows sold for 15-25 guineas, suckler heifers for 11-27 guineas, bulls for 14-24 guineas, the total amount realised being almost £2,000.

The smoky-faced cattle story lingered on into the 20th century with a comment in C.H. Mate's *Shropshire, Part 1, Historical, Descriptive, Biographical* published in 1906:

> At Lydham Heath there still survives a herd of aboriginal cattle of the district as old as the white cattle of Chillingham. They belong to the nearly extinct smoky-faced breed of the border country of Montgomery. According to a local story a red calf with a white face was born among this breed and the farmer ordered it to be killed. His daughter begged for its life and from it descended the Herefords.

The conformation and hardy qualities of the smoky-faced Montgomeryshire cattle may have survived through the following years of cross breeding with Herefords but the famous white faces of the latter breed proved to be overwhelmingly dominant in the process and the distinctive smoky-faced cattle of Montgomery vanished completely.[4]

In other aspects of agriculture advances were made without such losses. New methods of improving soil fertility were practised. Cheap tile drains became available and the use of guano and bone meal spread. Later in the century new markets for meat and milk were opened up by an expanding rail network. It was the era of the birth of the local agricultural society and it was the age of the agricultural labourer.

In 1847 the Shrewsbury Cattle Market Act was passed to establish the Smithfield on land known as Raven Meadows. It was opened in November 1850 and marked by a big banquet presided over by the Mayor of the Borough.[5]

In 1846 the Hereford cattle Herd book was opened to establish a record of breeders and cattle.[6]

We had Hereford and Shorthorns and crossbreds years ago. We never sold milk at Ackley, it was all beef. We made a bit of butter. We sold the stock at Welshpool and Montgomery and walked them there. It was the only way. (Mr. Henry Evans, Ackley, 2007)

The farming industry in 1841 in Marton township was the direct means of livelihood for one farmer owner (possibly more), four tenant farmers, several smallholders, 18 female farm servants, and 56 male agricultural labourers, either single and living on the farm or married with a separate household.[7] If this latter situation was the case, the most fortunate had cottages with gardens and three or four small fields (closes) on which to pasture their animals, keep a pig and a few hens and at least one arable plot. (It is worth noting that anyone on the census with 30 acres, which is a small acreage in modern terms, was classified as a 'farmer', and was living and supporting a family on this land.) There are several instances where fathers and sons in the same house were both agricultural labourers.

The land had always required men in numbers to perform the seasonal tasks. At the top of the hierarchy were the ploughmen and their teams of horses, and the horsemen who cared for the power source; there were stockmen, shepherds, dairymaids and plough boys; gangs of men were needed to harvest hay and corn, to cut and reap within an uncertain length of fine weather; boys to lead the horses, pick stones and to scare off birds from the newly seeded fields; there were hedges, fences and ditches to maintain and weeds to clear from the arable fields.[8] The work was time consuming and labour intensive. Consequently, the agricultural labourers and their families by long tradition were allowed or encouraged to set up homes in the marginal land in the township, as evidenced in the Enclosure Award when it was proposed that the cottagers paid rent for their homes and plots of land. (In other areas the enclosures led to extreme hardship, loss of homes and there was no substitution for lost grazing rights). In the census of 1841 the statistics show that in Marton the agricultural labourers made up a fifth of the population, but a sobering fact is that 25 years later in 1869 a government enquiry found that labourers' cottages in Shropshire were in worse condition than in any other English county except Dorset. Families lived in wretched, dilapidated hovels containing only one bedroom, and with little hope of improvement.[9] The only period in which an agricultural labourer might be moderately well off was in his fit middle age when his older children were contributing to the family income, but in his old age he might be unfit for work, homeless, without family support and destitute – a pauper with the threat of the workhouse a permanent fear.

At the end of the 18th century oxen were still used to draw wagons on the roads around Marton, particularly heavily loaded vehicles. The toll gate fees on the Montgomery / Westbury road included a charge of 3d. for every oxen drawing a carriage. The same amount had to be paid for every horse drawing a vehicle. But horse power had many obvious advantages over oxen – the new machines could be pulled faster by horses and consequently functioned better, oxen took longer to eat and digest their food and needed more compared with a horse who ate high energy food at the beginning and end of the day's work. Inevitably the days of oxen power drew to a close, but at a slower rate in the more remote rural areas. Throughout the 19th and into the 20th century horse power reigned supreme.[10]

## Horse power as recalled today

The memories of the days when a farm's most valued asset was its horses are still there to be appreciated, as the reminiscences we collected proved.

It was all horses then. Everything was done with horses. One horse was worth as much as eight or ten cows. The railway needed horses to take stuff from the station to the towns. They were the best buyers of good horses. A horse three or four years old could make up to £100; you were lucky to get £15 for a good cow then. We bred all Shires for working and ponies for travelling on the road. All the ploughing was done with horses. You just drove them with lines, two horses to one plough and one furrow. You would have to work hard to get an acre a day done. You walk about 20 miles if you've an 11-inch furrow. (Mr. Henry Evans, 2008)

Ploughing was only one job, then you've got harrowing, sowing, drilling and the binder to lug around. There were generally four people working on the farm with my father. Not much more than now like, but they were working all the time. Now you can plough 30 acres or more in a day with a tractor. Then you were lucky to plough one acre and you were ploughing all the winter pretty well like. Some days it would be cold and wet but you would have to carry on. We had one or two men living in. (Mr. Henry Evans, 2008)

The threshing box would go from farm to farm. Everyone would have to send a horse and a man to move it. Do you know the corner from Fir House? It's a nasty corner; it's very narrow but it's better now. To get a big machine like that around the corner, well, horses didn't always work together. Some people were violent with horses, some were gentle. There were arguments: 'What are you doing to my horse?'

You had to get extra coal for the engine and make beer for the threshing day. They'd drink a lot of beer; 12 men they'd have for dinner when threshing in the winter. It was better for the stuff to be in the barn to sweat. They used to comment on the different catering round the farms. I think Lower House and Red House were quite well known for good meals, but at the Mulsop they used to cut an egg in half. (Mrs. Lil Richards, 2008)

*Pryce and Ann Bowen at Fir House, Trelystan, with children John and Margaret*

The threshing box was drawn by a portable steam engine. To start off it was drawn by horses, then we had a traction engine, then we went to a tractor in the early part of the war. We were lucky in the 1947 storm. We'd just had a couple of days threshing before the storms started. They took the threshing box to the Malthouse. They had a job to get it there because of the ice. I think they threshed and didn't get it to the Church House Farm. It was there for weeks, months. So we were right lucky with the threshing. Eight or ten horses pulled it. It was 4 or 5 tons see. Red House lane was awful muddy in those days. In winter it was bad. When they had the threshing box at Red House one man got on the front horse, riding, and one man on the shafts. That's how they took it up the lane. The rest of the men walked up the fields topside the lane because it was so dirty. It was a real bad lane. The War Ag. got the council to do our lane and Lower House, stone it. They made a firm road of it then. It was a big improvement. (Mr. Elvet Richards, 2008)

There are big farms down there near Montford Bridge, some up to 500 acres. Each farm had three teams of three and a 'cag' team, a jobber. The other three teams did all the ploughing and sowing and all that. I enjoyed the work. (Mr. Dick Roberts, retired blacksmith. 2007)

Sustaining the 19th-century farming industry in Marton were the skilled tradesmen and craftsmen most of whom lived within the village bounds and close to the toll road. The immediate needs of the small farming community could be met by the blacksmith, the carpenter/joiner, the wheelwright, the cooper, the mason and the bricklayer. Each of these trades had at least one practitioner living in Marton in 1841.

**Blacksmiths**

There were three blacksmiths in the village: John Gardner, William Rogers and Sam Roberts.

The Gardner family lived The Smithy, opposite The Sun Inn, where they were tenants until they purchased the property in 1862 for £165. It was then described as 'A comfortable cottage, smithy, cowhouse and garden containing 19 perches.'[11] This was the Gardner home on every census up to 1911 and thereafter as several current village residents can recall.

> The post office used to be part of the blacksmith's shop. Sam Gardner, the blacksmith, was getting older as I remember. He had three or four cows as well. His sister used to run the post office in a little place in the side of the kitchen. (Mr. Bob Jenkins, 2007)

> Mr. and Mrs. John Gardner moved into the Blacksmiths, they had a son and daughter, their son Sam took over from them. One of his first jobs was to fix ironwork to a drill to make a roundabout for the children at Marton sports. My father made the wooden animals for the children to sit on. My father was the carpenter and wheelwright. Emma Gardner, the daughter, married Ernest Davies who was a bricklayer; he also painted the scenery back then for the Marton pantomime. (Tom Butler's memories contributed by Mrs. Glenys Broxton, 2007)

In 1796 one of the other smithies named as such on the 1843 Tithe Map was destroyed in a fire:

> John Roberts of Marton, blacksmith did lately erect and build at his own costs and charges a dwelling house, smiths shop and cowhouse on a quillet of land (2 roods [*sic*]) where formerly stood a smith's shop which burnt down in Marton.[12]

He, and his wife Joyce, and their daughters Mary and Catherine, were given a lease of 99 years by the landowners – Robert Lloyd of Oswestry, Jenkin Parry of the County of Montgomery, Rev. Thomas Edwardes of Frodesley, Pryce Jones of Glansevern, John Smith of Dysserth, John Stephens of Welshpool – at an annual rent of 5s. 6d.

In the 20th century, this smithy became the site of a garage owned by Mr. Cyril Jones, but in due course the land was sold for building purposes. There are now three houses on the site with particularly fine views over the valley.

> Mr. and Mrs. Jones came from Rorrington to live at the Garage, they had stock wagons and used to take stock to market. My Father [Tom Butler] fitted a bus body and seats to one wagon. Mr. Jones used to run it to Welshpool on a Monday. We used to go on our yearly Sunday school trip to the seaside in the charabanc. It took us nearly all day to get there. Everyone piled on the bus, they were not too fussy where they sat, inside or out, as long as they got there. (Mrs. Glenys Broxton, 2007)

*This is the last cart, built in 1956, made by Mr. Dick Roberts, blacksmith and wheelwright at Montford Bridge. It is a Scots tipping cart used for carrying turnips, muck etc.*
*The back board is loose and can be removed for the tipping process. It has loose boards on the sides for extra height for bigger loads. It was made for Lewis Edwards of Leaton (whose name is in the side of cart). Such carts would have been a familiar sight on the lanes and fields of Marton*

William Rogers, a 65-year-old blacksmith in 1841, had a house, a garden and a smithy at the southern end of the village, but after 1841 neither this blacksmith nor his smithy are mentioned in any subsequent census.

The blacksmith's shop was often the hub of village affairs, an informal meeting place for the exchange of news and gossip especially if it was located near the village shops and the local Inn. There's not been a working smithy in Marton since the second half of the 20th century, though the name with the memories remain to identify the site of Sam Gardner's old smithy. The work of a blacksmith had its challenges as recalled by Mr. Dick Roberts, who practised his trade at Montford Bridge before retiring to Marton:

In the morning there'd be nine horses sometimes waiting to be shod. They'd come early, seven o'clock, to try and get first. I used to go to work some mornings at six o'clock. We used to have to make all the shoes, but after a good many years a firm called Rogers and Jackson used to send a salesman round. They started to make horseshoes then. Almost all the farm horses wore six-inch shoes. You measured a horse's foot for his shoe across the hoof and three times that. If he wanted toeing and heeling you had to add two inches more. If you had shoes from the firm you only had to toe and heel them. I made some shoes for a mule in the war but never got them on him. He'd kick the life out of you. He had an arrow stamped on his backside. A smallholder had got a mare and I never got any shoes on her, nor nobody did, on the back feet. I got kicked once on that knee, I feel it a bit now. But they get used to it after they've had a set put on. (2008)

## Wheelwrights and Carpenters

Equally important in this age of carts, carriages, wagons, drays, traps and all the other two and four wheeled horse drawn vehicles in general use, were the village carpenters and wheelwrights. William Rogers, aged 50, was a carpenter living in the village next door to Richard Hammond, joiner. Matthew Edwards, aged 45, a wheelwright lived at Ryecroft with his family, one son John being an apprentice wheelwright. John Evans, aged 50, was also a wheelwright in 1841. Thirty years later Thomas Butler and his family appear on the Marton census:

> My Grandad was a wheelwright, carpenter, undertaker and blacksmith at Chirbury before we moved back to Marton where he continued his trade. When we took over Jubilee House in 1920 it used to be a Butchers and slaughter house, also a stores and a cobblers shop. Jubilee House was built at the time of Queen Victoria's Jubilee, thus the name. It was built by a Mr. William Hughes and my grandfather, another Mr. Thomas Butler. My grandfather had a carpenter and wheelwright's shop at the back of Upper Shop, Marton. He made a rack saw bench that we used to saw coffin boards, also a lathe for turning a block of wood into a stock for a wagon wheel. (Memoirs of Tom Butler)

If one conclusion is obvious from the censuses in the 19th century, it is that frequently the skills of the father were passed on to the son, often to the grandson, sometimes to a fourth generation. This inevitably created a stable community, a trusted workforce and an assured place in society for those sons willing to step into their fathers' shoes.

*Jubilee House, built at the time of Queen Victoria's Jubilee and in its time a butcher's and slaughter house, stores and cobblers and home of Tom Butler, wheelwright*

Plate 1  *The village of Marton and Marton Pool seen from the air.*
*(Photo courtesy of Maldwyn Colley)*

Plate 2  *The 1908 log boat found at Marton Pool is in the foreground of this picture*

*Plate 3  A group of items (burial urns and food vessels) from the Trelystan dig now in the Powysland Museum, Welshpool. (Photo courtesy of CPAT)*

*Plate 4  Trelystan Bronze Age Burial site, Long Mountain, during excavation in 1979. (Photo courtesy of CPAT)*

*Plate 5  The earthworks of Stockton Iron Age hill fort seen from the air, with Pentrenant Farm in the foreground. (Photo courtesy of CPAT)*

*Plate 6  River Camlad and Rhyd-y-Groes flatlands looking towards Marton*

Plate 7  *St Mary's Church, Trelystan*

Plate 8  *Thomas Bray 1658-1730, founder of the Society for Promoting Christian Knowledge. (Photo by Picture Partnership, reproduced by kind permission of SPCK)*

Plate 10 Hatchment in St Michael's Church Chirbury relating to the death of male
member of the Pryce family of Gunley showing the coat of arms in his ancestry:
1 - a lion passant between three fleur de lys; 2 - two crescents and three annulets
on a bend; 3 - three nags heads argent erased (the link with the Lloyd family);
4 - three boars' heads. The blank (sinister) side indicates he leaves a surviving wife.
The motto reads 'There is peace in Heaven'

Plate 11 A bold cross is landowner John Bowdler's signature on the Enclosure Award
document drawn up by the Commissioner Mr. William Jones of Garthmyl in 1815

Plate 9 (opposite) The sundial erected by Richard Lloyd of Marrington in 1595 now
in the Lodge garden at Marrington, inscribed 'from dai to dai these shades do flee
and so this life passeth awaie'. This sundial incorporates several coat of arms, one of
which is the arms of the de Boulers (Bowdler) family

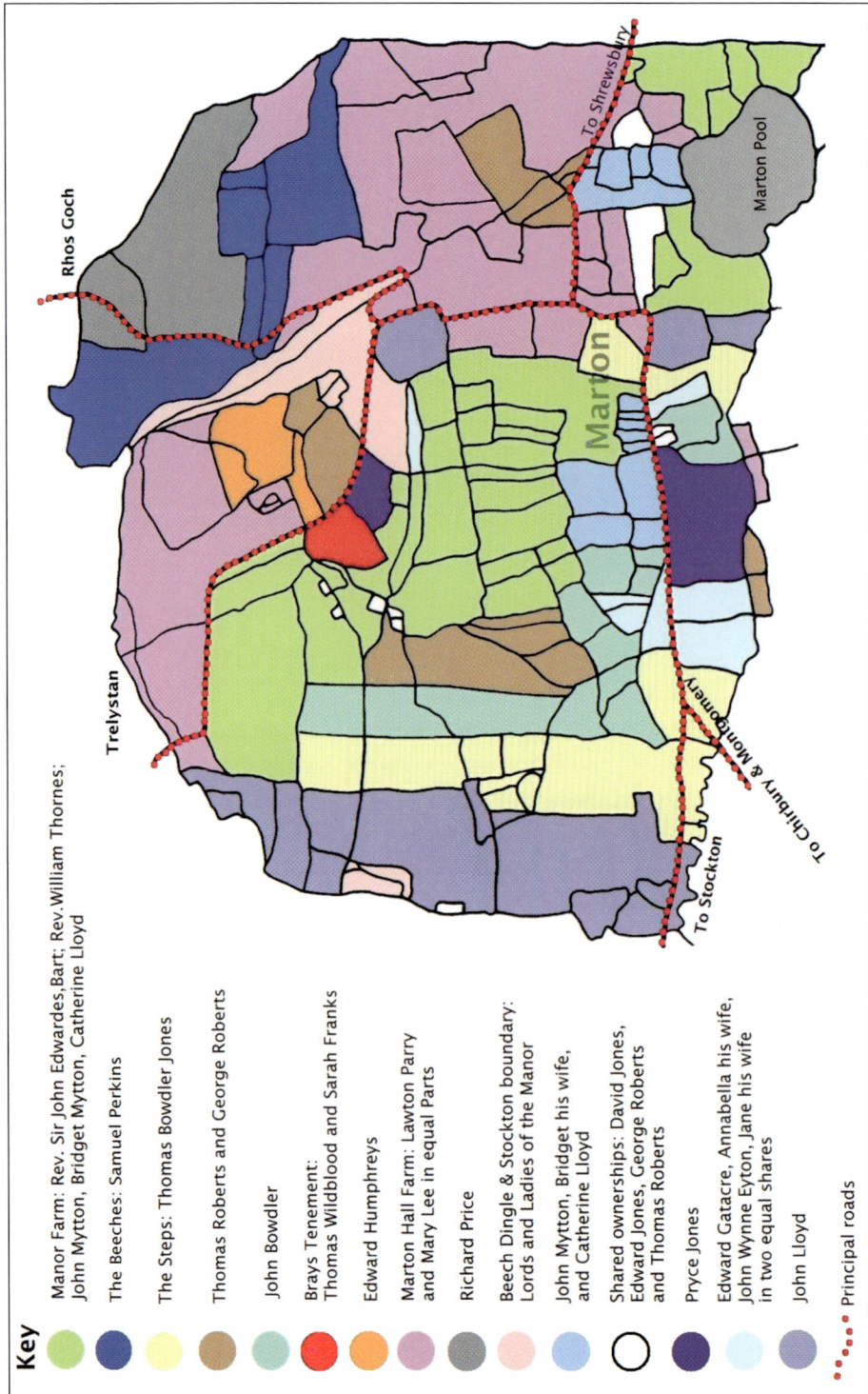

## Key

**Manor Farm:** Rev. Sir John Edwardes, Bart; Rev.William Thornes; John Mytton, Bridget Mytton, Catherine Lloyd

**The Beeches:** Samuel Perkins

**The Steps:** Thomas Bowdler Jones

Thomas Roberts and George Roberts

John Bowdler

**Brays Tenement:** Thomas Wildblood and Sarah Franks

Edward Humphreys

**Marton Hall Farm:** Lawton Parry and Mary Lee in equal Parts

Richard Price

**Beech Dingle & Stockton boundary:** Lords and Ladies of the Manor

John Mytton, Bridget his wife, and Catherine Lloyd

**Shared ownerships:** David Jones, Edward Jones, George Roberts and Thomas Roberts

Pryce Jones

Edward Gatacre, Annabella his wife, John Wynne Eyton, Jane his wife in two equal shares

John Lloyd

Principal roads

*Plate 12 Land Ownership following the 1815 Enclosure Award*

*Plate 13  The Manor House shown on Mr. Meredith's map of Mr. Thorne's estate in Marton 1806*

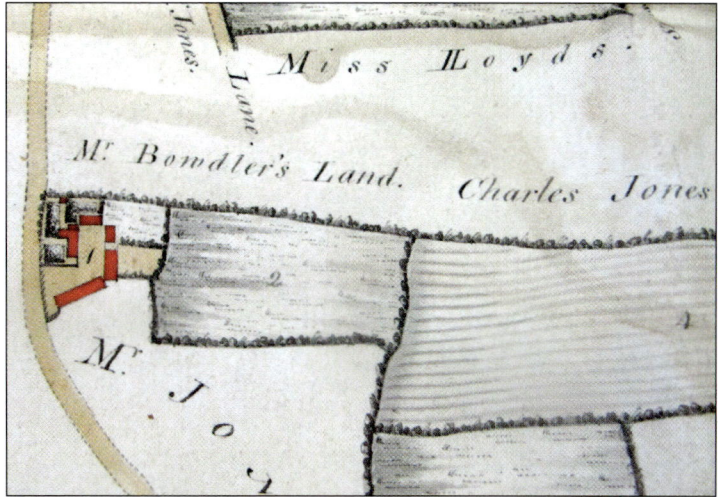

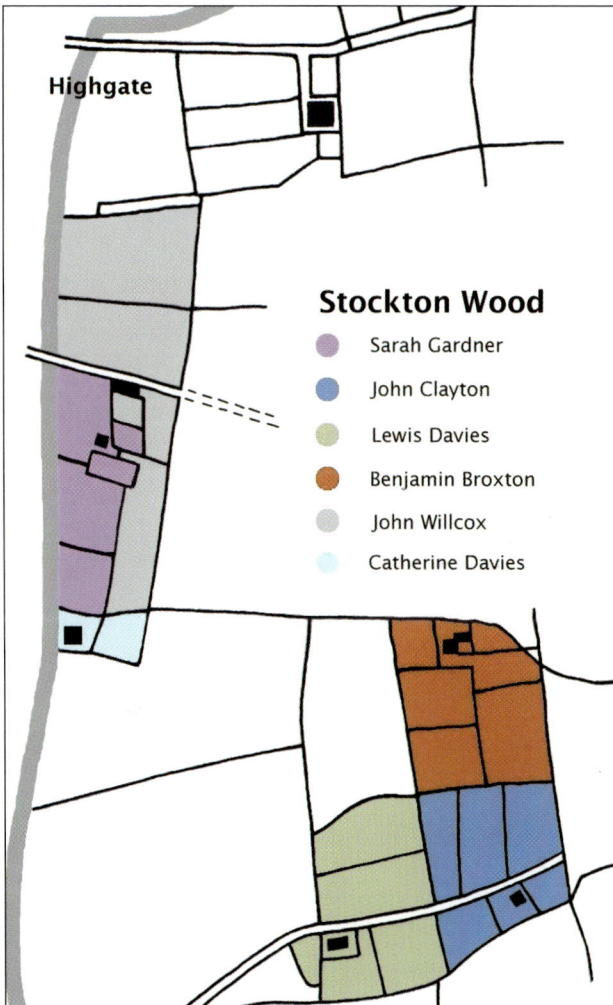

Highgate

Stockton Wood

Sarah Gardner

John Clayton

Lewis Davies

Benjamin Broxton

John Willcox

Catherine Davies

*Plate 14  Stockton holdings, one of three settlements now deserted shown on the 1843 Tithe Apportionment Map*

*Plate 15  Beach Dingle, one of three settlements now deserted shown on the 1843
Tithe Apportionment Map*

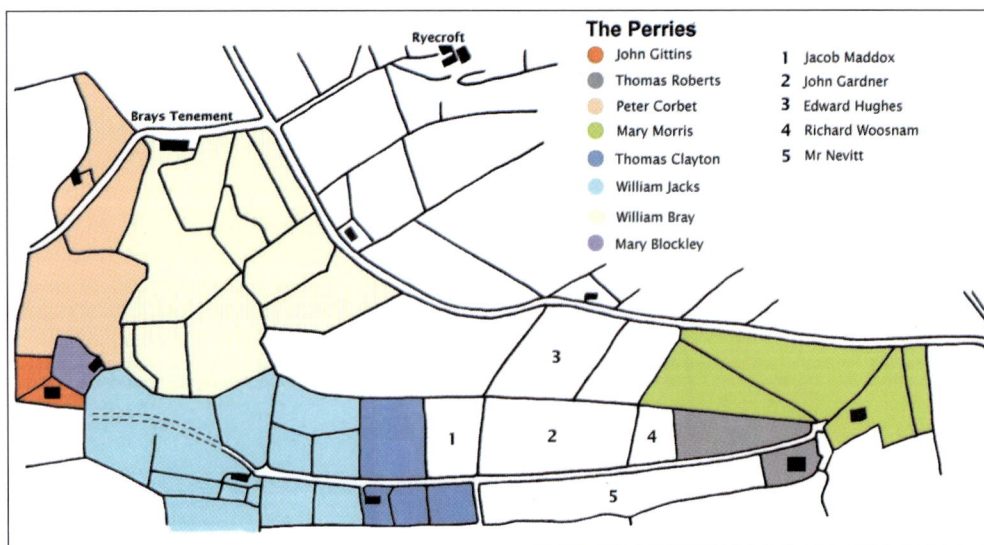

*Plate 16  The Perries, one of three settlements now deserted shown on the 1843
Tithe Apportionment Map*

*Plate 17  Perrys Cottage, now unoccupied*

*Plate 18  Now a private house this building was once the 'Upper' Shop
kept by Dick Oliver and his family*

Plate 19 From: 'A New Map of the county of SALOP, Divided into hundreds. Printed for C. Smith. No 172 Strand January 6th 1804. 2nd Edition, Corrected to 1808.' The turnpike road and milestones from Shrewsbury to Montgomery are clearly marked

*Plate 20  The Lowfield in the late 19th century, then known as the New Inn*

*Plate 21  The Lowfield shortly before demolition started in 2007*

*Plate 22  Marton Village Hall prior to demolition, 2009*

*Plate 23  New Village Hall*

*Plate 24  The Congregational Church Manse*

*Plate 25  Peter White is welcomed home to Marton*
*at the end of the Second World War. Photograph taken outside The Sun Inn*

*Plate 26  Following a slap-up tea in the Village Hall senior citizens enjoy a singalong. At the back, left to right, are Doreen Bowen, Audrey Evans and Laura Yapp. In the foreground are Lil and Elvet Richards*

*Plate 27  Chirbury and Marton Young Farmers, Dan Powell, Richard Breeze and Huw Thomas at the West Mid Show 2008*

Plate 28  Members of Chirbury and Marton YFC in the 'Magic Tractor' 2006.
Left to right: Gary Hockly, Harry Trow, Huw Thomas, Kathryn Lewis, Chris Davies,
Ian Millington, Katie Wyke, Rachel Mountford, Dan Powell, Tanya Francis,
James Jones, Richard Breeze, Andrew Evans

Plate 29  David Trow,
Maureen Jenkins, Christine
Richards and Liz Tuffin

*Plate 30  After much hard work
and commitment Marton's Lottery
bid is successful, 2009.
From left to right:
Hilaire Pugh, Graham Sheen,
Maureen Jenkins and David Yapp*

*Plate 31  The tranquil waters of Marton Pool*

## Coopers

The family of coopers in Marton were in 1841 led by David Oliver, aged 60. His son John was also a cooper. The barrels or casks were produced in varying sizes: firkins, kegs, butts, churns, tubs and pails were required for storing, carrying and packing goods for everyday use and for travel thus ensuring a constant demand which a successful cooper could turn into a relatively comfortable lifestyle. All manner of goods required safe storage: dry goods, flour, eggs, cereals, fruit and liquids like milk beer and oil. A cooper might specialise in producing one type of cask for wet goods (tight work) or casks for dry powdery items (dry tight work). An experienced cooper would measure by eye, test a finished cask by ear and use as many as 25 tools in the production of a single cask.[13] It may have been a natural progression for the cooper's shop to eventually become the village grocer's shop, for in the census of 1861 John Oliver's occupation is given as grocer. Another ten years on and he has a different occupation, that of 'relieving officer' (an official responsible for the welfare of the poor, both collecting money and distributing it to the needy). The other family members were still running the grocer's shop which, in 1901 also included managing the post office. The property was one of 12 lots sold in 1862. It was described thus:

> A commodious messuage or dwelling house and shop, bakehouse, large oven, convenient stabling, yard and garden containing 15 perches or thereabouts be

*A wedding party leaves Marton Villages Stores in April 1887, on the occasion of the wedding of Arthur Jarmen and Amelia Jane Oliver. In 1891 they were living in Kingston upon Hull where Arthur was secretary to the Hull Rope Works Company. The building, excepting its modern extension, is much the same as it is today*

the same more or less, in the holding of Mr. John Oliver and is situate opposite to the Sun Inn in the village of Marton.[14]

The village stores continued to be run by the Oliver family and their descendants until the late 20th century:

> On Fridays we delivered groceries up Marton Hill, by the Perries to Church House, across the top and then back down the Beeches. That took us from 10am until 4pm. We started with a car, then later we had a van.
>
> On Saturdays we did Brockton and Rowley. That was a very big round. It took until 5 pm or 6pm to finish. Wednesdays you were getting ready for Thursday. Thursdays you did Friday's orders and so on. There were always three or four people working in the shop, never less than two unless it was just me. Wednesday morning there was just one person on but I was in the house doing the Post Office accounts.
>
> Monday we went off shopping all day. The girls would clean the fridges and the shop while we were shopping. On Tuesday we would have to put it all away. Different people came to help us, including youngsters on government schemes, but we couldn't really afford to give them a full time job afterwards. We had quite a few local part-time staff. Usually we fed everyone at home and took turns to do the cooking. (Mrs. Sally Pugh, 2007)

*Marton Stores in the 1960s*

This Oliver family has a long connection with Marton and members of the family continue to play a large part in village life today. The shop however has changed hands twice in recent years and is currently managed by Mrs. Margaret Evans from Lake View, Marton and her sister, Mrs. Barbara Morris from Brockton. There is a part-time hosted Post Office service and a range of groceries, fruit, vegetables, meats, takeaway snacks and daily papers available in the shop.

## The Upper Shop

Returning to 1841, the census shows there was another shopkeeper in Marton, Thomas Evans, and subsequently *Bagshaw's Directory* in 1851 mentions Joseph Gough and in 1881 William Hughes, as grocer and builder. In the next census in 1891, John Oliver, his wife Harriet and their family are noted as village residents and his occupation that of grocer. (A relationship between the two Oliver families of Marton has yet to be proved.) John and Harriet lived at the Upper Shop (see plate 18) which is set back from the road on high ground, with sheds and buildings alongside for storage of 'bag stuff,' a general term used to describe animal feed which their son Dick began selling in the 20th century.

Old John Oliver baked bread in a wood-fired oven in the kitchen. The shop had a zinc-topped counter on which everything was weighed on a large brass

*Sally and Hilaire Pugh are presented with gifts and a certificate on leaving the shop in 1997. Left to right: Hilaire Pugh, Sally Pugh, Pat Davies and Angela Bishop*

*John and Harriet Oliver, and later their son Dick kept the 'Upper' Shop selling animal feed and groceries*

scales – sugar (wrapped in blue paper), butter, cheese, lard etc. The Olivers ran a smallholding and also a thriving animal feed stuff business, One of the excitements of the week was to watch the Foden steam engine of Peate's the Millers of Oswestry reversing up the steep slope from the road to the granary. (Mr. I. G Griffiths, 2008)

Auntie May and Uncle Dick Oliver were both single when I knew them. We used to come for holidays. Uncle Dick used to come to Welshpool on the Monday we were coming over to Marton with his motor bike and sidecar. Then we'd both get into the sidecar with our little cases or whatever we'd got our clothes in and off we'd go to Marton. There we were with our hair blowing all over because there was no shield or anything. We'd get to Marton and Auntie May would say 'You be careful Dick, now you be careful'. Making bread, well, it was chaos then. He used to 'tice us to go down. He'd slice the dough and then say 'Now you smell how nice that bread is'. Well, of course the gas went up your nose. He'd hold your head down 'till you had a good sniff. It would nearly knock your head off. He used to sprinkle a bit of flour on us. We being naughty would get a handful and throw it back. Bang. Poor Auntie May would come in the middle of it. She'd be beside herself. (Miss Nesta Lewis, 2007)

He decided one morning that we should take the horse up to the field up Mill lane. So he gets both of us and sits us on this horse. 'You know where to go, don't you? Because I've taken you before up there'. 'Yes', 'Well, just put it in the field'. 'Right'.

So he starts us off from the shop, Auntie May saying, 'You shouldn't do this with them', and wringing her hands, 'They'll come to harm'.

Off we went jigging and jogging up to Mill Lane. Then we had to decide who was going to get off to open the gate, or how otherwise we were we going to open the gate. So we'd got to fall off or get near enough to the gate to undo it. Anyway unknown to us Dick had gone up the field at the back of the shop to see we were all right. He was killing himself with laughter at us trying to open the gate. Anyway he had to come to our rescue in the end and opened the gate himself to let the horse in. (Miss Nesta Lewis, 2007)

There was a bread oven at the back of the house. That's where we used to start our Pantomime practices. We used to think it was lovely to go in the bakehouse than to go down to the old hall in the cold. There was always heating in the bakehouse. (Miss Peggy Pryce, 2008)

## Village Carrier

The variety and number of craftsmen, tradesmen and women living within the township is typical of 19th-century village life. Almost all the needs of the farm and individuals could be met within the small population of Marton. It was village self sufficiency with one notable exception – the village lacked a working mill, the nearest being at Worthen, Stockton or Chirbury.

Usually there was one individual who was equipped with a sturdy horse and cart to make the difficult trips to collect or deliver people and goods between Marton and the towns of Shrewsbury, Welshpool and Bishop's Castle.[15] In the 1840s John Oliver had added this sideline to his main occupation, Welshpool being his destination on Mondays and Saturdays. By 1850 his itinerary included Shrewsbury, his drop-of and collection point being The Queens Head, Churchstoke, Chirbury and Newtown (The Raven). Moving forward ten years, the job had become a fulltime occupation for local carrier and 'higgler' John Edwards.[16] The higglers were middlemen – they went round the farms of the local area, buying up produce such as poultry, rabbits, eggs and cheese to sell in the market. In return they supplied goods the household needed. Some of the trade was done by barter rather than by money changing hands, but all of it involved haggling hence the term 'higgler'.[17]

## Shoemakers

Three shoemakers and one apprentice made a living in the village in 1841. William Turner, aged 40, lived near the village centre, then there was the elderly William Bray, and the very young Thomas Corbet, aged 15, whilst Samuel Willcox, aged 12, was a shoemaker's apprentice. After 1841, the role of the village shoemaker was taken on by Richard Wilcox from Kerry who employed three men, one being his brother, also from Kerry. Richard was described in a later census as a shoe manufacturer. This family was still in Marton in 1901 when Edwin Wilcox's occupation was a boot- and shoemaker and they lived at Jubilee House. William Jacks was also a boot- and shoemaker in Marton at the turn of the 20th century. He lived at Holmwood House before moving to Wotherton. His great-granddaughter Diane Jacks (now deceased) recalled the following memory in her book, *Growing up on a Shropshire Farm*:

I think he had a club foot, but I'm not sure. When he was a boy they lived at Middleton and his mother used to borrow a donkey to take him to the Royal Salop Infirmary in Shrewsbury. She walked and he rode the nearly 20 miles each way.

## Poverty and the Forden Union

There must have been families living in Marton who existed in destitution in the early part of the century, but not until the 1861 census is there an example of such poverty – a child born in the Forden workhouse but living with grandparents. Ten years later there are five paupers living in Marton township, three in 1881 then no more paupers are mentioned, although the description 'no known occupation' is often used in the case of elderly spinsters or widows living alone. The lot of Thomas Bishop, a 90 year old former agricultural labourer noted in the 1881 census is perhaps typical. At the end of his life he lived alone in a poor rented cottage near Jubilee House dependent on the assistance of the retired local vicar, Rev. Pulley, who noted: 'As long as we were at Marton we looked after him. I have just been ordering him 8cwt of coal for next Monday.' As it happened the coal was not required, for within a day or two the

*Dated 1886 this letter to Mr. Bowdler reflects the poverty of the time particularly among farmworkers. Thomas Bishop, aged 90 on the 1881 census will end his days in the workhouse. His neighbour, Mr. Jones, is very keen to have first refusal of the old man's tumbledown house. (Courtesy S. Pugh)*

roof collapsed on Thomas Bishop's house. In spite of Thomas' great age he survived and was taken to the Union workhouse at Forden by Mr. Oliver, the Relieving Officer, where he ended his days. Thomas' tragedy was seen as an opportunity by another Marton resident, Mr. Jones from Chapel House, who immediately applied to the landlord to take over the tenancy of the cottage.[18]

In the early years of the 20th century the Forden workhouse was the ultimate fate for the destitute in Marton and elsewhere, not merely the elderly or ill. As a child Mr. Henry Evans walked from Ackley to Forden to attend school and remembers meeting several of those who had stayed overnight in the workhouse, or hospital as it was known in later years:

> We walked of course and we were never late for school. It took an hour to get there. Morning and night we met the tramps, people who had been for a night's lodging at Forden Hospital. There'd be forty or fifty people on the road coming in droves. They'd got no homes and no work. They couldn't stop at the same place for two nights running so they walked to the next place at Craven Arms or Bishop's Castle or Newtown. At night we would meet them coming to Forden. There were whole families, children and all. It was a terrible thing to see. They would work if they could get it but people could not afford to pay them. There was only agriculture or the railways. (Mr. Henry Evans 2008)

Poverty continued to rear its ugly head well into the 20th century, and the following extract from the School Log book in November 1930 is salutary:

> Letter from office stating that neglected or shoeless children are not to be refused admission but should be brought to the notice of the Relieving Officer. One family is a constant source of worry in this respect and a considerable hindrance to the work of the school in mornings. I had frequently to supply footwear to the girls before they can sit at their desks and therefore thought I was justified in excluding them. Boots have twice been provided for them.[19]

## Dressmakers, tailors and milliners

On a lighter note, Marton had its full share of dressmakers, seamstresses, tailors and milliners from 1841 onwards. The seamstresses and tailors were professional women and men who had served an apprenticeship to learn their trade working alongside a master tailor and usually living with the family while doing so. The Powell family were in Marton in 1841 making a living in this trade, and in 1861 William Powell was described as a master tailor employing two men. The art of the tailor was in taking the client's measurements accurately, pattern making and in hand sewing until the Singer treadle machine came into common use in the second half of the century. Both sexes would visit their tailor for formal suits and coats and jackets. Men wore best or Bedford breeches in tweed or drab cord, sometimes with a particular type of pocket with a flap to hold cash, barathea trousers and also army breeches – to name but a few of the various styles and materials the local tailor could manufacture.[20] In the early

20th century the well-turned-out farmer could be seen in breeches, polished leather gaiters and boots driving a smart pony and trap to Montgomery, accompanied by his wife with eggs, butter and cheese to sell in the market or to the Co-op where she would buy the necessities to supplement her home-made bottled, salted and otherwise preserved produce stored in her larder and dairy. Often the farmer's wife depended on the sale or her eggs and other produce for the week's housekeeping money, so the journey to town to sell her wares was essential whatever the weather and road conditions. When Marton could boast of its own charabanc for the weekly trip to market, the ladies quickly took the opportunity to travel in relative comfort.

> Jack Jones from Holmwood had a bus. There was no other way of going into Shrewsbury. He used to run the bus on a Saturday. It was a great but rickety old thing. There were no cars you see. Cyril, Jack's son had a garage lower down the village. Mother used to go to market and take eggs and butter on the bus, bread as well. It picked people up on the way to Shrewsbury, all the farmers' wives. (Mrs. Ruby Bourne, 2008)

> Montford Bridge, 1947 winter.
> We were cut off for three weeks so we walked to the bakery to collect a bag of loaves. All the women were waiting in the square by the church. We emptied them out and they all went. There was none left for us so we had to go back again. There were no snow ploughs. They did buy an old tractor and got some sleepers, put them together and cleared the road down to the A5. We had a lot of hard winters without snow so we had to put frost nails on the horses so the farmers' wives could go to market on Saturdays and Wednesdays to take their eggs and butter to Shrewsbury. (Mr. Dick Roberts, 2008)

> My Grandfather John Jones was a baker. His family owned the village shop in Rorrington and had done for many years. Eventually he opened the garage in Marton and ran it until he retired and sold it to Potters in about 1954/55. I lived at The School House in Marton from 1945 to around 1953. (Mrs. Diana Coles, 2009)

Lydia Jones, dressmaker, and Ann Blockley, seamstress, also plied their trades in Marton in 1841, but oddly 20 years later, when the Powell business was in full swing, there was neither dressmaker nor seamstress in Marton but there were five washer-women. In 1871 the dressmaking trade was flourishing again, perhaps because the Powell family had moved their business to Chirbury. Harriet Maddox was one of the three lady dressmakers for the fashionable ladies in Marton but the enterprising wife of John Oliver at the grocer's shop, Amelia Oliver, had started up a millinery sideline in her spare time that was taken over in later years by her two daughters, Lucy and Isabel. Either the demand for posh hats faded away or the grocery shop business expanded, because by the end of the century both ladies were working in the shop as assistants. Unrecorded but presumed are the many mums and daughters who made up their own clothes out of necessity or choice. Sewing was a skill girls learnt both at home and in school through plain sewing and making samplers in which they could practise a variety of stitches.

Diane Jacks gives a vivid description of her grandparents' life on the farm at Stockton between 1912 and 1918, and of her grandmother's childhood clothes she says,

> The girls wore white pinafores with frills and yokes to go to school and dark pinafores at home. These dresses were made at home but they were the best dressed children around except those from Marton Hall. Underneath the pinafores were starched petticoats, calico chemises and knickers all frilled and flounced. They had liberty bodices and knitted stockings. In summer they had tussore silk dresses for best and in winter they had tailor made grey coats from the Royal Welsh warehouse in Newtown from cloth made in Newtown. They would be taken there to be measured and fitted.[21]

A last word on the subject is fittingly from a direct descendant of Amelia Oliver.

> We used to make our own clothes from a very early age. Mum would take us to Welshpool to the Town Hall market and buy the material. We made our own skirts and dresses, which kept us busy and saved money. We were dab hands at running up a skirt. We used to make those net petticoats, layers and layers of them. (Mrs. Sally Pugh, 2007)

**Early education**

The Dame schools of the 19th century have a poor reputation for teaching reading and writing skills at a very rudimentary level. The 'Dame', often elderly, taught children who were too young to work in the fields in a corner of her own home for 3d. or 4d. per week. She provided more of a child care facility for parents who were obliged to leave their children whilst they went to work in the fields, than a good grounding in the three Rs. But this is a generality and there were exceptions. In 1841 there was a schoolmistress in Marton, Susannah Jones, aged 35, who lived with her five children aged nine and under, an elderly independent relative, Evan Jones (her brother?), a Dissenting Minister and a servant girl. The quality of the education she provided is unknown, but the household situation bears little resemblance to the general description of Dame schools of that period. But the family moved on and by 1851 the parents of Marton who wished to give their youngsters even a basic education locally had a choice between Mary Matthews, aged 50, living alone and Sarah Jones, aged 75, also living alone but both better candidates for the 'Dame' qualification. Those parents who had the means could send their children to Chirbury village school by pony trap or horseback, and in later days by bicycle.

Rev. John P. Jones from Denbighshire was minister of the Independent Church in Marton. Providence House, the church manse, does not appear on the census until 1861 when yet another Welsh-born Dissenting minister, the Rev. Richard Lloyd and his wife and family were living there. The next decade produced Forster's Education Act and elementary education for children aged between 5 and 12. This Act became law in 1870 a few years after the foundation, in 1864, of Marton School, which was a church school. The headmistress in 1871 was Sarah Bayliss from Halesowen and the school had a boarder, John Bunner. By this year the Anglican church in Marton had been constructed together with a comfortable vicarage overlooking the pool. Rev. Harry Pulley from Middlesex was the first incumbent. Following the usual tradition of the era, the Congregational church minister was a Welshman, the Rev. William Bowen.

# Chapter 16

# Highways

When the Bishop's Castle Turnpike Trust was set up in 1768[1] the improvements made along the section of the road from Montgomery to Westbury would have encouraged better communications, more travellers and consequently more investment in hostelries alongside the turnpike road to accommodate the increase in traffic (see plate 19). The Trusts also erected milestones along the highway to facilitate travellers. The later type of milestones were often made of stone with a cast iron front plate, two of which have survived on the outskirts of Montgomery marking the distance to the town and to Shrewsbury in the opposite direction. There were two milestones in Marton township, one near Lukes Cottages and the other near the Lowfield. These would have also only marked the distances to Shrewsbury and Montgomery.

The Act of Parliament establishing the Trust empowered Trustees to build toll-houses and gates and charge passing travellers to raise money for the road's improvement. Tollhouses were built on the Chirbury road on the outskirts of Montgomery and at the first road junction on the south-west side of Westbury, where the Montgomery section joined the Westbury/Shrewsbury turnpike road.

Anyone refusing to pay the tolls or evading the tollgate was dealt with severely. Any animals involved could be seized and sold, the charges deducted and the 'overplus' returned to the owner. Charges were:

1. For any horse, mare, gelding, mule or ass drawing a carriage    4d.
2. Every ox or cattle drawing a carriage    3d.
3. Every horse, mare, gelding etc. unladen    1½d.
4. A drove of oxen or cattle    10d. per score.
5. A drove of calves, hogs, swine, sheep or lambs    5d. per score.

The Bishop's Castle second district Act allowed Trustees to improve the section of road from Gunley through to Marton. This was probably the Act which produced the Tollhouse on the Marton / Stockton boundary. Three of the Trustees of this Tollhouse were Thomas Thornes, Lady Edwardes and Mrs. Catherine Lloyd, all lords and ladies of the Manor of Marton.[2] To qualify as a Turnpike Trustee a man or woman had to have a yearly minimum income of £80 from rents or be the owner of real estate to the value of £2,000. (These qualifications varied between Trusts.) The Aylesford Gate as it was called, made returns for 1860 of £85 and in 1866, £60.[3]

A further Act of Parliament divided the area covered in the first Act of 1768 into three districts. The Montgomery / Westbury road through Marton which was originally in the Bishop's Castle Second District was included with the Montgomeryshire Second District in the annual returns to Parliament for Montgomeryshire. New trustees were appointed, among them John Lloyd, George Lloyd and Thomas Jones of Marton. The toll gate charges increased also:

| | |
|---|---|
| For any horse, mare gelding, mule or ass drawing a carriage | 6d. |
| Every ox or cattle drawing a carriage | 4d. |
| Every horse, mare gelding etc. unladen | 2d. |
| A drove of oxen or cattle | 1s. 8d. per score. |
| A drove of swine, calves, sheep | 10d. per score.[4] |

Ideally the annual sum of the tolls in a district should have been used to pay, firstly, the interest of the debt incurred in setting up the Trust at the outset, secondly, the salaries of the officers of the Trust and thirdly for repairs and maintenance of the roads. All the roads in a district should have had a fair share of the funds. If the funds did not stretch to repairs, the local magistrates could resort to the tithes or the highway rate introduced in 1835.[5] Though this was the ideal scenario, often the Turnpike Trusts were in debt and obliged to borrow further sums of money from their trustees to balance their budgets. Tollgate keepers were not popular in their local communities. Understandably travellers resented having to pay tolls for previously free passage, particularly if the journey was a weekly or twice weekly necessity. In some instances the gate keepers were scorned by their neighbours and ostracised. Nonetheless it was a paid position and added an extra income into the family budget if the lady of the house was prepared to take it on.[6]

The Tithe map and schedule of 1843 show the Aylesford toll house in position on the Stockton township boundary. The census of 1861 states that Edward Williams, an agricultural labourer, and his wife Mary, the tollgate keeper, lived at Aylesford Gate. In 1871 Richard Broxton, another agricultural labourer, and his wife lived at Aylesford Gate, and again it was the lady of the house, Mrs. Broxton, who was the tollgate keeper. After 1871 the tollhouse disappears from the census. Today a lay-by is the only indication that there was a tollgate cottage on this site.

When the royal mail coaches were introduced in 1784, the average speed of coaches was 7-8 mph in summer and 5 mph in winter. The turnpike trusts gradually improved the roads and communications so that averages had risen to 10 mph by 1837. This rate of travel was a killing pace for the coach horses who would often be sold on after their prime years. In London a dealer named Hobson collared the market in ex-coach horses, buying up all such and giving his own customers little choice, hence the phrase 'Hobson's choice'. Mail coaches required a change of horses, usually four, every ten miles, but for steep gradients and notoriously bad going more horses joined the team. There was only one post office employee on the coach and he was armed and carried a horn to warn other road users to keep out of the way and to signal to tollkeepers to open the gate and let the coach through. The other travellers were paying passengers. As the coach passed through villages where it didn't stop, the guard threw out bags of letters to the letter receiver or post master.[7]

There was no shortage of opportunities for journeying along the turnpike road in Marton, to and from Shrewsbury or Montgomery, providing the fare was paid and a certain degree of discomfort endured. A traveller in 1815 complained, 'Once you crawled and were overset gently; now you gallop and are bashed to atoms'.[8] Speed and time keeping were a matter of pride for the coachmen and the companies that employed them. *Pigot's Directory* for 1828-9 records that a post coach to Montgomery and Worthen left The Talbot Inn in Shrewsbury every Saturday evening at 4pm. The same directory for 1835 mentions the *Sovereign* coach that left The Dragon Inn, Montgomery, every Saturday morning at 7am for Shrewsbury. The *Post Office Directory* of 1856 notes that a coach (Powell's) that ran from Newtown to Shrewsbury passed through Marton every Monday, Wednesday and Friday, returning on alternate days. Carriers between Newtown, Montgomery and Shrewsbury also passed through the village, and Marton had its own carrier for many years.

*This milestone stands exactly one mile from Montgomery and marks the route of the Turnpike Road through Chirbury and Marton to Shrewsbury*

> Sam Gardner had a carrier's cart, so I was told, and he used to take it to Welshpool. They would go up Rhyd-y-Groes on the way there and back by way of the Vron, because it was too much for the pony.
> My father-in-law was the Lengthsman on the road from the Marton turn to Hockleton Farm. He used to have two red flags [to act as a warning], a handcart,

broom and shovel to keep the roadside verges tidy. It was his job to paint the white lines and clean out the drains. The other Lengthsman was Percy Hughes from the Chapel House in Marton. (Mrs. Gwen Evans, 2007)

# Chapter 17

# The Village Inns

### The Sun Inn

The sign of The Sun is one of the oldest inn signs with its origins deep in the past. It appears to be synonymous with the bountiful gifts of the earth derived from the life giving heat of the sun. The rays spreading from the sun's circumference are traditionally wavy, designed to show that light and heat spread out from the centre.[1] The Sun sign is particularly appropriate for one of local hostelries in Marton in a

*Lloyd Day, named on the sign above the door, was licensee on the 1891 census. A harpist and fiddler entertain visitors and passers by outside the Sun. (Photo by permission of Llyfrgell Genedlaethol Cymru/ The National Library of Wales)*

community where for centuries the success or otherwise of the harvest depends on the seasons, the weather and the sun playing their due part. The Sun sign in Marton is very similar to the sun sign carved on the Lloyd sundial at Marrington Lodge. As a symbol it has changed very little over four centuries.

The earliest known record of The Sun Inn in Marton is in 1804 when an agreement between four parties is mentioned in a schedule attached to a later sale. The four parties are: Watkin Williams; Jane Lloyd, widow, Annabella Lloyd and Jane Lloyd, spinster; Lawton Parry; and William Wynne.[2] The Sun seems to have been the established venue for the Manor Leet before 1812, when the enclosure process was legalised at a Leet called by Mr. Jones, the Commissioner, and Mr. Richard Pryce. After the demise of the Manor Leet, The Sun Inn continued to be used on a monthly basis for the Petty Sessions, every second Friday at 12 noon except during October, until at least 1891.

As the road improvements were carried out the traffic passing through Marton increased. In 1861, The Sun employed an ostler to manage the care of their clients' horses.[3] When the property was sold in 1862, it had stabling for 12 horses with a house and building 'equal to new'.[4] Perhaps the earlier hostelry had recently been replaced by the current solid stone building and stables to meet an increasing level of business. At that time it was managed by Mr. Richard Morgan and was sold for £756 10s. The sale details mention The Sun's advantageous position on the 'Turnpike road'. In 1871, Richard Morgan, his wife and two adult sons combined

*A selection of old documents relating to the Sun Inn in the possession of the Gartell family. The underlying conveyance states that Mr. Medlicott paid £756 10s at auction for the Sun in 1862, together with its crofts and lands, to Orlando Bridgeman and Edward Williams. The landlord was Richard Morgan. It was agreed at the sale that the title deeds which related not only to the Sun but to other property of greater value should be kept by John Hamer who promised to produce them if needed. His signature and seal are visible at the top left corner. (Documents courtesy Gartell family)*

*In the late 1950s the Sun sells petrol as well as Burtonwood Ales*

inn-keeping and farming 48 acres of land with access to Marton Pool, in a family business that had lasted 20 years and which had benefited considerably from lying adjacent to the Turnpike road.

The returns of licensed houses in 1901 show Elizabeth Carryer as occupier and manageress, when the premises consisted of a kitchen, bar, bar parlour, sitting room, five bedrooms, back kitchen and cellar. There was stabling for eight horses all in good condition, and the inn itself had a clean record.[5]

The lakeside access and fishing rights on Marton Pool became a valuable asset to The Sun's proprietors during the early 20th century. A wooden boathouse was constructed on the shoreline to store several punt-like boats which could be lowered into the water within the boathouse, and paddled out onto the pool. In these peaceful surroundings, anglers enjoying a few days fishing holiday at The Sun could be sure of a catch and perhaps a tale to entertain the evening's clientele in the bar. When the water level in the pool fell later in the century, the boathouse was left high and dry, several yards from the water. Alder trees and vegetation have quickly taken root in the boggy terrain making access to the water difficult, until recently when the proprietors of The Sun Inn cleared the area and reopened their inlet to the pool.

In 2010, The Sun Inn is run by the Gartell family who have a restaurant with a reputation for fine food, and a pleasant bar.

> It is said there are very big pike in the pool. There was a pike's head hanging up in The Sun Inn for many years. It weighed 22lbs. (Tom Butler's memoirs)

When mother married they went to live at The Sun. There they had the fishing on the pool and a boathouse which I think is still there. They used to have fishermen at The Sun and mother did the catering. Dad put an advert in the *Birmingham Post* and everybody went to The Sun for the fishing and for the lovely meals. I can remember a chap called Charlie Boden. He came from Birmingham for years for the fishing. My one sister and two brothers were born at The Sun. I was born at Middle Farm, Rorrington. (Mrs. Ruby Bourne, 2008)

I loved Middle Farm I used to walk to the school at Middleton; the others went to school in Marton. Mum and Dad had Middle Farm and The Sun Inn. Do you know how far it is from Marton to Rorrington? Mother used to close The Sun early and then walk to Rorrington with the children. It was too much for her. Eventually she had double pneumonia and very nearly died. The doctor gave her 20 minutes to live but she survived. So they packed The Sun up. (Mrs. Ruby Bourne, 2008)

Marton Pool is famous for its pike. There's one in Rowleys Mansion that was caught in Marton Pool years ago. But mother remembered the pool being frozen that hard that they went across it with a wagon and horses. That's what she used to say. (Mrs. Ruby Bourne, 2008)

When we took The Sun Inn we had fishing guests in the summer. We had five boats to hire out for 8 shillings each for a day on the pool. I remember we charged £1.25p for bed and breakfast. The fishing and boats were separate. (Mrs. Rogers [née Bolderston], Wotherton, 2009)

We had two shops in Marton and a bakehouse at Dick Oliver's, a garage and petrol pump at The Sun. When the garage shut we went up to The Sun. (Mr. Bob Jenkins, 2008)

Auntie Belle from The Sun sat up with her dog, Nell Gwyn, all night when he was ill. She gave him a teaspoonful of brandy every hour but he died all the same. Peter White's wife, Fay, wrote a book called *Ian has a shilling to spend*. It was a children's story book. The tall brass bell they used to keep on the bar was given to John, my son, when he was young. He tied it on his tricycle until it fell to bits. (Mrs. Edith Humphreys, 2009)

## The Lowfield Inn

The history of the Lowfield Inn was neatly summed up in a framed document which used to hang on the wall of the old hostelry (see plate 20) together with other conveyances and historical documents and photographs. The following is the content of that account.

The story begins with a conveyance dated 29 September 1806 in which the freehold of three separate parcels of land known as Town Meadow, The Lower Field and a close or enclosure known as Questeous measuring in total some 19¼ acres and then in the occupation of one John Bowdler, were conveyed to Thomas Roberts and his heirs forever, with the tenancy of the property going to

John Maddock. In the same year Thomas Roberts erected a dwelling house on the piece of land known as The Lower Field.

In March 1811, Thomas Roberts assigned the property to his son George and his heirs for ever out of his love for him – and the payment of £60 per annum. At this time the property was described as a house, barns, stables, cowhouse, orchards, garden and land. Two years later the lease was transferred to Thomas Barnfield and his heirs, by which time the existence of a malthouse was also noted.

Thomas Barnfield died in 1816 and the owner of the freehold, George Roberts, sold the lease to Samuel Taylor for £1,540. Unfortunately a commission of bankruptcy dated 15 August 1818 recorded George Roberts' descent into bankruptcy.

William Nevett, gentleman of Swan Hill Shrewsbury, acquired the property from the trustees for £1,550 in 1824 after the death of the founder, Thomas Roberts.

William Nevett died in 1856 and the inn and surrounding land was sold at public auction at The George Hotel, Shrewsbury, to Thomas Smout of Bayston Hill for £1,850. Edward Gittins was then the tenant and licensee. It was sold again at public auction in 1901 to the son, Gilbert Smout, John Roberts having been the tenant for some years at this time [see the photograph below].

*The Roberts family at The New Inn (The Lowfield). John Roberts, licensee in 1901, (died in 1911), seated. On the left is daughter, Annie Maude Roberts; other family members and staff are also shown*

When John Roberts died in 1911, the tenancy of the New Inn, known to the locals as the Lowerfield, passed to Robert Northcote Vaughan who married the daughter of the house, Jessie Roberts, in the same year. Robert Vaughan held the licence from then until his death in 1946, first as tenant and from 1918 as owner. He grew the barley, made the malt, brewed the beer and dispensed it from a barrel. [See the photograph below of Robert with his second wife, Edith in front of the inn in 1925.]

Harry and Ethel Yardley bought the property in 1947 following the death of Robert Vaughan, and it was subsequently acquired by Frank Bithel in 1964. He made many changes including creating fishpools at the rear and renamed the inn the Marton Pool Hotel. Mr. Bithel moved abroad in 1969, selling the inn and the farmland as separate units.

My mother was born at the Lowfield in 1884. Her name was Annie Maude Roberts (Sis). I only know what my mother used to tell me. In those days they used to have what they called the Marton Club. [This was possibly the Druids Club, see p.173.] Those ladies on the photograph are the people who helped at it. My Mum is wearing a long skirt on the left of the photo and one is an aunt. I think the others were workers. My mother was the first person to have a bicycle in Marton. She always used to say that they said to her, 'Which would you rather have, a sewing machine or a bicycle?' and she said 'sewing machine'. But she must have had a bicycle after.

*Robert Northcote Vaughan, wearing plus twos, landlord from 1911-1946 and his second wife Edith. On the right is an unknown sporting gentleman*

My mother used to make malt in the malthouse from barley which the farmers brought in. It was always called the Lowfield. Bob Vaughan married my mother's sister, Jessie, and they carried on running the Lowfield. They had one son John. He did very well. John Vaughan built the bungalow down by the pool for his stepmother but I don't think she ever lived there. (Mrs. Ruby Bourne, 2007)

I remember being at the Lowfield once. A brook runs across the top. Something happened and the brook was going down past the Lowfield like a river. It looked very big and frightening to me. Uncle Bob used to milk at the Lowfield; he was a great big man. He had a bit of land by the pool called the Ghisleys. It's a nice name. I don't know now if they still call it the Ghisleys. It reminded me of geese. That's what I always had in mind. (Mrs. Ruby Bourne, 2007)

When the Second World War broke out the landlord of the Lowfield was advised by the authorities that he must reduce the specific gravity of his beer. As recorded by Edmund Vale in *Shropshire, The County Books,* published in 1949:

He wrote in reply pointing out that he brewed in the old traditional way and could use no other, and that if he reduced the gravity of his brew it wouldn't keep at all. He stated at the same time what was implied by his traditional method and a very comprehensive process it was. He grew his own barley on his own land. Then he was his own maltster. He germinated the grain on the stone floor of his malting house and killed it in his kiln. These were part of the Inn building and the traditional wooden cowl with its wind vane was perched on the roof. Thus having produced his own raw material and malted his malt, he brewed his beer.

The outcome was that he was allowed to continue brewing perhaps because the whole process was carried out in one place on his own property.

The Lowfield Brook they used to call it. We took our own barley there, seven bags to have it malted. … Vaughan had it at that time. They lay it out and spurt it. I'm not sure how it's done. Then heat it up and cook it. We had it back like and put it through the roller mill to grind it up to make our own beer. We used to make 60 gallons every six weeks in the summer. You put the malt in a 60 gallon barrel then pour this boiling water on it, stir it up, drain it off into a cooler then put it back in the boiler and boil it up for I don't know how many hours. Then you put a second lot of boiling water on the malt again, like to make more. But that wouldn't be so strong. You'd have to mix it somewhere in the procedure. Then you used to put a stick across the top of the boiler and hang the hops in this bag down in the boiler when it's boiling. Lift that out, run the second lot of water out into the cooler, empty the boiler with buckets back into the mashing tub as we called it, then put that back out of the cooler into the boiler and boil it up with the hops again. Then get the malt out of the tub. Then put that lot that's in the boiler back in the tub. Then you had to put the barm [froth on fermenting malt liquor] to it. It was supposed to be a certain temperature when you put the barm to it like. That would work it up for a day or two. Skim this barm off. Put it in the barrels then overfill the barrels a little bit and the barm would come over the top then you could seal it. The barm would all be out of it then. You had to add sugar to it sometime. A fair performance like. Mother was the brewer at Red House. At Lower House, Llettygynfach, Pentrenant they all brewed. It was nice stuff like. But the funny thing about it was everybody's beer was different. Pentrenant's was a different taste altogether. Llettygynfach's was nearer ours. I suppose the water made the difference. They've still got a spring like. It was good stuff. The funny thing about it now is I've never drunk or gone out from home. The postman used to have a pint, more than a glass when he came by, even the blokes in the van used to have one. Watkin, the postman, he wrote in the magazine sometime about my Dad giving him the pint of beer... Lloyd, the blacksmith, from Forden used to do the posting when they were walking from Forden up round Llettygynfach, our place [Red House], down through the Dingle up the Stubb. He always had a pint of beer by our place and talked about it, 'Oh you could go up that bank, up the Stubb after it.' You'd get the barm from a pub usually. You'd have a tin of barm then you used to go round the farms with it. (Mr. Elvet Richards, 2007)

In the late 20th century the malthouse was used as a venue for dances and as a restaurant by the licensee of the inn. Then the complex was bought by S.J. Roberts Construction Company. In 2008 the old Lowfield with its half thatched roof and its adjoining malthouse shell were demolished (see plate 21) and a new purpose built inn on the site of the original building was erected.

# Chapter 18

# Changing Times,
# From the 19th Century to the Present Day

**Estate Sales**

Comparisons between 19th century Marton and the village in the early 21st century are irresistible. The most significant change occurred when the estates were fragmented and sold by auction on the open market in the early 20th century when land was considered a poor investment. Farming had fallen into a depression in the late 19th century following imports of cheap food from North America, Australia and New Zealand which had undermined a whole range of home produced products and hit cereal prices particularly. Beef had fallen from 6.4p to 5p per kg in price, whilst wheat had more than halved from £12.95 to £6.08 per tonne. The First World War gave rise to a temporary revival in the fortunes of farmers, to be followed by an even greater slump between the wars.[1] Estate owners were obliged to reduce rents, to sell off their property piecemeal, or to offer individual farms to sitting tenants at reduced prices in an effort to keep their estates ticking over for a few more years.

The Marton Estates, which had for many generations belonged to the lords and ladies of the Manor – the Lloyd family from Marrington Hall, Chirbury and Stockton and their descendants, then in the 19th century to the Humphreys from Walcot, Chirbury, and the Edmunds from Edderton Hall and their descendants – were finally dispersed in the early years of the 20th century. The sales brought to an end a system of land management which had grown out of the feudalism that had been introduced by the Normans. In the good times, when corn prices were high and the seasons mild, it might have seemed a God-given way of life, especially when also under benevolent paternalistic landlords. But in hard times neither landlord nor tenant prospered and the farm labourer prospered least of all. The agricultural labourers had no choice but to leave the land for better paying occupations in towns, cities or opportunities abroad. In those changing times the tenant farmers who knew their land, crops and animals, had an inbred love of the farming life and were willing to take on the risks financial and otherwise as well as the years of hard work, now took their opportunity and bought their farms. Under their vigorous private ownership the farms eventually experienced a new, more prosperous future.

> These places [near Ackley] used to belong to Gunley; all the farms around here belonged to Gunley. The Mostyn Pryces of Gunley died out one after one, then the Devizes from Wolverhampton bought the estate for a while, then they came out just after I started farming. I took over from my father. They gave us the chance to buy it and we bought it in 1939. These others round about had the chance like Llwynyrhedydd, but they didn't take it then. Rent was just over £1 per acre. The Pryces from Gunley were a very tidy, a nice family, and they gave tea parties for the tenants at Gunley. They used to come around very often, they were very homely. The agent called for the rent. We were lucky then to buy the farm. People said we were daft because it would come cheaper. Well it looks like it, doesn't it? (Mr. Henry Evans, Ackley)

> A number of landowners in Marton were too hard up to carry on after the First World War and land had to be sold. Farmers in Marton competed among themselves to buy up land, sometimes buying fields which were in the tenancy of their neighbours. Some local squires were killed in the war such as Mr. Pryce of Gunley. (Dr S. Nethercott)

> Old Mr. Humphreys who lived at Walcot, Chirbury used to send his best shirts to London to be laundered. They came back to Montgomery station by train where they were collected by the Chirbury postmistress and then delivered to Walcot. (Anon.)

The final sale of the Gunley estate, which had been the seat of the Pryce family since the 15th century, came in 1950 when it was sold to Messrs J.R and J.E. Price who in turn sold the hall to Mr. D. Glyn Pryce in 1965.[2]

The outbreak of war in 1914 was fortuitous for a few who were quick to adapt to changing circumstances and seize new opportunities.

> Talking about money, my husband's father came home from America to claim £100 he had lent his auntie. It was a lot of money then. His father and mother had gone to America when he was nine years old where you could have a piece of ground if you had a little shack and you had smoke going through the roof by morning. They did that. But they went to keep pigs and everything was going great, but they had swine fever, wiped all the pigs out. They were broke so they had to come back. He went back to America later to work on the trams then came back again to claim the money. He got the money and he was going to go back to America but the exchange rate altered. There weren't so many dollars to the pound. So he stayed in this country and the war broke out, the 1914-18 war. You see he didn't want to go to the war, so he bought a little farm called Llydcoed Mill near Aberhafesp and that's how he started farming. He had two older half-brothers who went back to America. They used to work in Swifts meat factory in Kansas. (Mrs. Mona Thomas, Woodmoor)

It could have been no coincidence that the two major landowning families in Marton decided to sell their estates on the same day in the same year by the same auctioneers at the same location, but the reasons for it can only be surmised.

Marton Hall Estate and Marton Manor Estate were auctioned by Morris Marshall and Poole on 1 September 1919 at the Royal Oak Hotel, Welshpool. The vendors of Marton Hall Estate were Miss Farmer, Miss Ludger and Mrs. Meredith, descendants of the Humphreys family from Walcot, Chirbury. There were five Lots in the sale including a quillet of land by Marton Pool and The Perries. Marton Hall Farm, which at the time of the sale was let out to Mr. David Hughes, was sold as 211 acres 3 rods 2 perches of fertile arable and pasture land watered by the Lowerfield brook. The Mill Cottage was included with the main Lot. The farmhouse was described as:

> Situate in the village of Marton, [the house] stands on the roadside, the main portion being stone built and slated with a wing of brick half timbered; it contains a Parlour, Kitchen, Back Kitchen, Dairy, Larder, Two store rooms, Cellar, Six bedrooms and a Box room. There is also an Out house containing a baking oven and two boilers.

The tenants of The Perries, which was sold as one Lot comprising two cottages and 14 acres of land, were Mr. Richard Evans and Mr. J.L. Evans.[3]

Marton Manor Estate comprised the Manor Farm; The Cottage Farm, including Birch Tenement; Lower Hill and Upper Hill Farms; The Den (a smallholding of approximately eight acres occupied by Messrs Gittins, Woosnam and John Evans); shops, cottages and gardens in Marton. It totalled 604 acres.[4] A cottage and garden in Marton village let out to Miss Sockett was Lot 9 in the sale. Lot 1 contained:

> Two cottages, Grocers and Wheelwright's shops situate in the village of Marton occupied respectively by Mr. D. Oliver and Mr. H. Butler, with Warehouse, Cowhouse, Traphouse, Piggeries and other outbuildings together with gardens and accommodation land 10acres. 3rds. 34ps.
> Each cottage contains Kitchen, Back Kitchen, Pantry and 3 bedrooms and is supplied by a Wash House and there is a joint Baking Oven. Water is laid on.

The vendor was Lieut. Col. H.J. Howell Evans DSO whose mother was Elizabeth Edmunds, only daughter and co-heir of John Edmunds of Edderton Hall (d.1858). She married Rev. Canon Howell Evans, Vicar of Oswestry.[5]

**Owner occupiers take over**
The beginning of the 20th-century history of the Manor Farm can be traced from the 1901 census. Mr. Jonathon Roberts, then living at the Manor Farm, was a Welshman from Cardiganshire and a single man described as a 'worker' on the census. However, the older generation of the Roberts family are known to have farmed here and their daughter, Mrs. Jenkins, a widow with two children, came to live with them in 1902. Subsequently Mrs. Jenkins re-married, and with her second husband, Mr. Gwilt,

*Mr. and Mrs. Roberts moved into Manor Farm in 1900. Their daughter Jane was the widow of Benjamin Jenkins and the four boys and one girl in the photograph are from that marriage: Jack, David, Annie, Bill and Dick. There were two daughters from Jane's second marriage to Robert Gwilt: Pattie and Lucy*

farmed at the Manor Farm.[6] Mr. and Mrs. Gwilt presumably purchased the property, perhaps in 1919, for they continued farming it until it was sold by the family for £24,000 following the death of Mr. Gwilt in 1962.[7] Three generations of the Evans family have successfully farmed the land since buying Manor Farm in 1962.

> My Dad came to the Manor Farm from Wern Ddu when he was nine. Then his Dad died. There were five of them but they weren't hardly old enough to farm it. Then my Granny's brother came and after him she had a bailiff. It was 200 acres but it was only rented. Granny married Mr. Gwilt and they had two more children. My eldest uncle went to America and stayed there in Texas. Then they bought the farm off the estate and Dad bought The Steps. (Mr. Bob Jenkins, 2008)

> When I went to the USA in 1966 with Ray Dale, Bob Jenkins' brother was dead and his widow was living in Amarillo on Route 60. We called to see her. He had a petrol station and supermarket called 'Jenkins One Stop'. It was a successful business. (Mr. John Francis, 2008)

For the past three decades Marton Hall Farm has been owned and farmed by Mr. and Mrs. E. Davies and their family. Their farming business includes a dairy herd, fat cattle, corn production, sheep rearing and suckler cows, a mixed farming enterprise which reflects the versatility of the land.

The other large farm in the village, The Cottage Farm, was taken over at the beginning of the First World War by Mr. and Mrs. John Francis and purchased by them between the wars. Since the Estate sale in 1919 the farm has been increased in acreage as the result of various purchases of neighbouring fields.[8] In the recent past it employed local labour in an egg production enterprise. Currently it is a dairy farm run by Mr. John Francis and his wife Sue.

Most of the common land which was enclosed in 1812 along the left and right side of the Trelystan road beyond Ryecroft and farmed in the early 20th century as Upper and Lower Hill Farms is now one autonomous farm, Lower Hill Farm, owned by Mr. Malcolm Trow. At the time of the Estate sale Upper Hill Farm (The Bytuck) amounted to approximately 84 acres with a brick and stone built two-bedroomed, slated house with a pump outside and a wide range of farm buildings. Lower Hill Farm was some 62 acres with a larger house, baking oven, four bedrooms and a dairy. The outbuildings were 'conveniently arranged round a Fold Yard'.

These farms still form the backbone of agricultural life in the community, surviving both the Foot and Mouth disasters, BSE and the vagaries of officialdom in the form of DEFRA. Much of the Beeches land has been absorbed by other larger neighbouring farms. The stone farm buildings are currently being converted into houses and the old farmhouse is undergoing a degree of interior modernisation.

*Planting potatoes at Cottage Farm c.1959. Driver Bill Jones,*
*sitting Arthur Francis, Bert Jones, Vaughan Davies*

**Smallholdings**

The survival of the smallholdings is significant. Several of them lie outside the village, surrounded by their own small fields which are sometimes precipitous or at best sloping and not particularly suited for modern farming implements. This may explain to a certain degree their survival. Often their description in the Tithe schedule mentions the existence of folds adjacent to the homestead, the inference being that sheep were a usual part of the 19th-century farming scene. By the middle of the century the Shropshire breed of sheep had come into its own. It was kept for both meat and wool, producing a fleece weighing between 5 and 8lbs.[9]

Today some of the local farmers still run flocks as part of their farming enterprise, but many of the small Welsh sheep seen in the winter on the dairy farms are on 'winter tack', returning to their own uplands in the spring. Commonly a mule cross breed such as a Border Leicester cross Welsh is a favoured local type, but at least one smallholder prefers using a black-faced Suffolk tup to produce a big early spring lamb. On the uplands in Trelystan, beef cattle and sheep are the main farming enterprises.

> 1947 and 1963 were rough winters. I don't know as ever we lost but one sheep under snow drifts and that was later than 1963. The sheep and lambs were up under the hedge by the house. On 29 March there were blizzards. Dad got a haw, he'd hook 'em out see. The little owd lambs were in the snow. He saved them. All night long he was at it. It was a bad time. We never went to bed for a fortnight. I remember another year. It was snowing all night. We got them in the patch that year by the stackyard. They lay there all night. When we got up in the morning there were holes where they lay and snow about that big right up to the top of their backs. They were all right like. (Mr. Elvet Richards, 2007)

The appropriately named Highgate property lies within its own fields much as it has for at least 200 years but the house has been pleasantly modernised. Upper and Lower Ryecroft, the latter which is now known as Seiffen, exist as smallholdings but with reduced acreages. Seiffen was so named after a village in Germany by Mr. Walter Lewis who arrived in Britain as a German P.O.W. and stayed on after the war ended, married, changed his name, and turned to farming for a living. The other smallholdings, Brays Tenement and Pen-y-Bank, have provided scope for the alternative interests of their owners. The grounds of the latter property have been landscaped and laid to lawns and gardens which are an added attraction available to their bed and breakfast guests. One of the two larger smallholdings in the village is the Steps Farm which is still in the ownership of the Jenkins family and farmed by them, although their residence is now a new bungalow overlooking the Rea Valley and Wilmington motte. On the edge of the village stands Maesderwyn, a substantial cream-washed house which has been extended and modernised. It was until recently a 30-acre farm identified on the censuses between 1861 and 1901 as Stone House. The good agricultural land previously attached to Maesderwyn has been sold to The Cottage Farm. The house has a cellar, very attractive polished oak upper floors and staircase and an inglenook fireplace.[10]

The other smallholding, The Parks, lies at the west end of the township. This bungalow does not appear on any census return before 1900 and only came into existence as a separate entity after 1901. The land, however, was bought by the Oliver family in 1879 when it was sold as a separate lot at the time of the Villa Farm sale. Marton Villa or the Villa Farm occurs in the census descriptions until 1901. In this year the occupier is John Gethin, farmer, and the name has changed to Cottage Farm. The descendants of the Oliver family currently own the land and let it out, but the bungalow is owned by Mr. Kevin Pugh who is also the proprietor of a log business.

On the edge of the township boundary is Parkers Tenement. In the 1891 census this property was included in Stockton township, not Marton. The current national revival of interest in native breeds of cattle and sheep is reflected in the recent appearance of a few Highland Cattle at Parkers Tenement and, in the summer, a small herd of pedigree Hereford cattle graze on the fields at The Parks.

### Electricity, mains water and the wireless arrive
Modern improvements such as piped water and electricity arrived in the mid 20th century within living memory of the older generation.

In 1955 we got electricity. It was blessing when Tilly lamps came in. They were different from the old lanterns. Dangerous those old lanterns were – an open flame apart from the dome. We had to go up in the hayloft with one hanging on your arm to put hay down for the stock. Then hang it on a nail then go back down with it on your arm. Dangerous wasn't it? But we never had any trouble. (Mr. Elvet Richards, 2007)

I remember when electricity first came around here. My Granny wouldn't have it. Under pressure we eventually had electricity, downstairs only – one switch, one light, one plug. Of course eventually she was the one who was putting the light on so we had to pay extra for the electrician to come and finish the job. Then we had television which she didn't want. So we had it put in our own little room yet she was the one who watched it all the time. (Mrs. Sally Pugh, 2007)

One Sunday evening the Chapel congregation was invited to go to Gwilts, the Manor House, to see and hear the wireless. I can still see that lamp-lit room with this enormous contraption of glowing valves, masses of wire and the loud speaker hanging on the wall with a squeaky voice announcing '2LO calling from Daventry'. (Mr. I.G. Griffiths) [In October 1922 the government granted the British Broadcasting Company a licence to operate and 14 November 1922 saw the official opening of the BBC London station 2LO, managed by Arthur Burrows, on a wavelength of 369 metres from Marconi House on The Strand. Captain Peter Eckersley was the BBC's first chief engineer. Eckersley had been an engineer and on-air announcer at 2MT in Essex.]

One hundred yards down from Red House, down the field there's a little spring in a hollow there. It would run all summer, even in them dry summers. It supplied all the water we wanted on the farm. Tom Bowen, Lower House Farm, lugged his clean water from there one year when they ran out of water. It kept going all summer. It watered animals as well. I don't know how it did it. There's a brook running down but that would dry up in a dry summer. We had to pump it by hand, a tankful at a time, 400 strokes to fill the top tank and 300 to fill the other tank. Then we had an engine to pump the water in about 1943. The pump was down the field and we had a lot of trouble with that Lister pump. The packings used to wear out. It was drawing water from the well so far up then it would draw air, it was easier than drawing water. We had to prime it again. There's an electric motor right down by the well now, that's where the Lister ought to have been. It was drawing the water up a 25ft rise and that was about its limit, see. We put it a bit lower, about 23ft, but it was still too much for it. When they brought the mains water down the top road about 1976 they wanted everyone to join so it would be worthwhile bringing it down. So we put our name and had a tap put on the end but we never use it. Our little spring does very well. (Mr. Elvet Richards, 2007)

[In July 1970] they connected up the mains water to Folly cottages. There used to be a well and a pump between the cottages. When it went dry we went across to the spout in the field. There was also a spring in Trow's field. (Mrs. Gwen Evans, 2007)

## Dairy Farming changes the landscape

The nature of farming is that the product can vary in response to the changing needs of the market, providing the land is suitable. The Tithe commutation schedule shows most of Marton land was producing arable crops in 1843 to supply the immediate needs of the local animal and human population in response to good wheat prices in the early part of the 19th century. Wheat, oats, barley and rye were grown in rotation with mangolds, swedes, potatoes and turnips. Bearing in mind that the small closes attached to cottages and small holdings were tilled by hand to produce vegetables and fodder for one house cow, sheep and/or pig and that the larger farms employed their own teams of horses and men in a year-round effort to cultivate their crops, the

*Percy Beddoes selling milk from the back of the Stores, c.1955. (Courtesy S. Pugh)*

dominance of arable farming in the 19th-century landscape is still surprising to anyone accustomed to the present largely pastoral scene. The change in the use of the land from arable to mainly pastoral was brought about by the growth of the dairy industry, which is particularly in evidence along the rich grasslands in the Rea valley.

In the early part of the 21st century there are three dairy herds in the township producing

114

milk from Friesian Holstein cows, with store and finished cattle for the meat market produced as alternative enterprises. Lower Hill Farm runs a suckler herd and sheep. Corn crops are still grown, particularly on the south-facing slopes and on the enclosed land in the north of the township, along with root crops such as stubble turnips for winter feed, but overall by far the largest share of the land is devoted to grazing combined with silage and hay production for winter cattle and sheep feed. There are indications from the censuses that dairying, with a surplus of milk which could be sold as cheese or butter to outside markets, existed in Marton in 1861, 1871 and 1881 when there were dairymaids employed at the Manor Farm and The Steps. The former farmhouse has a commodious dairy laid out with cool slabs and drains for butter and cheesemaking. A heavy stone cheese weight makes a solid gatepost in the yard fence. (The long oblong kitchen table from Marton Manor which could seat 20 people at one time is now in the village hall where it still serves a useful purpose.)[11]

**Population, Houses, Barns and Businesses**
Since the introduction of strict planning regulations, new settlement is generally allowed only within the village confines. In the 20th century two council house developments were built and more recently a Housing Association complex of cottages. The modern houses and bungalows which infill along the main road are the result of private development. All except two of those 20 plus cottages which in 1843 lay scattered around the township in the Perries, the Beach Dingle and on the township perimeters have disappeared, leaving very little trace of their existence. The two that have survived are The Perries cottage and Parkers Tenement. The decline in the numbers of agricultural labourers towards the end of the 20th century, their emigration into local towns and alternative employment and the availability of better accommodation, were all reasons behind the desertion. One of the more significant improvements in the life of the farmworker occurred in 1908 when Lloyd George and the Liberal government introduced the 5s. a week old age pension for those over the age of 70 and with an income less than 12s. per week. This must have been a great relief to those without family, facing a penniless old age or the workhouse. Something of this feeling is reflected in this poem written in dialect by an observant Radnorshire Headmaster in 1909:

### The first Pension day

On this memorable morning
Folks were sid with faces beaming
To the Post Office streamin
It was Penshun Day.
Arter years of ekspectashun
Years of toil and half starvvashun
Now they come with ecksultashun
For the Penshun Pay.

115

Ay, in spite of jibes and jeers
'Twill make bright the closing years
and remove some hauntin fears
For Auld folks today.
'Mong the toilers and the landless
Clouds of misery and sadness
Will give way to joy and gladness
On the Penshun Day.

Good old stajers bent and hoary
Bid goodbye to cares and wurry
They be all agog and merry
On this Penshun Day.
This grand stroke of lejislashun
Now be hail'd with acclamashun
For 'twill drive the wolf privashun
From the door today.[12]

In 1901 there were 39 Marton residents involved in agriculture either as farmers, retired farmers, farmers' sons, labourers, waggoners or carters, compared with 56 male agricultural workers in 1841. Those cottages anonymously identified as on Marton Mountain in 1871 numbered 14: each one was inhabited by a farm labourer and in most cases his immediate family. In 1901 only one cottage in this area appears on the census, presupposing the others were either uninhabited or derelict. The population figures show a corresponding decrease from 246 to 180.

Trying to assess the number of people involved directly with agriculture in Marton today reveals one or two similarities with past scenarios. There are those retired and semi-retired, together with those whose main non farming occupation is outside the village who 'farm' a few acres either owned or rented on a part time basis. Secondly, some land within the township is farmed by individuals whose main farm lies outside Marton. A third group consists of farmers/farmworkers living within Marton whose sole livelihood is the business of agriculture, either as employers or employed. A fourth group are the part-time relief milkers/farmworkers/contractors who travel into the village to work. Taking all these variations into consideration a figure of 30 individuals, men and women, with a 'hands on' connection with agriculture in Marton is arguably conservative.

All the land which is strictly within the old township boundaries is devoted to supporting traditional farm livestock. There are at the time of publication some horses kept for pleasure at Upper Ryecroft and at Groton which is outside the bounds of the old Marton township.

Farming methods and agricultural vehicles in this millennium need purpose-built farm buildings; the old barns and wainhouses of past eras are no longer suitable. Inevitably this change has led to a multitude of barn conversions in villages all over

*Vehicles from John Jones Haulage in a photograph taken early in the 20th century*

Shropshire. Marton today is one of those increasingly rare working agricultural villages with several of its old barns unconverted, protected by listed status and still in use for farming purposes. There is a fine old weather-boarded 17th-century barn at the Manor Farm, along with stone-built sheds and a 17th-century cartshed/granary, timber-framed with brick infill. Marton Hall Farm has some old farm buildings of stone and cart sheds constructed with mellow orange/red brick in Old English Bond.

Six houses in the village are Grade two listed buildings: Mill Cottage (late 16th century), The Beeches Farmhouse (late 17th century), the Manor Farmhouse (17th century), Marton Hall Farm (early 17th century), Yew Tree Cottage, formerly

*Mill Cottage (Photo courtesy of Rev. Ralph and Nina Wilkins)*

a farmhouse, is dated 1634, and The Steps Farmhouse (probably 17th century). The Church of St. Mark is also a Grade two listed building. With the exception of The Beeches, which is a stone building, all the listed houses are timber-framed. The three substantial stone buildings in the village are The Sun Inn, Holmwood House and Maesderwyn. A later 19th-century brick building phase produced Jubilee House, The Villa's Victorian wing, and the Village Shop. Each of these has its own unique, 'built for purpose' features or decorative embellishments. Some smaller cottages within the village, Rose Cottage for example, may contain early features. Cartref has a splendid twisted Tudor chimney built in an era when such an extravagance indicated a degree of status. Yew Tree Cottage has three star-shaped chimneys in a stack similarly indicative.

Whereas in the 19th century most of the tradesmen lived in the village and the farmer brought the item to be repaired into the workshop or smithy, today the skilled tradesman either travels to the farm to effect repairs or the item is transported to a central workshop located in a nearby town such as Welshpool or Montgomery. There are two notable construction firms based in the area which provide valuable work opportunities within Marton, in south Shropshire generally and over the Welsh border: S.J Roberts Construction Ltd. and P. Hockley, Builders. Coincidentally, the 19th-century Hughes family from Ryecroft were equally well known for their building work, work that included Montgomery Baptist Chapel, Jubilee House and Tre-Llydiart, Montgomery. Other home-based businesses in Marton and Ryecroft are Chiltern Electrical Services, Jones Refrigeration services, Colley Construction, motor mechanical repairs at Seiffen and at Seiffen Barns an agricultural contracting business.

> I left school and went to work on the farm but left, there was more money in driving. I saw an advertisement for a milk churn lorry driver and took the job for the Milk Marketing Board. (Mr. Bob Jenkins, 2008)

# Chapter 19

# Gathered Together – Two Churches and a Hall

For centuries, come rain, wind or snow the inhabitants of Marton had walked or ridden the three miles to Chirbury to attend the parish church. Some went under a sense of duty, some were obliged to attend, others were borne along by conviction, but whatever the reason, the church in Chirbury was at a distance and outside their normal daily round. From the 17th century onwards, those who disagreed with the teaching and authority of the established Anglican church gathered strength under their particular dissenting denominations and in rural areas met to worship initially in their own homes. In 1851 the Primitive Methodists in Marton met in a farmhouse at Marton Beachs where the afternoon congregation averaged 20. Edward Jones, John Clarke and Joseph Davies were members of that group.[1] But there was no Methodist chapel constructed in Marton, perhaps because Congregationalism had already taken a strong hold in the village.

In 1809 Thomas and Priscilla Roberts, who were connected to the Independent church in Minsterley and committed Dissenters, moved to Marton but continued to worship in Minsterley every Sunday, walking both ways, a distance of 14 miles. Some years later they persuaded the Independent minister from Welshpool to preach in their house. When the numbers in the congregation increased, services continued to be held in a barn fitted out with seats and a pulpit until the Roberts family moved closer to Marton six years later. At this point the smith's shop in Marton became their Sunday worship venue. On their journey to worship they often had to suffer the jeers of their neighbours or dodge the eggs and stones thrown at them.

In 1823 Mr. William Nevett of Shrewsbury moved into the neighbourhood. He was not only a wealthy landowner purchasing Vale Cottage (Marton Villa / Cottage Farm) but also a man of faith in the tenets of Congregationalism which maintain that each congregation has a right to govern itself independently of higher human authority. Each member of the local church has a part in the government of his own church, where the emphasis is on the sacraments of baptism (both infant and adult) and the Lord's supper.[2]

Mr. Nevett appears to have been a man of Christian conviction who was moved by a perceived need in Marton to personally provide a place of worship for local people. He, together with the small group of practising Dissenters, was the driving force behind the construction of the Independent Church in Marton in 1823. In the first instance he bought the land from Thomas Roberts Esq. of Wilmington, then financed the building of the chapel and finally, in 1834, gave the whole as a gift to the Trustees.[3]

> Thomas and Priscilla Roberts went from Minsterley to live at Geyfors Cottage in Marton in about 1810. Thomas was a labourer and they had a son Samuel. They hired a barn on the Long Mountain to hold services and a minister from Welshpool led them. Mr. Nevett and two more gentlemen joined them in the barn. Later they held services in the blacksmith's shop in Marton where Thomas Roberts lived. Then it was decided to build a chapel on ground bought from Thomas Roberts Esq. The second son, also called Thomas, went to Snailbeach in 1844 and built a cottage and a blacksmith's shop. The family still own the land. (Mrs. Sybil Lewis, 2008)

> At Marton the earliest written record of Dissenters' activity is in 1809 when a Roberts family came from Minsterley to live in the area but continued to walk to Minsterley to worship there. A family named Watts and others joined the group and they began to worship in the smithy. (Mr. I.G. Griffiths, 2009)

The meeting house was built on the south-west end of Marton Town meadow and William Nevett set apart a small portion near it as a burial ground. This latter was fenced by walling, a hawthorn hedge and a bank. He granted the premises to trustees under certain conditions, the main one being that the chapel should be used for divine service by Independents, or Congregationalists as they came to be called, of the Calvinistic persuasion holding the doctrine in the assembly's catechism and Westminster Confession of faith. The burial ground was only to be used for members of the chapel.[4]

The Chapel Trustees in 1834 were:

> William Nevett jnr. of Marton, gent.
> Francis Nevett of Shrewsbury, cordwainer,
> The Rev. Thomas Weaver of Shrewsbury, Minister of the Gospel.
> The Rev. John Jones of Marton, Minister of the Gospel.
> John Bickerton Williams jnr. of Shrewsbury, gent.
> Richard Phillips, farmer of Marton.
> Benjamin Williams, shopkeeper, Marton.
> John Meddins jnr. farmer, Marton,
> Thomas Roberts, labourer, Marton.
> Samuel Roberts, blacksmith, Marton.
> William Culham of Stockton, miller.
> Thomas Jebb of Bin Weston, farmer.
> Thomas Ward of Shrewsbury, grocer.

By 1881, just three of the original Trustees remained:

Wm. Nevett, now of Yoreton Villa, Salop.
John Bickerton Williams, now of Birmingham.
and Samuel Roberts.

They had been joined by:

The Rev. Rd. Lloyd, of (blank) Minister of the Gospel.
Wm. James Powell, jnr. of (blank) tailor.
Richard Wilcox of Marton, shoemaker.
John Roberts of Llanderfel, Co. Merioneth, stationmaster.
John Oliver of Marton shopkeeper.
Richard Lewis jnr. of Wotherton, farmer.
John Meddins of Hem, Forden, Mont. Farmer.
David James of Marton, farmer.
Edward Watkins of (blank).
William Thomas Watkins (son of sd. E. Watkins.)
Edwin Henry Wilcox (son of Rd. Wilcox).

Further changes had occurred by 1897:

The Rev. William Bowen of Marton, Minister of the Gospel.
John Gethin of Marton Villa, Marton farmer.
John William Gethin of the same place, farmer.
Edwin Henry Wilcox of Marton, shoemaker.
Nathaniel Watkins of Stockton, farmer.
William James Powell of Chirbury, tailor.
John Powell of Montgomery, tailor and draper.
Edward Watkins of Marton Hall, farmer.
Thomas James Woosnam of Marton, farmer.
Job Watkins of Stockton, farmer.
Robert Roberts of Nantcribba Farm, Forden, Mont. Farmer.
John Blockley of Marton Mountain, farmer.

The Rev. John Jones of Marton, named among the trustees, was their first minister. The deed of 1834 stated that the subscribers of the society, both men and women being members, should elect a pastor or minister, although the business relating to the property was to be conducted solely by the male members of the chapel. Should the number of trustees become as low as three they were to make up the number to 12. This they had to do in 1897 when the Rev William Bowen became their minister.[5] In the religious census of 1851 it is recorded that 100 people attended morning worship and 130 in the evening. Morning Sunday school had 38 pupils and 29 attended in the evening. However, an added comment is also enlightening, 'there are never a hundred at this chapel except at a Christmas tea party'.[6]

The original church deeds specifically mention a 'meeting house' being erected and a 'burial ground' being set aside, but no mention is made of an attached building or cottage for a minister or caretaker, and by omission it seems there was none.

*A ticket, priced 1s. to attend the laying of the new Congregational chapel's
Foundation Stone in 1874*

Neither does a chapel cottage occur by name in any census until 1881. However, this cottage, known as Chapel House, is currently an integral part of the solid stone building apparent today. It appears that the original building erected by Mr. Nevett in the early part of the century was replaced in 1874 with a new Congregational Church with its attached caretaker's cottage, at a cost of £450. Certainly, the laying of the foundation stone for the new Congregational Chapel of Marton in Chirbury took place at 2pm on 22 July 1874. After the ceremony, performed by William Nevett Esq., son of the first William Nevett, there was a Tea Meeting to celebrate the occasion, entry being by ticket only for one shilling each.[7]

The church wall plaques commemorate members of the Nevett and Gwilt families and several items of furniture have been donated to the church as memorial gifts by surviving family members. The Jenkins family provided a Communion table in memory of Mr. Will Jenkins of Texas USA 'who was brought up in this church and became its worthy benefactor and by his generous gifts made it possible to beautify this house of God.' The brass reading lectern was given in memory of the Rev. and Mrs. T.G. Griffiths who served the community between 1913 and 1929, and a brass vase was presented by Edith L. Jones in memory of her husband Edward Jones and brother Arthur James Powell. Mrs. G.A. Oliver donated a pulpit lamp in memory of her parents, Mr. and Mrs. J. Bennett, and the communion rail was presented by the children of Mr. and Mrs. John Oliver, Upper Shop, Marton in April 1927.

In 1972 the Congregational Church in England and Wales joined with the Presbyterian Church in England to form the United Reformed Church (URC).

122

*Marton Congregational church Sunday School outing to Corndon, 1920s.*
*Seated in the centre row seated wearing a trilby is Rev. T. Gibbon Griffiths;*
*Mrs. Griffiths is on his left, their son Haydn Griffiths kneeling in front.*
*Three to the right of Mrs. Griffiths (looking at the photograph) is May Oliver,*
*Top Shop. Behind Mrs. Griffiths and slightly to the right is Lillian Richards from*
*Stone House, (Maesderwyn). Behind her, with only her head showing, is Edie Powell*
*from Chirbury. The gentleman in the back row is possibly Eddie Evans of Ackley.*
*Standing on the left in the back row are the Colley girls.*
*In the very front lying down is Linda (surname unknown).*
*(Photograph courtesy of Mr. I.G. Griffiths)*

Some congregations, Marton and Forden among them, resolved not to join the new denomination and remained a Congregational church which to a large extent is independent and self governing. (Mr. I.G. Griffiths, 2009)

Every year the children in the Sunday school anticipated the annual outing with great excitement. The expeditions were not too ambitious initially. The distance was limited to that which a horse and dray could accomplish in a day, perhaps a picnic on Corndon or a visit to some other local beauty spot, until the arrival of the village charabanc opened up a new world of possibilities.

Mr Jones ran a garage/transport business. He had one 5 ton truck which was incredibly multipurpose. It served as a cattle wagon and having been hosed down, also a sort of charabanc. A primitive bus body was lowered on to the lorry, attached by some bolts, some benches were put in and it was ready to take the Sunday school the 60 miles over Plynlymmon to Aberystwyth for their outing. I remember many heads hung out of the windows, adults and children leaving a trail of Marton breakfasts in the wake of the vehicle. There was no means of communicating with the driver so you just had to get on with it. (Mr. I.G. Griffiths)

*A chapel outing in the early 1920s. Some of the group have been identified: a young Dick Oliver is the man at the extreme right of the picture; Edie Powell (Chirbury) and Miss Roberts from Maesderwyn are the two women on the left of the centre row; May Oliver, sister of Dick, is behind them in the back row*
*(Photograph courtesy of Mr. I.G. Griffiths)*

*Marton Congregational Chapel in 2007*

In 2009 the church no longer has a resident minister in the village and is served by the Rev. Debbie Martin from Swan Hill Congregational church in Shrewsbury. Services are held at 2pm on the first and third Sundays in the month. The church secretary is Mrs. Heather Thomas, of Woodmoor.

In 1859 a plot of land was given by Mr. Richard Beaman, a gentleman of Marton, for the erection of a manse. He had bought this land in 1845 from Richard Newcombe and it formed part of a piece called Stockings. The piece he gave was 486 sq.yds and adjoined the turnpike road from Marton to Chirbury. This was conveyed to the trustees to erect a house with powers to repair, enlarge alter or improve it. The house now called Providence House (see plate 24), is still the property of the Congregational Church. It provided accommodation for the minister and his family until the church no longer required it. Subsequently it has been let privately.[8]

Finally a church hall was added to the above property in 1926, on land gifted by the Hughes family of Marton Hall.

> Mr. Hughes from Marton Hall gave the ground for the village hall. He was Chapel. I helped fence it. I remember him saying, 'It inna that much ground!' They used to have whist drives in the granary at Marton Hall but I don't remember that. (Mr. Bob Jenkins)

**The Congregational Church Hall**

When the school was built in 1864 there was one large classroom, 42ft long. The village adopted this indoor space to hold a variety of functions particularly at the weekends, with the permission of the school managers and for a fee.[9] St. John's Ambulance classes were held here, and church council meetings. Socials, dances and the scout meetings all took place in the school. From time to time there were complaints from the schoolmistress that those using the building had not cleared up and prepared the room for its proper use on the following Monday, or had caused some minor damage or breakages. It was an unsatisfactory situation and pointed to the need for a suitable venue for village social events. In due course a meeting was called to assess the support for a Boys' Club room. Whatever the outcome of this discussion was, the first mention of The New Hall in the *Corndon Magazine* is in 1927 when the schoolchildren were entertained to tea there by the 'people'. But it was the members of the Congregational Church who took on the responsibility of providing the much needed building, both for their own use and for the use of the village.

> On 19 January 1926 a special meeting of the Congregational church was held, presided over by the Pastor, the Rev. Gibbon Griffiths. Two objectives were proposed:
>
> To erect additional premises for the Church's Sunday School and social activities,
>
> To adopt the envelope system of weekly contributions to improve the finances of the church.
>
> A building committee was formed: Mr. Job Watkin, Mr. John Oliver, Mr. T. Woosnam, Mr. D. Hughes, Mr. E.B. Roberts, Mr. A.J. Powell. All above were

13th July 1926

A meeting of the Building Committee was held at 8 p.m. when the following members attended.

Mrs. Colley,
Mrs. D. Davies.
" Y. J. Woosnam.
" D. Hughes.
" J. Oliver
" E. B. Roberts.
Rev. Y. G. Griffiths
A. J. Powell.

Minutes. The minutes of the last meeting were read & adopted.

Legal. On the advice of Mr. Ferrington, Solicitor, Oswestry it was decided to ask Mr. Hughes, upon whose land the Hall is being built to estimate the value of the site so that same

may be included in list of subscriptions as his donation and deed of purchase be drawn up accordingly. This Mr. Hughes kindly agreed to do.

Seating. The secretary submitted estimates from different firms for chairs & forms. It was proposed by the chairman, Rev. Y. G. Griffiths & seconded by Mr. J. Oliver that we purchase 200 chairs from Messrs. Mealing of High Wycombe vis: 150 of no 80 on list + 50 of no 18.

Opening of Hall On the motion of Mr. E. B. Roberts Sept 9th was provisionally fixed for Opening the Hall. The chairman undertook to write and ask Miss. Davies of Gregynog, to perform the opening ceremony.

*Facing pages of the chapel minute book detailing arrangements, including the proposed opening of the new hall in September 1926*

Deacons of the Church. Mr. R. Jenkins, Mrs. Colley, Miss Davies (Cottage), Mr. Jones (Lower Stockton), Mr. W.B. Oliver, Mr. Eddie Evans, Mr. John Owens, Mr. Evan Roberts, Mr. Pryce Bowen.

They agreed that £100 should be promised by the members of the church before proceeding further. At the end of the meeting £55 had been promised.

An estimate of £455 for the new hall was put forward by Messrs. Harbrow of London in March and accepted. Mr. Maddox from The Steps was asked to put in the foundations. A bank account was opened and an application for a loan to the Congregational Union refused. An overdraft of £650 was allowed by the bank after the site had been valued and the valuation added to the list of donations. Miss Davies of Gregynog performed the opening ceremony on 9 Sept. A tea and a concert followed.[10]

The opening day of the new Congregational Hall in 1926 was celebrated with a Grand Evening Concert featuring artistes from Shrewsbury, Newtown, Llanfyllin and Welshpool and an elocutionist, Miss Ena Davies, from Four Crosses. Dr. Du Pre from Worthen was the chairman of proceedings and Miss Olive Davies, also from Worthen, was the pianist. Selections were from Vaughan Williams' folk song arrangements, Verdi, Joseph Haydn and other songs suitable for tenor, soprano, baritone and contralto voices. On the back of the evening's programme there was a reminder of the next event in the hall – a Grand Bazaar – taking place in October.[11] Thus began the long and continuing tradition of bazaars, socials, coffee mornings and craft fairs held in the hall for the next 83 years. Inevitably there was a two-fold purpose to the

*Children from the Rebel School, taught in the Village Hall between 1949 and 1953, run out to play*

social events: repayment of the debt and keeping up with the running costs of the hall, as well as having a good time with your neighbours and friends. Another money spinner was *The Marton Congregational Church Recipe Book* which went to print in 1927. Every lady of note from near and far – Marton, Chirbury, Trefeglwys, Clun and Churchstoke – contributed a favourite family recipe.[12] The village hall survived one crisis in 1985 when funds were not sufficient to pay an outstanding electricity bill, and three committee members, Messrs. Meyrick Holloway, Albert Roberts and Tom Evans, each put a £100 into the kitty to save the day. This was followed rapidly by a coffee evening hosted by Mr. and Mrs. David Evans from Marton Manor which raised £450, more than enough money to put the hall back on a sound financial footing. At this point monthly whist drives were re-introduced. These continue to be a regular monthly fund raising event (see plates 22 and 23).

**St. Mark's Anglican Church**
Although Mr. Nevett had been diligent in supplying a place of worship for the people in Marton in 1823, that is not to say that the parish church in Chirbury, its vicars and church wardens were indifferent to the situation of their parishioners in Marton. The first attempt to remedy the situation occurred in the 1840s when the

Rev. Wilding became anxious about the spiritual welfare of the village. He mooted plans for an Anglican church to be built in Marton and launched an appeal for money. One benefactor (Sir Offley Wakeman?) gave 100 guineas, but otherwise there was a limited response to the appeal. The appeal money was banked and the matter allowed to drop for the time being. In 1852 the issue was raised again with a public statement and within a year a considerable amount had been raised:

> Some years ago the spiritual destitution of Marton, a hamlet in the parish of Chirbury, Salop, three miles and more from the Parish church induced anxious enquiry whether this painful state of things might not be removed, or, at least, relieved by building a church and placing a resident Minister there … One day at the beginning of last year 1852 the donors [of the original appeal money] felt themselves called upon to take an onward step of making fresh exertions and enlarging their donations. That very same day the Rev. Wilding received a cheque for 100 guineas by post which he devoted to the contemplated church in Marton. And since then the sum of £989 13s. ½d. has been collected from people of all ranks, down to cottagers. The contract accepted for the building is £600. The surplus namely £389 13s. ½d. is reserved for a repair fund and towards an endowment. This statement has a double aspect – of explanation to those kind friends who have already aided us, and of appeal to others.
>
> Subscriptions are received for Marton Church Endowment fund by the Rev. the Vicar of Chirbury, Salop, or Messrs. Hoare, 37 Fleet Street, London; or Messrs. Beck and Co., Shrewsbury and Welshpool.[13]

> The site in the middle of the village was given by Mr. Edward Humphreys from Walcot. Mr. Haycock of Shrewsbury was appointed architect and Mr. Henry Thomas of Shrewsbury the builder. There was to be room for 120 free seats. As the first stone was laid near St. Mark's Day 1855, it was agreed to dedicate the church to St. Mark. The day of the consecration, 6 March 1856, was reported at great length and in glowing terms by the Shropshire press. Those attending included the Lord Bishop of Hereford, the Earl of Powis and his retinue, the local landowners and their wives. The collection at the service was £66 3s. 7d. Afterwards a large party 'partook of luncheon' at the residence of the Rev. R.M. Pryce at Gunley.[14]

> Chirbury was originally a very large parish. Marton folk would have attended Chirbury church sometimes three times a day. They had to go whether they wanted to or not. But from Marton to Chirbury was a long distance to walk once or even twice a day. Not everyone had a horse. The mines at Wotherton were open so the population increased. Eventually Marton built its own Anglican church. The vicarage was built in 1856. It was renamed Caledon House which has South African connotations. (Dr. Stephen Nethercott)

> My Grandad Hughes was a great churchman. He lived to be 90 something. One Easter Sunday they were getting ready to go to church but it was snowing. So mother got up and looked through the window, there was Grandad going down

*St Mark's Church on 19 April 1887, with a decorated gateway on the occasion of the wedding of Arthur Jarmen and Amelia Jane Oliver*

the path to church. So she thought, 'If he can go, I can go.' They had an organ and he carried it from Worthen to Marton on his shoulders. He used to play a bit and sing. We went to church but the chapel and church always did get on well. (Mrs. Ruby Bourne, 2007)

At the time of the consecration Marton was a Chapel of Ease of Chirbury. In 1859 however it was decided Marton should become a separate parish. Much discussion took place and many maps were drawn. Eventually the parish was delineated as Marton with Stockton, Highgate, Ryecroft, the Perries, Lower Malthouse, Marton village and half Marton Pool.[15]

The church originally had a wooden turret which housed the bell but this began to show signs of deterioration by 1946. In the next year the PCC were offered two choices by the consultant architect: repairs and restoration at a cost of £775, or replacement with a type of arch bell-cote in stone. The latter proposal, which was slightly cheaper, was favoured by the architect and taken up by the PCC. £150 was available from the church accounts plus another £53 from invested money for the project, but the village was advised in the *Parish magazine*: 'We must be prepared for a great effort. In the meantime – do not miss services because the bell is not being rung.'

Today St. Mark's, Marton is a very attractive and welcoming little church. The interior is elegant and well proportioned. It is light and airy and the stained glass windows are of pleasant muted colours unusual for the time when the church was built, as the trend then was to use the heavy strong colours of the German glass makers. The east window is of Christ baptised, Christ crucified and Christ risen. The south window is believed to be of the infant Samuel and his mother.

In 1993 it was necessary to launch an appeal for the refurbishment of the church. More than £20,000 was raised (with only £2,000 in grants) from among local people and well wishers in the space of two years, and the work was completed in 1995.[16]

In August 2008 an appeal went out from the parochial church council to the village when it was realised that the church needed a new roof, estimated to cost £45,000. To date £15,000 has been raised. After 20 years serving the parishes of Chirbury, Marton, Middleton, the Marsh, Trelystan and Leighton, the Rev. Philip Harratt and his family moved in July 2009 to become Vicar of Embleton with Rennington and Rock in Northumberland. The churchwardens are currently Mr. John West and Mr. John Francis.

A list of the names of past incumbents of Marton church hangs on an interior wall. The list begins in 1861 five years after the church was consecrated:

> 1861-1862 .. Rev. G. Horn
> 1862-1886 .. H. Pulley
> 1887-1912 .. A.C.Higgins
> 1913-1941 .. G.W Hounsfield

*A postcard from a series published by the* County Times, *Welshpool, at the beginning of the 20th century, before the church tower was replaced with a bell turret*

| 1942-1965 | .. | S.W. Roden |
| 1966-1968 | .. | M.J. Peel |
| 1968-1970 | .. | C.G. Barker |
| 1970-1980 | .. | R.J. Colby |
| 1980-1988 | .. | K.J.F. Bradbury |
| 1988-2009 | .. | P.D. Harratt |

The churchyard is spacious and well kept. A register of the graves and monumental inscriptions was compiled by Marton WI and donated to the Shropshire Archives. In 1966 a faculty was obtained to remove neglected gravestones from the eastern part of the churchyard when a garden of remembrance was made.

The vicarage was built about the same time as the church. A spacious grey stone structure it stands on the sloping ground overlooking the pool adjacent to the Worthen parish boundary. The vicars were never very well off, with a stipend of £80 per year and four acres of glebe land to maintain the Vicarage, stable and horse, a cook, a housemaid, and a groom as well as the vicar and his family. There were constant appeals for the stipend to be increased and there was considerable correspondence between the Rev. Hounsfield and the Church Commissioners for repairs and improvements to the Vicarage, including the installation of a bathroom. An appeal was issued by J. Clarke Davies and Robert Gwilt, churchwardens of Marton, Edward Powell and W.H. Morris, churchwardens of Chirbury, and J.B. Reed, Vicar of Chirbury[17] to increase the stipend to something like a living wage, to which Sir Offley Wakeman promised the sum of £200 on condition that a similar sum was raised within three years. A sum of £50 was promised by E.S. Mostyn Pryce Esq. of Gunley on condition that the parishioners of Marton raised a similar sum. The churchwardens issuing the appeal felt it was quite impossible to raise that amount in the parish 'which is exceptionally poor, as its population of about 200 consists almost entirely of small farmers and farm labourers.' However, the church in Chirbury proposed to hold a summer bazaar and anticipated raising £100. Other sums of money from the Diocesan Society for

*The Vicarage possibly in the 1930s, as depicted in an appeals leaflet*

the Augmentation of Benefices and from the Ecclesiastical Commissioners would hopefully help produce a total of £1,200 that would generate an annual income of £120 which was still considered hardly adequate. Whatever the outcome of this appeal was, in 1938 it was proposed to re-unite Marton and Chirbury once more, and despite many pleas from Marton parishioners, this took place in 1943. The Rev. Roden, then Vicar of Chirbury, took over the benefice and the Vicarage was sold.

# Chapter 20

# Schooldays and a Rebellion

### The village school

The Marton 1841 census did not provide a classification for schoolchildren or scholars. Children are simply recorded, their age is given and relationship to the head of the family and birth place, in or out of Shropshire. Nonetheless there was a schoolmistress in the village in 1841 providing some kind of education for some children.[1] The situation was different 20 years later in 1861. Sarah Jones, aged 52, who lived in the schoolhouse, the location of which is uncertain, was head of the household and her occupation stated as schoolmistress. It's quite feasible to presume that she taught many of the 54 children classified on this census as scholars. Their ages ranged from 1 to 16. Robert Arthur Oliver from the grocer's shop, aged 15, was listed as a scholar as was Sarah Ann Gardner, aged 16, from The Smithy, but it's possible that their education took place outside the village. Some children on the census were not listed as scholars and since there was no compulsion to educate children, presumably they grew up with a minimum of literacy skills or were educated to some degree at home by a parent or parents. However, the families who attended the Congregational church may have attended Sunday School as well, where literacy was taught alongside Biblical stories and precepts, with some history and geography.

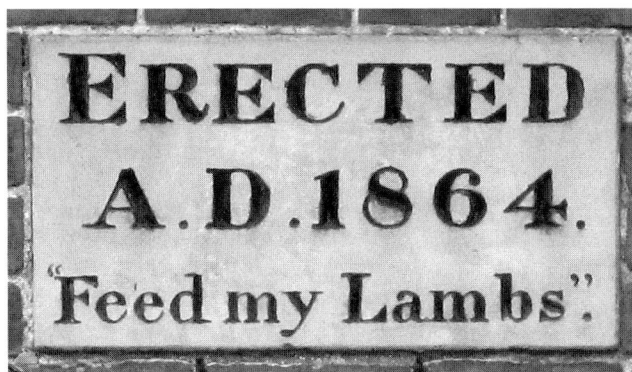

*The plaque set into the wall of Marton's old school building*

In 1864 the time was ripe for the worthies of the village to take matters into their own hands and provide a purpose built school large enough to accommodate all of the children in Marton and to set forth the philosophy upon which the school was to be based. An account of the foundation of the school was printed in the *Corndon Magazine* in 1922:

The Title deed dated 29 February 1864 conveys a piece of ground in the District or Township of Marton in the Parish of Chirbury as a site for a Parochial School. Mrs. Mary Edmonds of Edderton Hall in the Parish of Forden conveys it to the Lord Bishop of Hereford and his successors to the Incumbent and Churchwardens of the District of Marton and to the Rural Dean and his successors. The land is bounded by the Independent chapel, two cottages and a ditch. The premises on it are to be used for a School for the education of the children of Marton in the principles of the Church of England and as a residence for the Teacher or Teachers of the said school. There are to be four foundation Managers, ie. one ex-officio manager, one nominated manager, two co-optative managers, one Parish council and one County council manager.

The ex-officio manager is the principal officiating Minister of the Parish and cannot resign.

The nominated Manager appointed by the Minister and Churchwardens is Mr. J.P. Francis, the co-optative Managers are Mr. J. Gardner and Mrs. Howell Evans of Edderton Hall. The Parish council Manager is Mr. R. Gwilt. The County council Manager is E.S Mostyn-Pryce Esq. of Gunley Hall.

The managers are bound to meet every three months. The school treasurer is Mr. R. Gwilt. The School House is at present let to the School cleaner, Mr. D. Lloyd.

The school has 61 children on the books. The Headteacher is Miss Graig, the uncertificated assistant teacher is Miss E.B. Yeomans, to whom an apology is due for her name having so often appeared in incorrect form in this magazine. The school correspondent is the Rev. Hounsfield.

Our readers will pardon these lines as they will show them the great interest the Church of England has always taken in our education as a Christian people.[2]

The school building of red brick consisted of the schoolroom, which could accommodate 80 children, and a house for the mistress. The datestone inset in the exterior wall is inscribed with a biblical precept, 'Feed my lambs' a choice of words which reflected the motivation of those moved to provide the school. The first head was Miss Alice Catherine Whitaker who was reported to be 'bright, informative and firm'.[3]

In *The Shrewsbury Chronicle* during the 1930s the headmistress of the time describes the building in unflattering terms as reported by the District Ranger (the name given to the paper's roving reporter) 'The pious founder of the school tried to make the house a kind of prison. It was built where it would be impossible for the governors to see anyone or be seen and to guard against possible frivolity in entertaining friends the teacher was allowed to have only one chair, one cup and so on. This scant furnishing was in those days supplied by the managers'.

The report made following the Education Act of 1902 describes the building, noting that it had three playgrounds, an enlarged cloakporch built in 1894 and a schoolroom with 'abundant space' and assessing the improvements required as drainage of the playgrounds, general repair and provision of a water supply. The head teacher, Mr. J.C. Main, was recorded as living in the schoolhouse and receiving a fuel and light allowance. The report recommended that the assistant teacher, Miss Maddox, received a rise of £5.

In 1902 the school managers – J.C. Davies Esq., Mr. W. Hughes, Mr. T. Butler, Mr. J. Gardner, all of them Marton residents – had been in office since the arrival of the Rev A.C. Higgins who had taken over his appointment 15 years previously.

The junior curriculum included English, Maths, Drawing (boys), Needlework (girls), Geography, History, Common things, Singing and Drill, whilst the Infants were taught Reading, Writing and Numbers, simple lessons in Common things, Needlework, Drawing, Singing and Drill.

The average attendance was 36 children, but the number on the school register at the end of the last school year was 52.[4] Regular attendance of their pupils was always a primary target for the school staff in the first quarter of the 20th century

In November 1909, Miss Millicent B. Martin took over the headship of the school and noted:

> Attendance has continued to be poor this week. Mr. Blakeman the attendance officer called during the afternoon on Tuesday and took the names of the most irregular ones.
> Dec. 11th. Attendance is very poor this week owing to colds being prevalent.
>
> 1910.
> Feb. 11th. The attendance is very irregular and very little improvement can be expected in the work of the school until this important fact is realised.[5]

In 1910, the School Inspector, Mr. C. Pawle, found some encouraging signs:

> The new mistress is bright and firm in manner and is paying attention to the chief defects. Although inevitably the children are still backward, sufficient improvement has already been made to justify expectation that the school will gradually be raised to a satisfactory level of efficiency.
> The assistant mistress is much to be commended for the improvement she has effected in her manner and methods of teaching.
> It is understood that the ventilation is to be improved.[6]

There was some improvement in attendance figures and in exam results by the end of the summer term, but illnesses such as colds, scabies and impetigo inevitably took their toll of the children. Many of the children were involved in seasonal agricultural activities such as harvesting when they stayed away for a week or more. Four boys were absent to assist at the shoot at Gunley. In other instances the school closed officially, such as for the Hiring Fair at Welshpool, a Sunday School treat or the use of the school by another organisation such as when the Druids Club Feast was held. At the conclusion of the First World War the children celebrated with a week's official holiday. Empire Day was celebrated on 23 May with a holiday, a tea and an address by the Rev. Hewson.[7]

February 26 Copy of Report made by H.M.J. Mr C.S. Pawle
after visit of 10th February 1910.

"The new mistress is bright and
firm in manner and is paying
attention to the chief defects.
Although inevitably the children
are still very backward,
sufficient improvement has
already been made to justify the
expectation that this school will
be gradually raised to a satisfactory
level of efficiency.

*Mr. C. Pawle, the H.M.Inspector in 1910, is impressed with the new schoolmistress*

In spite of the difficulties holding back their children, both parents and teachers would have seen progress in the school over those early years. On 7 July 1911 the Headmistress, Miss Stoessiger, wrote in the School Log book:

> The school was closed on account of the Nature Study Exhibition at the Shrewsbury and West Midland Agricultural Show. Miss Maddox and I with twelve children visited the Show in Shrewsbury and went with interest through the school work department.

Some changes in class organisation and teaching content suggested by the school inspector were adopted and bore fruit. It was noted by H.M.Inspector in 1913:

> The headmistress has drawn up a good scheme and has written a discriminating appreciation of the work in her terminal report. It would be advisable to teach the older scholars in two groups for nearly all subjects so that the junior children may be able to receive instruction better suited to their powers of comprehension. The teaching of arithmetic might be somewhat simplified. The junior children need a thorough grounding in the methods of calculation and the older children need practice in exercising their individual intelligence in dealing with simple practical problems.

*An early 20th-century photograph showing chapel, school
and well turned out scholars*

The mistress manages the children pleasantly and takes much trouble with them. The written exercises are very fair as regards accuracy and neatness though punctuation might receive more attention. The children are very nicely mannered but it seems to be a matter of great difficulty to train them to express themselves orally with any confidence and fluency and many make little or no attempt to do so. Recitation however, shows improvement; the modification of organisation suggested above and more attention to the form of questioning to elicit answers at length and methodical checking of chorus and indiscriminate answering should prove effective measures. It is interesting to note that 'Handwork' has been introduced and seems to prove an attractive subject.

The Physical exercises are performed with some keenness though more vigour and accuracy are desirable. Full advantage should be taken of the many hints and directions given in the Official Syllabus.

The younger children and Infants are taught in an earnest and painstaking fashion.                                                               HMI Mr. C.D. Pawle[8]

*The Corndon Magazine* of 1914 contains a religious report by Harold Mason, possibly a Diocesan inspector, who recommends the good teaching and high tone of the school at this stage. The Catechism was satisfactorily written and Division Two did very good work in all its subjects. However the School Inspection report of 1926 reveals some problems had developed during the early part of that decade:

The headmistress was appointed to this school a little over a year ago when conditions were not satisfactory. She has made a commendable effort to create a different atmosphere and to encourage the children to take an interest in school life … but there was much more to be done before the attainments and application of the children were satisfactory. Many of the children come to school at a late age but satisfactory progress in being made.                HMI H.A. Hinton[9]

137

*Younger schoolchildren in 1921*

In 1926 five pupils sat the Bible and Prayer book examination: Mabel Mellings (1st class pass), Melinda Davies, Irene Hughes and George Blockley (2nd class passes) and Harriet Lewis (3rd class pass).[10]

*Senior children in 1928*

Eight years later the school has a glowing report from HMI. The headmistress was complimented on the marked progress in the school in all areas:

There is a good tone in the school and it is evident that the children are enjoying their school life. They are much more responsive and interested in their work.[11]

The school was closed at Whitsun in 1937 (12-18 May) for the Coronation of King George V:

The children have been engaged in Coronation activities for some time, handicrafts for decoration etc., plays, poems and songs with lessons based on the Coronation – its history and meaning. The school was decorated for the occasion. Every effort was made to make the occasion memorable for the children. They attended the tea and sports in charge of the head teacher. Through the kindness of Miss Hounsfield mugs were distributed to children up to 16 years. Mr. Fenton, a visitor at The Sun Inn presented a Coronation medal to each school child. They received gifts of sweets, money etc. from the local Coronation fund committee which also financed the trip to the cinema at Welshpool [arranged by the head teacher] to see the Coronation film. The majority of the children had never been to a cinema before.[12]

*Marton School 1931-32. Teachers: Miss Grovenor and Mrs Turner*
*Back row left to right: Harry Evans, Geoff Evans, Charlie Hughes, Harry Trow, Garth Maddox*
*Standing next row: Linda Maddox, D. Moss, Mary Francis, Susie Trow, Hilda Evans, Venice Lewis, ?, ?, ?, ?, ?*
*Next row: ?, Esther Gittens, ?, Gwen Lewis, Betty Mostyn, Joan Phillips, Joyce Lewis, Joan/Nora Hamer, Bert Price, Percy Trow*
*Front row: John Francis and Charlie Lewis (kneeling), Tom Trow, Henry Lewis, ?, ?, Doug Evans, David Phillips, ?, ?*
*On the photograph but not recognised: Jessie Vaughan, Ruby Hughes, Jane Vaughan, David Evans and Vaughan Davies*

As a result, the following letter addressed to Miss Hounsfield appeared in the *Parish magazine*:

> The Den, Marton, Montgomery. 28th May, 1937.
> Dear Madam,
> I am writing to thank you for the beautiful mugs. We were sorry to hear that you were ill and couldn't come to give them to us, and hope you will soon be better. Mrs. Fenton presented them to us and Mr. Fenton gave us medals and we also received a three penny piece each. We had a lovely tea and afterwards we went out in the field for the sports. We enjoyed ourselves very much, running races and playing games. Afterwards we went to the Hall for the Social. On the following Saturday we were treated to the pictures in Welshpool and we saw the film, *Mary Queen of Scots*, which was followed by the Coronation film. It was the first time I had been to the cinema and I enjoyed myself very much. Yours truly Esther Gittins.

As a Church of England Primary school it was also subject to regular inspections by representatives of the diocese. In 1939, the Rev. A.R. Vincent from Minsterley made such a visit and another good report was filed for posterity:

> The discipline and tone of the school are excellent. The infants were as usual eager to answer questions and showed by their answers that they enjoyed the subject. Although the seniors have always done well I think it is true to say this year they answered questions more readily than ever before. It is a great pleasure to visit the school.[13]

**The Rebel School**

In 1946 Marton school was one of those small rural village schools nominated for closure by the Local Education Authority (LEA) under the county development plan. Many changes in the education of the nation's children were introduced by the Education Act of 1944 in a determined attempt to standardise and improve the quality of education and make it universally available and free up to the age of 15.

At the time Marton School was essentially an Anglican church school under local management in all respects but subject to Diocesan authority. The Act provided a choice of two alternative ways forward for such schools. The managers could either elect to become a controlled school, in which case the LEA assumed full financial responsibility for maintaining the school and its daily management, or it could choose to become a state aided school, in which case the state paid half the cost of running the school and maintaining its buildings, and the church paid the other half; could appoint teachers professing a particular faith and were free to allocate the number of school hours spent on religious education. After considering their choices it seems that the managers of Marton chose a third option which was to close their village school, and duly sent in notice of their intentions to do so. However they had every expectation that Marton children would attend a new school at Chirbury paid for by the LEA but which could be managed as a church aided school. It may have been the case that

Marton School's building was in need of considerable improvements to bring it up to standard, a daunting prospect perhaps. It's not known what part the diocese played in their decision but as managers of a church school they were obliged by duty and conviction to ensure their children had the education along the guidelines set out by the Anglican church. They were convinced that the LEA would close Marton School anyway so that the Chirbury option, a new school which was church aided seemed the best course to take. The decision was reported in the *Parish Magazine*:

> Under the new Education Act if we do not carry out our reorganisation ourselves soon it can be done for us whether we like it or not and we may lose our chance of getting a 'Controlled School' which would be more or less our own. The managers of Church Schools are under an obligation to preserve their schools as far as possible as Church Schools and cannot rightly evade it.

The managers quickly scotched the rumour that the old POW camp at Woodmoor would be used as a school. Their preferred course of action was to construct a new school on a site midway between Marton and Chirbury which would be attended by the children of both villages. But their hopes for this new school in the near future were disappointed when the LEA produced the final proposals in the next year and the closure of Marton appeared to be inevitable. A report in the *Parish magazine* of 1947 stated:

> The School managers have now received the proposals of the LEA for the future of our school under the new Education Act and they are now in the hands of the Diocesan Council for Education. According to these, the school is to be

*Children attending the 'Rebel School' are taught in the Village Hall*

closed and the children transferred to Chirbury. This will be a disappointment to many who hoped the school might be retained; but it seems to be, in any case, inevitable, for we are told that the Board of Education has ruled that single-teacher rural schools are only in exceptional cases to be retained and Marton has no chance of keeping two teachers with the number of children attending the school (including infants under 5) what it is at present, or is likely to be in the future. No date has been proposed for the change; but, whatever may be the case for the rest of the scheme, it is highly improbable that the new school at Chirbury will be built for some years.

On 21 June 1947 the managers submitted to the Ministry of Education two years notice under section 14 of the Education Act 1944 of their intention to discontinue the school. The managers also indicated that they were unable to continue to maintain the school until the expiration of the notice.[14]

It was proposed that the children be transported by bus to Chirbury School three miles distant, and in July the parents met to consider the scheme. After much discussion eventually it was decided by a large majority to oppose the closure of the school. It's not clear what part the managers played in this decision; it's possible that the full force of village opinion may have made individuals revise their views. In spite of letters to the LEA and a petition to the MP, the only concession gained was by a deputation sent to the LEA in January 1948 which successfully persuaded the authority to keep the school open for the two years of notice given by the managers. However the school provided only for the education of the infants during this period. The juniors were taken to Chirbury.

At this point the parents refused to accept the situation. They did not want their children moved to Chirbury, at least not until new school buildings were provided. The current school at Chirbury was, they considered, too small and the extra children would lead to overcrowding. The only spare space in Chirbury, an upstairs room, was not suitable for a classroom. The outrage was keenly felt in the small community particularly after the LEA stated that Marton School was being closed because of the retirement of a teacher, yet afterwards it was discovered that the teacher had been given another post. In the first instance their disapproval was demonstrated with a strike. The school managers responded firmly, as reported in the *Parish Magazine*:

We earnestly hope that Marton parents who are still supporting the so called strike will change their minds. The present absurd situation is doing no good to anybody, least of all to the children whom it is only harming and who are the chief sufferers. Its only other result has been to provide certain people with cheap publicity. Is it worth it? It is foolish to suppose it will bring about any change of decision with regard to closing of the school. And every right minded person (and we are assured there are many in Marton) can judge for himself the value of an agitation which has been accompanied by so much personal animosity, bitter unchristian feeling and misrepresentation.

Church people should remember what is at stake. Unless the three schools Marton, Chirbury and Middletown are amalgamated by the action of the managers and the Diocesan Council of Education by the middle of next year, they can under the Education Act be taken over by the Ministry of Education and amalgamated as a Council School. By acting in time the managers have secured the retention of a Church Controlled School in the district to serve all three parishes. So far as the Foundation managers were concerned it was their duty to see to this. If they had not done so they would have been failing gravely in their duty, and it was in the interests of the children, both from the point of view of religion and that of their general education, that they acted.

However the parents' protest gathered force to become a total refusal to comply with the plans of the LEA. They were determined to provide for the education of their children themselves regardless of the disapproval of the diocese and some school managers and against the wishes of the LEA. It was a unique development. Faced with the revolt, the LEA could do little except lock the school doors and observe events as they unfolded. The outcome was an Independent School in Marton managed and financed by the parents.

For the first three days the small rebel school of six junior children were taught in the vicarage in Marton which was at the time the home of Mrs. Nethercott. Miss Mary Kinsey (later Mrs. Holgate) cycled over from Chirbury to teach them in the small study, but the room proved to be inadequate as the number of children attending increased. An alternative venue was required with space enough and within the village confines, and the village hall was the obvious choice. The school met here regularly during term times under the authority of several different teachers over the five years it existed. Mrs. Husson replaced Miss Kinsey, followed by Mrs. Cicely Jones and finally Miss Rowlands (later Mrs. M. Taylor). Mrs. Alice Oliver, a qualified teacher who lived in Marton, acted as a supply teacher in emergencies. She was also chairman of the Rebel School committee. The teachers were appointed by the parents and paid directly by them from a school fund raised by donations from the parents and village fund raising events that included whist drives, jumble sales, the annual pantomime and raffles. Mr. Arthur Francis sold draw tickets in Welshpool cattle market every week. One buyer told him, 'I've bought enough tickets to build a new school, never mind fund it'.

During the years the school existed, funds were barely sufficient to pay teachers at the national scale, and purchases of paper and books were stringently monitored. Parents took turns in cleaning the hall, lighting the stove and transporting the teacher morning and afternoon to her home. Miss Kinsey was paid £2 a week, Mrs. Jones £4 per week. But against all expectation, including that of some of the parents, the school thrived, the number of children increasing from the original six to 24 in 1954. Two of these were from Montgomeryshire and four from the Middleton school catchment area.

Despite all the effort, the problems of running this independent school in a village hall with few facilities soon became apparent. On a windy day the stove in the hall would smoke and the children had to be moved into the small room behind the stage. Most of the children lived at a distance from the school and had to bring their lunch with them and a hot drink, although those that lived in Marton could pop home for lunch and perhaps take a friend. The lack of piped water in the hall was solved by having a portable wash basin with soap and towels and a parent prepared to carry in buckets of water daily for drinking and washing. There was one closet which was kept clean. Whatever problem arose the parents rose to the challenge and dealt with it, determined to continue educating their children in the village. The daily third of a pint of milk provided by the LEA was discontinued for two years until the parents realised their children were entitled to it and applied to have it restored.

> One morning a child who arrived late said there was a crate of small bottles outside labelled Marton. This was the third of a pint of milk that we were entitled to and which I hated except in the coldest weather when few children attended and the teacher would heat it up in a saucepan on the black stove and even sometimes make us cocoa. (Mrs. Jean James, pupil)

The daily timetable followed a normal course.

> The three Rs were the main subjects plus history and English, painting, acting, handiwork and five a side football gave light relief. The room was big enough for games when it was too wet to use the outside yard. (Mrs Cicely Jones, teacher).

> I lived at Leighton at the time with my mother when I was offered the post at Marton. It suited me rather well, it was a challenge but I found the children well behaved and no trouble. The parents set up a rota to transport me to and from

*A 'Rebel School' photograph taken in 1950*
*Standing left to right: John Wainwright, Diane Pryce, Eileen Jenkins, Cyril Jones,*
*John Francis and Bill Jenkins.*
*Seated: Leonard Bennett, Jean Barker, Robert Jenkins, Robert Davies, Ann Buxton,*
*John Jenkins and David Owen*

School. Often the husbands would be roped in to drive me home in the afternoon. We were allowed to use the school yard for PE which we did. We were having a PE lesson one day and I noticed we were being watched by a gentleman outside the yard. It turned out he was a School Inspector. The parents were very keen to keep the school going. I particularly remember Mrs. Oliver and Mrs. Jenkins. (Mrs. Muriel Taylor, Head of the Rebel School, 2009)

We did not have proper desks. They were in the school. I can remember climbing up and seeing them through a window. We also had make do cupboards and shelves. I think we provided our own exercise books although we must have had textbooks for reading and maths. I don't know where they came from. The County Library van visited us termly. I can remember having books from the brown box. It was kept on the stage. There was a piano. (Mrs. Jean James, pupil)

The school attendance book for 1951 has survived. It was meticulously kept and includes records of the children's progress in tables, arithmetic and reading. Their attendance was regular even in the winter months. There was only one day in January and February when there was less than 20 of the 24 children in school. The school was closed for six days while repairs were carried out to the hall and also for three days when it snowed and the coal had run out. The Rebel School was still obliged by law to undergo a regular school inspection. This took place in 1951 and a full report was issued after the event. Extracts follow:

The premises provide adequate space for indoor Physical Education in wet weather and the small school playground nearby is used on fine days. The natural lighting in the hall is reasonably good and electricity has been installed. The children work at trestle tables. There is a reasonable supply of books and an adequate amount of stationery. In formal work adequate progress is being made. The normal range of reading ability is found. In written work progress is somewhat slow in free composition. The children seem to have quite a good understanding of numbers… more work of a practical nature would be useful at all stages.

 The pupils are very friendly, responsive and keen to learn and they are being trained to be self reliant and helpful. They do not seem to have been affected by the changes of teacher during the past year. The school has been fortunate in obtaining the services of trained teachers. (HMI 1951)

Mrs. A.G. Oliver who was a Clun District councillor defended the Rebel School with determination and was often quoted in the local press:

The village school is the backbone of village life. When the child is taken away to learn – though only to Chirbury three miles away – he or she loses his interest in the village. (Mrs. Oliver, 1953)[15]

In 1953 the LEA produced an alternative solution with a recommendation that Marton School should be re-opened as an annexe of Chirbury School. The two schools together would cater for 41 children, infant and junior, and have an annual budget of £815. After four years of independence and huge struggle this decision was seen as a moral victory for the parents and was reported in these terms in the *Express and Times* on 17 October 1953. Not only did the local papers take an interest in the

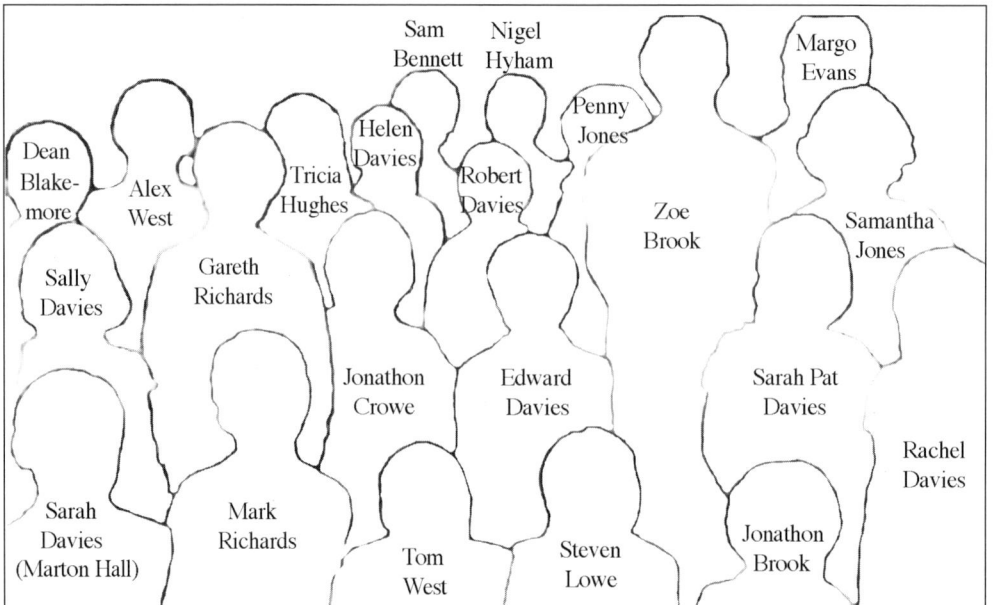

*Schoolchildren in 1984*

146

school's progress but the parents' fight to keep their little village school in Marton alive made news in the national press. A local councillor, Mr. Derek Jones, was in London attending a meeting and was astounded to notice the headlines of a newspaper 'Marton village rebels against council'.

However, not everyone was pleased with the proposal that Marton school should be re-opened as an annexe of Chirbury, but nonetheless it went ahead and Mrs. I. Davies assumed the headship of both schools, dividing her time between the two. Marton School doors opened again and 23 children resumed their education in the school building. A new school building at Chirbury for all children in the area was a further suggestion by the LEA, but the reprieve for Marton School extended for another 30 years, allowing the next generation of children to receive their education in their own village. The school complex eventually closed in 1984 and was converted into three cottages with a fourth built on the playground. Marton children are now taken in the yellow taxi bus to attend Chirbury School. When Marton School finally closed its doors in 1984, each of the children were given a commemorative stainless steel spoon inscribed: 'Marton School 1864-1984'.

> I was one of seven children. I went to the old school in Marton to start. Then they shut it and I went to the Rebel School. Then they opened it up again and we went back. We had school dinners which they brought from Worthen. Robert Davies and Len … were in school with me. I remember running home from school one day and hiding under the chicken house because I didn't like one of the teachers. They couldn't get me out. (Mr. Bob Jenkins, 2008)

In 1986 Miss Paula Davies (later Mrs. Brayford), at the time a 5th year pupil at Bishop's Castle Community College, produced a school project called 'The Rebel school of Marton 1949-54, How a village snubbed the Education Committee'. This careful and thoroughly researched account of the events of those five years has provided much of the detail included above. We record our grateful thanks to Paula for the use of her material.

## The best days of your life. Memories of childhood days
These reminiscences tell their own story, the tales of childhood when school itself was a necessary daily event, dutifully attended but unremarkable. Whatever background forces moved the adults the children sublimely lived out their childhood following their own priorities, enjoying all the freedom and opportunities of rural life in post-war England.

> I used to attend the local church, perform in the pantomime, go fishing on Marton Pool, go mess about with the other children when Mr. Oliver used to do his harvesting, play tennis on the local tennis court and ride my bike with the other kids all over the village. I also started school in Marton and finished there. (Mrs. Glenys Broxton, 2007)

I can remember playing tennis on the road and cricket and roller-skating especially when the tarmac was all nice and smooth. We used to go fishing in the Folly brook. We had to make our own nets before we went; find a piece of wire and an old stocking and sew it altogether. It took us half a day to make the net. We caught minnows, bullheads, and tiny eel things. You could sit in the water and play it was so clean. (Mrs. Sally Pugh, 2007)

I made a fishing rod out of a withy stick and made a stand over a withy bough and fished from there. Sometimes we'd catch an eel. They're hard to kill. There used to be a lot of fishermen coming for the summer. They'd stay at The Sun and go out in a boat. The water in the pool used to come up to the stile by the boathouse. (Mr.Bob Jenkins, 2007)

Us kids used to go for conkers to the Old Vicarage. Mr. Morton Evans was 83 and he went up this conker tree to get us these conkers. He was 83! He always used to walk up to the Manor with a can to get milk. (Mr. Bob Jenkins, 2007)

Those were the days when everyone walked to school or rode a bike, sometimes with one or two extra passengers on board, risking a few cuts and grazes and even the occasional brush with the law.

We used to sell milk to the school in Marton. We used a great big can. My brother used to take it down to school and I was supposed to carry the empty can back. I always remember there was three of us, Doug Evans was one, three of us, and we had such a fight with this can and it was all bent. I got into such trouble. My brother used to deliver milk and poultry to Gunley Hall, then I would walk down to Leslie's and he'd pick me up on the bike on the back. (Miss Peggy Pryce, 2007)

When we were young coming home from school I used to pick Edward Windsor up and Elizabeth Gethin and .... So I got this bike with a carrier on the back and I'd got one on the seat, one on the carrier on the back and one sitting on the handlebars. I got ready to pedal and looked round and here was the policeman. He frightened us to death. He said, 'Now miss, how many is this bike built for?'. He took our parents' names. Well, we were so scared. Every morning… 'Has the policeman been?'… 'No'. (Mrs. Doreen Trow who attended school in Montgomery)

Thunderstorms used to worry us going to school. We were told never to get under an ash tree or an oak tree. I don't know why. We used to run from one tree to another, frightened to death. I've heard since it's a spiky tree you should get under. (Mrs. Lil Richards, 2007)

Walking home from school in the summer was the worst because of the flies. In the winter we cut across the fields, across the cow pasture. If it was really bad with drifts we didn't go. Mr. Perkin Davies used to take his old tractor down to the Beach Dingle and leave it in a shed there, then catch the bus in Marton. If we were lucky we would cadge a lift in the link box on the way back up. When Mr. Perkins died his ashes were buried across the field here under the oak tree. (Audrey Evans, 2007)

## Sports days

Stepping further back in time to the early 20th century, the village children were occasionally entertained to tea on the lawns of the Vicarage or Gunley Hall by the lady of the manor or the vicar's wife. After tea the children played games and, as a special treat, scrambled for sweets. This social occasion gathered momentum, becoming an annual event taking place on the field near the village hall. It was for several years combined with the harvest home celebrations. In itself the day-long events – tea and sports followed by a social evening in the hall – must have been a marathon of organisation and effort. The children competed in races, boys climbed the greasy pole, there were coconut shies and, in later years, the hobby horses provided memorable excitement for the younger children.

> We used to have a sports day in the village when I was in school. It was held on the field by the village hall. I remember the hobby horses, I think they were ducks, or they could have been swans, which you sat on, then Sam Gardner would wind a big handle and they went round and round. (Mrs. Audrey Evans, 2007)

> When there was a sports day in Marton, Sam Gardner brought a hobby horse which he had made himself. He used to wind it up. It was at The Smithy for years after that. There was something like a horse's back with a seat like a merry-go-round. (Mrs. Gwen Evans, 2007)

## Food and home-made remedies

There were always the simple remedies for colds and coughs which were passed on from mother to daughter in each generation. A spoonful of homemade blackcurrant jam in a cup of hot water tasted good and relieved the symptoms of a cold; jam on a spoon disguised a pill. Another cold cure was an onion cut in half and placed on a bedside table. Eating carrots would make you see in the dark and clearing up the crusts on your plate would make your hair curl. As a child of the times how could you separate fact from fiction or clever parenting from scientific truth? But the children of the Second World War and of the immediate post war years were a slimline healthy generation – a product of food shortages and rationing, free school milk and daily doses of cod liver oil and malt.

> Elvet's father lived on fat bacon. He lived til he was nearly 90. I would prefer dripping to butter now. (Mrs. Lil Richards, 2007)

> We used to go after whinberries on Stapeley Hill. They were lovely days, very happy days. We never seemed to go short of anything. (Mrs. Ruby Bourne, 2007)

Back in the 1930s homemade remedies were not dismissed lightly:

One day I had terrible asthma in the middle of the night so I put some goose grease on my chest. The doctor came at seven in the morning. He said, 'You should have rung me in the night.' I said to him, 'I'm sorry but I do smell of goose because I've got goose grease on my chest.' 'Well,' he said, 'that's the best thing you can rub it with.' It was terribly smelly. It used to smell the place out. We used to keep a lot to rub the cows' udders with for mastitis. (Mrs. Doreen Trow, 2007)

We never had the Doctor come out, only if you were very, very poorly and, of course, you had to pay. (Mrs. Hilda Francis, 2007)

We didn't go to the doctors very much. We didn't send for the doctor like you do now. The nurse used to come to school to look at your head but you doctored yourself as best you could. I've got a home remedy for gout. We laugh about it now, but when we were at Rorrington mother had the gout. She could hardly walk with it, so my Dad got a bowl and poured hot water as hot as she could bear it into the bowl. Then you put your foot in the hot water. The water cures it. Just keep adding hot water as hot as you can bear it. It's terribly painful. That's one thing I remember. (Mrs. Ruby Bourne, 2007)

We used to go to Mr. Camp, the dentist in Welshpool. He always used to give us a sixpence and of course it was wonderful to have a silver bit. He used to have a cat. We were thrilled to bits with this blessed cat. (Mrs. Hilda Francis, 2007)

I broke my leg when I was in school. I went to the doctor and he made a splint for me and bandaged it up. But I had to go to Welshpool Hospital because my mother was bad in bed. I was 12, you see. I lost my mother soon after. I was the eldest at home. I had an older sister but she was with my grandmother and she never came home. She's in Australia now. My father was very good with us. (Mrs. Mona Thomas, 2007)

I had asthma very badly. The doctor used to come out. He would stay with me for an hour and a half, two hours and inject me. Dr. Stewart used to put a tent over my bed of a white sheet and boil this big kettle for the steam. I had a brass bed and it went real rusty from this steam. But it was marvellous. I could hardly get my breath like. They were very good in Montgomery. (Mrs. Doreen Trow, 2007)

I was allergic to some things I ate. I was going to choir practice one day and had a little bit of beetroot. I could hardly breathe. I said to Nicky, 'I doubt you'll have to take me to the doctors'. I rang the doctor and he said, 'We'll stop in till you come up, but I've got another lady doctor practising'.
    So I went up. My eyes were all shut and my face swollen.
    So me, like a fool, said, 'I'm sorry but I think I've got myxomatosis'.
    The young doctor said, 'What's myxomatosis?'
    The doctor said, 'It's the same as what this girl's got. You can expect anything with her'. (Mrs. Doreen Trow, 2007)

# Chapter 21

# Lest we Forget ... Two World Wars

Both the memorial in St. Mark's Church and the commemorative plaque in the Congregational Chapel record the names of those nine young men who gave their lives for King and Country in the First World War. For a small close-knit community such as Marton their loss must have been a bitter blow. One of the present day residents in Marton, Mr. Ernie Breakwell, has spent many years researching the stories behind the inscriptions of both Marton and Westbury war memorials. The following details concerning Marton men are largely the result of his research and are given in the order that they fell.

**William Stanley Bowen** signed up in Canada where he was working as a waiter, and served with the Saskatchewan regiment in the Canadian Infantry. He was killed on 23 May 1915, aged 36.

He has no known grave and his name, together with 11,166 other Canadians, is commemorated on the Canadian Memorial to the missing at Vimy Ridge which is situated about five miles from the town of Arras in the Pas de Calais area of northern France.

His father was the Rev. William Bowen, minister of the Congregational church in Marton in 1901. His mother was Hannah Bowen. William's wife was Rhoda Ellen Hughes, formerly Bowen, of 3 Betly Villas, Lythwood Road, Bayston Hill.

**Francis Maddox** was a regular serving soldier having enlisted into the First Battalion Kings Shropshire Light Infantry at Shrewsbury before the outbreak of the war. He was killed on 19 August 1915. He has no known grave, and his name is therefore recorded on stone panel 47-48

*Francis Maddox*

on the Menin Gate Memorial to the missing at Ypres with over 45,000 others who have no known grave and were killed nearby.

He was born in Marton but his residence recorded at the time of his death was at Minsterley. (A number of the men born in Marton and killed in the war are not shown on the Marton War memorial because they lived elsewhere at the time of their death.)

**Evan Morris** was aged 31 when he was killed serving as a private with the 1st/5th Battalion of the Welsh Regiment on 26 March 1917. He was the son of Mrs. Phoebe Parsons of Ryecroft, Marton and was killed in Palestine fighting to capture Jerusalem. His death is commemorated on the Jerusalem Memorial to the missing located inside the Jerusalem War Cemetery. Evan has no known grave and is one of 3,300 servicemen so commemorated. The War Cemetery itself contains 2,514 burials.

**Walter Maddox** was a private soldier serving with the fifth Battalion of the King's Shropshire Light Infantry. Walter was killed on 10 April 1917, aged 30, on the second day of the battle of Arras in northern France. He was the son of Mrs. G. Maddox of The Steps, Marton and husband of Edith Perry (formerly Maddox) of Milford Street, Splott, Cardiff. Walter is buried in Warlincourt British War Cemetery near Saulty in the Pays de Calais region of northern France between Arras and Doullens, together with 1,285 others.

> Walter's father, Cornelius Maddox born 29 January 1854 appears on the 1861 census at Jacobs Ladder, Marton with his parents Jacob and Mary. Jacob was an agricultural labourer, with four children: Cornelius aged 7, Jacob aged 3, Martha aged 10 and Harriet aged 13. They later lived at Birch Cottage. Cornelius went on to marry Ann, either from Stockton or Trelystan, we think they had six children. One of the children was Walter Richard Maddox who was killed in the First World War. His brothers and sisters were as follows: Harry John, George Edwards, Arthur Jacob, Albert Cornelius, and Annie Maddox. Cornelius died in 1928 at the Steps, Marton and is buried at Marton. (Mrs. Helen Hatton, 2009)

> My father was Albert Cornelius Maddox. He was in the First World War at the Somme. He didn't talk about his experiences, didn't want to be reminded of it. He was a bricklayer and carpenter working for the Offley Estate at Rorrington. He used to say that he volunteered to fight the Germans because they all thought it was better to fight them over there in Germany than let them get to England and have to fight here. (Roy Maddox, 2008)

**John Griffiths** served with the First Battalion King's Shropshire Light Infantry. He was killed on 17 April 1917, one week after Walter Maddox. He is buried at Dud Corner Military Cemetery, Loos together with 683 other fallen comrades The cemetery is near the Lens Pas de Calais region of France which is a coal mining area. In this cemetery is the Loos Memorial which commemorates over 20,000 men who fell in the area who have no known grave.

**Edwin Whittall** was just aged 21 when he was killed on 10 November serving as a private soldier with the Royal Welsh Fusiliers. He was the son of Arthur and Ruth Whittall of the Crest, Marton. He is buried together with 239 others in Estaires Communal Cemetery, approximately 7 miles from Armentieres in northern France. The cemetery is an extension of the civilian cemetery. It also contains 10 British burials from the retreat to Dunkirk who were killed in May 1940.

**Henry (Harry) John Oliver** served with the Thirteenth Company of the Machine Gun Corps with the rank of Second Lieutenant. Always known as Harry, he was one of five children of John and Harriet Oliver of the Upper Shop, Marton. Harry was wounded at the beginning of the German offensive of March 1918 and was brought home to the 54th casualty clearing station at Aire, a town about 8 miles from St. Omer in the Pas de Calais in northern France where he died on 23 April. He is buried in the Military extension to the Aire town cemetery with 920 other British war dead.

*Harry Oliver*

**Samuel Arthur Mills** was a gunner serving with The Royal Field Artillery when he died of wounds at the casualty clearing station at the village of Proven in Belgium. He is buried at Mendinghem Military cemetery nearby with 2,434 others.

'Mendinghem', like 'Dozinghem' and 'Bandagem', were the popular names given by the troops to the group of casualty clearing stations in the area. Samuel was awarded the Military Medal for distinguished service and brave conduct. He was the son of James and Ellen Mills. His wife Elizabeth lived at North Ploypup, Washington, U.S.A. (A lot of men who had emigrated returned to join the army).

We have not been able to discover exactly what action he was involved in when he died but reading the history of the First World War the date matches the last big German 'push' when we lost most of the ground in the third battle of the Somme. (Mrs. Diana Coles, née Price, 2009)

In Ever-loving Memory
OF
**Samuel Arthur Mills**
(Gunner, 87th Brigade, R.F.A.),

Died of wounds received in action April 18, 1918,
and buried at Mendinghem Military Cemetery,
Proven, Belgium.

Aged 31 Years.

"Somewhere in Belgium" his body lies
Amid the battle's din,'
But a spirit freed death's power denies,
And leaves a world of sin.

Somewhere at home a tear is shed
And sorrow rends a breast;
But a trusting soul, by pure faith fed,
Just whispers, "God knows best."

*Arthur Mills*

**Private F.C. Lawrence** served with the 10<sup>th</sup> Battalion King's Shropshire Light Infantry. He died on 20 September 1918 and is buried at Doingt Military Cemetery, northern France. He was the grandson of Mrs. E. Brown of 4 Hillside Cottage, Horton on the Hill, Stanford le Hope, Essex. His age at the time of death is unknown.

**Marton War Memorial**

At the beginning of the 20th century the Vicar of Marton, the Rev. G.W. Hounsfield contributed a monthly column to *The Corndon Magazine*. This was a collection of similar reports about parish events from several of the vicars in the surrounding villages printed in a leaflet and distributed to all parishioners on a regular basis for a small charge – a form of parish newsletter. It contained whatever the vicar chose to include about such matters as details of church services, school tea parties, social events, financial accounts and so forth. In some way it reflected the life of the community of that time with particular attention paid to events relating to the Anglican church. In 1914 an item states:

> The following are amongst those who have enlisted or volunteered for the war: Albert Cornelius Maddox, Mont. Yeomanry; Henry John Oliver, Cheshire Regiment; Henry Morris Pottle, R.H.A.; John Lewis, Mont. Yeomanry; Henry Pritchard, Shropshire Light Infantry.

Entries on the theme continued:

> 191? Soldiers on leave have duly visited us: Pvts. J. Whittall, W.J.Whittall, J. Jenkins, Gunner S. Clarke, H.G. Blockley, W.C. Jacks, C.E. Lloyd, and our two prisoners of war have come home feeling the effects of their captivity.

> 1915 The following letter has been received from Bedford Barracks, Edinburgh, 2nd January. 'Please thank the boys and girls of Marton School, Chirbury for their very kind presents. The mufflers and helmets will be given to the men composing the next draft to France. Twenty Officers and 500 men have gone from this Regiment [K.S.L.I.] to France and through the kindness of the people of Shropshire and Herefordshire I have been able to give every man a muffler and pair of mitts. With best wishes T. Dicken. Lt. Col.'

> 1919? We hope shortly to see the Memorial Tablets adorning the walls of our two places of worship; the subscribers would do well to give as freely as they can; any surplus will be available for a Testimonial to each of those who returned home safe and sound from the Great War; while the homes of those who gave their sons will receive a like recognition from the village.

> 1920? The Rural Dean kindly came over to dedicate the War Memorial Tablet to the Fallen … It is well to have Memorials dedicated to the Fallen; though they had died in vain, if we did not make the England they died for a better place to live.

1920 The War Memorial committee announce that they have collected some £25 in addition to the £10 balance from the Soldiers Supper that was kindly left in their hands. The one Memorial tablet has been placed in the Congregational Chapel and duly opened at a service on Ascension Day.

**They also survived**

One local man who survived the First World War, **Harrison Richard Powell**, from The Sun Inn, managed to keep several diaries describing the horrors of the war in France which his daughter, Miss Mary Powell, transcribed and published in 2003.

Harri and his mother Elizabeth moved to Marton in about 1909 to take over the lease of The Sun Inn following the death of his father. They had only a few years in Marton before moving to Montgomery, but they were the light-hearted years of pre-war Britain. In those days Marton could boast of a number of local celebrities all able to muster an amusing or musical item for a social evening in the schoolroom for a worthy cause. In January 1912, Harri played a violin solo and a duet with Miss Stoessiger in a packed programme to raise money for the church heating system. Dancing to music by Messrs. Clayton of Forden completed the evening's gaiety.

> I remember my father saying he enjoyed his life in Marton. He was keen on painting, playing the violin and dancing. He would cycle to Minsterley and dance all night and cycle back again. They kept hens and grew most of their own vegetables in Marton. (Miss Mary Powell, 2007)

During the war letters and parcels from family and friends arrived regularly for Harri and he replied just as frequently whatever the chaos around him:

> Shells all around Mess. Had a hellish time 4 o'clock. 7 o'clock sheltering in Mess when shell hit it. Buried one fellow – tried to get him out but couldn't. Ran to Officers dugout for help through shell fire. All Battery ordered to keep under cover.

The next day he wrote in his diary:

> Wrote to Gill and Mrs. Lovelace. Letters from Doll Jeffs and L. Did cooking in Major's dugout.

Between bouts of frenetic action on the battlefield there were long sessions of waiting and inactivity which Harri filled with reading books he had received from home, letter writing, painting and drawing. A few of his paintings and sketches have survived although many were stolen when he was in hospital.

Among his Marton contacts were Emmie Gardner and Jack Grice. He notes in his diary the death of his Marton friend, Harry Oliver:

> Saturday 11 May 1918. On water fatigue. Wrote AWP and BA and G in green. Bought green from Jock Chisholm. Heard Harry Oliver killed.

Harri Powell served in the war and survived. He was simply grateful to escape a fate 'like those things that lay about – horrible shapes which only two hours before had been men.' He wrote to a friend who had been with him during the war:

Talking about the war – but this much I knew, those fellows who were not lucky enough to go out and share the great gamble, have absolutely no idea of the good things which came out of the general chaos; they have not one hope of realising the friendship which existed between two pals, who, no matter what came, stood always together, and how that friendship will always remain.

You have to stand beside a fellow when death is simply howling to get at the both of you to know what the other is made of. Bob and I have done that and we know.[1]

## The Second World War

*John Evans*

In just over 20 years another generation of young men left homes and family to fight for their country. This war became a desperate battle to defend British air space against overwhelming odds and many brave young flying officers went missing, presumed killed in action. One local man, **Lance-Corporal John Evans**, failed to return from a flying mission. A report in the *Montgomeryshire County Times* on Saturday 20 April 1940, contained a copy of the letter from John Evans' Wing Commander which had been sent to his parents, Mr. and Mrs. William Evans, The Stores, Marton following the news that he was missing presumed dead after failing to return from a mission over the North Sea. 'I had the good fortune to know your son and appreciate his work as a flying member of the unit. His unfailing cheerfulness and resolution were always present and his passing will leave a sad gap amongst his comrades.'

Corporal Evans was within a few days of his 21st birthday. His parents formerly lived at Woodmoor, Chirbury and whilst there John Evans attended Chirbury School. Later he was a pupil of Ashby de la Zouch Grammar School and left at the age of 17 to join the RAF as a wireless operator. He had since qualified as a gunner and it is understood he was about to have a further promotion.

Lance-Corporal Evans and all the other men and one woman who fought in The Second World War are remembered on the memorial placed in the Congregational church:

Lance-Corporal John Henry Evans. RAF
D. White. Flight Lieut. RAF
Belton Tipton. Corporal. RAF
Garth Maddox. LAC, RAF
Elizabeth Mostyn. LACW, WAAF
J. Stanley Mellings. Private. RAMC (The Folly)
Herbert Forgham. Driver. RASC (Stockton)
Philip J.M. Nethercott. Sergeant. RA
Charles Lewis. Craftsman. REME
Henry Lewis. Private. Paratroops
George Evans. Private. Pioneer Corps
Geoffrey F. Evans. Private. Welsh Guards
W. Harry Evans. Private. RASC
David T.R. Phillips. Sergeant. RA
Stephen Nethercott. Captain. RAMC

Though there was a real possibility that the enemy would invade the country from across the Channel, simultaneously dropping thousands of paratroopers from the air, the inhabitants of Marton were not subjected to the bombardment experienced by city dwellers. A few bombs dropped on the Stiperstones, however, and are remembered.

> The Stiperstones were on fire. I remember that … going up the steps and looking down. Peter White, who lived at The Sun, we had a big party outside for him coming back from the war. (Miss Peggy Pryce, 2007)

It was a quite different experience for Mr. and Mrs. Ron Smith who retired to Marton 30 years ago.

**The Smith War**: London, 1939

> Teenagers expect to have fun, both of us were in that age group when the Second World War started. We all had to sign on for war service – I was drafted into the British Red Cross as an auxiliary nursing service member. Trained and 'ready for action' as it was put, my first all night duty, with a friend, was down to a big tube station called 'The Archway' at the bottom of the famous Highgate Hill. One thousand people were on that station, all ready for a good night's sleep away from the bombing of London. Many incidents took place, as you can imagine, but one in particular brings back a memory: 'Can you come nurse, shift this old chap next to me, he's crummy'. Whether I was totally ignorant (or too well educated) I had not a clue that it meant he was almost alive with lice.
>
> When the 'All clear' was sounded you came up from the underground not knowing of course if your home was still there or that your parents were O.K. Most Sundays were spent in a hospital ward helping staff bring in bomb victims and cycling home with only a tin hat for shelter, praying that a flying bomb or a rocket did not explode nearby (you never heard them coming). Off to work everyday. Six long years - how did we survive I shall never know. I thank God

I did as I got married to the other half of the Smith story. Ron was called up (as were most young men) and drafted into the army. For a few weeks he traipsed around the Isle of Wight in gas mask and heavy kit (he'd never go there on holiday for many years), eventually he trained as a tank driver mostly on the Yorkshire moors. Considering he was born and bred in London how he managed to be sent to a Scottish Regiment remains a mystery to this day. However the Fife and Forfar Yeomanry was his regiment for the rest of the war.

In 1944 the invasion of Europe began (D-Day it was called, 6 June, never to be forgotten in our minds). Over the Solent they went, landing eventually, after being terribly sea sick, on the beach at Normandy at a little place called Port en Bessin that we visited many years after. He'd only been in action a few hours when the whole of the track on the tank was blown to pieces. He survived, was given another tank and on again. Through Bayeux and on to Caen where a terrible battle took place to try and capture the city. He was in the 11th Armoured Division and how strange to find that fighting alongside were men of the Shropshire Light Infantry. The battle of Caen cost many lives but the grateful people after the war issued a medal (of which he is a proud owner).

Again blown out of another tank they drove on to cross mined bridges to free the city of Antwerp – they drove 700 kilometres in 9 days, fighting all the way – the thunder of tanks and the noise of battle was tremendous, but they eventually freed the city of Brussels. Then on to Germany but battle worn and weary he was taken out of line but not out of the Army. At the cessation of hostilities he was given the task of looking after the Brussels garrison with a staff of 2,000. There were buildings to be sorted out and the task of getting men back to their rightful quarters for transfer back to Britain from Germany. He was by this time a Squadron Quarter Master Sergeant – apparently a force to be reckoned with. After demob he spent a few months with his sister on the farm at Forden and so came to love the surrounding area. When it came to retirement there was only one place to go, near the beautiful countryside of Shropshire. This old soldier was a wonderful husband for over 50 years – laid to rest last year in Marton Church grounds at his request. (Mrs. Connie Smith, 2007)

## Reminiscences of The Home Front

At home the task ahead was laid before the farmers in plain terms. The land had to produce more food to feed the population and it was the duty of all farmers to take up their responsibilities and 'dig for victory'. Instructions from the newly formed War Agricultural Committee promised £2 for every acre of grassland over seven years old ploughed and cropped. Reluctant farmers could be compelled to plough suitable land. Potato production was encouraged by a guaranteed minimum and maximum price. It soon became obvious that the amount of land turned over by a horse-drawn plough could not compete with the acreage covered by a tractor and plough. Hence every effort was made by the government to increase tractor production and get them to the workplace, not always successfully.[2]

Pryce, my brother, was the horseman. He was the waggoner at Red House. In 1943 we got a tractor. It took some getting! We had it on order for months, months and months. Anyway a chap used to come to Pentrenant Farm to see Aunty Jessie, a relative from Manchester. Anyway we were talking about it and he said, 'I've got a brother working at Dagenham where they make these tractors. I'll have a word with him', And, by gum, we had a tractor afore long. The bloke at Welshpool was letting someone else have them all the while see, when they came through, £175 for a Standard Fordson and £7 10s. delivery from Dagenham. We used it a lot. The first implement we had was a trailer plough, a Massey, a heavy old plough. We wanted a lighter plough but we couldn't get it.

Sometime in the war we got a mowing machine. Our binder, a Dearing went down in the Atlantic somewhere. It was a foreign make and it was sunk. Dad found out off the dealer at Welshpool, Denbigh's, that the Dearing had gone down. Uncle George at Pentrenant Farm had a Dearing, and Lletygynfach and Lower House and Red House all used the same binder. But it got to the stage when there was too much corn to go round so Dad ordered another one. We ended up with an International binder but it was too heavy for the horses. It was all right when we had the tractor.

We had to grow potatoes in the war, about two acres our lot was. We used to dig them by hand. We used to clamp them and get them out in the spring. A lot of ours went up to north Wales to the Army camps. Probert used to collect them. If you grew any wheat you had to sell it all bar the tailings. You could keep that … the small grains that came through the screen on the threshing box. You had to sell a percentage of the barley but you could keep all your own oats. (Mr. Elvet Richards, 2007)

The Evans family farmed at Wotherton Hall for three generations. During the Second World War farming was critical. Farmers were compelled to plough up and grow wheat and reduce their livestock breeding. There was an urgent necessity for food. At Wotherton 40 extra acres were ploughed for wheat and cereals, six acres of sugar beet were grown and three of flax. The latter proved to be a dead loss because it was full of docks. Mary Bunner's father-in-law was a seedsman. Mort Evans used to grow seed crops which were harvested in August and the seed sold to Bunners. A good seed crop was Montgomeryshire red clover but it had to be sieved to clean it.

During the Second World War the story goes that Mr. Vaughan, the landlord of the Lowfield Inn, was one of only five brewers in the country who were allowed to grow their own barley, malt it and make beer on their own premises. The War Ag. had the final word. If you did not do as they said you could be turned off your farm. (Dr Stephen Nethercott, 2007)

The first tractor we had was in 1941. It was a spade lugger with iron wheels. We had to wait about 12 months for it to come because the war had started. That was the first one we had for ploughing. It was a Standard Fordson. You didn't get spinning with those wheels, it would dig into the land but you didn't want to get your toes underneath it. It's good land here, seven or eight inches of soil. It's dry land too, no flooding and plenty of sun. My brother Tom drove the tractor, he was older. (Mr. Henry Evans, Ackley)

To sell produce from the farm a licence had to be obtained from Clun Rural Office in Bishop's Castle and ration books were issued to all adults for weekly rations of fats, cheese, bacon and sugar. Coupons were issued for petrol, so travelling was limited. Social visits were curtailed but at times one had to find an excuse to visit friends or go to the pictures because life was pretty grim. At night all lights had to be covered so travelling was difficult with only a slit in the headlight giving a dim light. Ploughshares were carried in the boot of the car at all times so if you were stopped by the police one had a legitimate excuse for the journey. (Mrs. Hilda Francis, 2007)

The increased production on farms resulted in the drafting in of the Women's Land Army to replace the male agricultural workforce, many of whom were fighting on the battlegrounds in Europe.

During the war there were land girls. There was one at the Manor House. (Mrs. Gwen Evans, 2007)

Besides the Land Army, there were prisoners of war who could be employed in food production.

I was working at Leighton. As you come up Leighton Bank there's a pool there, that was frozen over, the path went straight up over it. I was walking back at 7 in the morning, the prisoners of war were walking up. I had to get off the path. They were at Buttington. (Mrs. Lil Richards, 2007)

There was also a POW camp on the site of the present day group of houses called 'Wayside' at Wotherton. It still held many prisoners of war in 1947 as they awaited repatriation to a homeland perhaps devastated by the war with their families widely dispersed, and the *Parish magazine* carried the following report:

We have been asked by the government department concerned to do what we can to relieve the monotony of imprisonment for the men at Woodmoor camp some of whom have been in captivity for years. A notice in the Post Office has appeared about this. If anyone has any suitable games or weekly or monthly periodicals they can spare when read please send them to the vicarage to be passed on.

During the war itself, rural Marton was preoccupied with the threat of invasion and prepared for the worst. The men who did not go to war had initially volunteered to join the Home Guard, or were conscripted from 1942 onwards.

The Rev. S. Roden from Chirbury was in charge. The 'Lookout Post' was on Corndon Hill. The men had to spend the night there and report any unusual happenings. They would often play cards to pass the time of night away.
    One night after we had gone to bed, at about 2am, a light kept on flashing at our window and someone was shouting down below. Arthur jumped out of bed

160

*The POW building at Woodmoor*

wondering what was going on; he threw open the window and on looking out saw Mr. John Pryce (Peggy's father) shouting, 'Arthur, come quickly bring your double barrelled gun, we want you to guard the Post Office in Marton (it was the Old Smithy then), the Germans are coming!' Large concrete blocks had been put across the main road. Arthur sat in the Post Office waiting with his gun loaded. At about 7am he went to look for Mr. Pryce and ask if he could go home as there was no one else to milk the cows. The cows got milked, and the Germans didn't arrive thankfully because what good would a double barrelled shot gun have been! At times when the British people felt the war was going badly the Prime Minister, Winston Churchill would give a rallying speech to boost everyone's moral. (Mrs. Hilda Francis, 2007)

The Home Guard was exactly like *Dad's Army*. They met on Sunday mornings and marched off to train. There were searchlights in Brockton and Chirbury running off generators. But they were manned by proper soldiers. The searchlights could pick out the German planes overhead. (Mr. Roy Maddox, 2008)

## Evacuees

Marton wartime memories would not be complete without including some information about the evacuees from Liverpool who were sent to the village in 1939 to escape the heavy bombing of their city. It was a strange rural environment for these young children from the city. Their homesickness would have been acute and exacerbated by the strange food put on their plates, perhaps more nutritious but not their familiar diet.

There wasn't enough room in the school so they used the hall. Evacuees were taught there. They came from Liverpool. Feeding them was the trouble. Cabbage and chips they ate. They would eat rabbit. They wouldn't eat the cockerel on the yard but Mum killed it, put the cockerel on the plates and said it was rabbit. We had no fat to cook chips, see. They'd been used to going out to the chip shop.

We had our own pigs on the farm. There were hens and rabbits by the thousand. We had butter but rationing went on so long Mum used to say she'd eke the butter out all week, then on Monday morning she's have more butter for breakfast than all the week. Monday was shopping day you see. (Mrs. Lil Richards, 2007)

The School Log describes the arrival of the children with their teachers and explains how the village hall was used to cope with the influx of children. Their education and that of the local youngsters continued with hardly a break.

1 September 1939. Evacuation of school children under the government scheme took place. The headteacher returned from holiday to give assistance with the reception of evacuees and was on duty all day in the hall which was used for evacuation purposes as repairs and painting etc. were being carried out at the school. Thirty-eight school children arrived in the charge of three teachers and two official helpers. Detraining took place at Craven Arms railway station. Arrangements were made for the reception of a considerable number of evacuees the following day but they did not arrive.

The children transferred here are from St. Francis de Sales Girls School (R.C.), Liverpool. They have amongst them a small boy and two girls from other departments. The teacher in charge is Miss E. Cousins, the Headteacher, Sister Gertrude Healey, being stationed at Plowden R.C. School.

The evacuees were assembled daily for social purposes and the staff of the visiting and local schools met daily for the purpose of obtaining records required by the LEA and to discuss procedures to be adopted.

In October 1939, a double shift school system was adopted to share the school building:

First Week
9am – 12noon Local school
1.30 – 4pm Visiting school

Second Week
9am – 12noon Visiting school
1.30 – 4pm Local school.

It is to be hoped that social and general activities can be arranged for each school when not in session (weather permitting).

Commencing on 9 Oct. by using both the Hall and school it has been found possible to provide full time instruction for all children of both schools including infants.[3]

Some of the evacuees found it impossible to settle down and adjust to their new life, but those who did have happy memories:

Several children came to Marton and also a teacher and it was most important that they attended Mass every Sunday. After a few months Pat returned home as he couldn't settle, but Tess stayed with us for nearly three years. To this day we keep in touch and when she married we were invited to the wedding and treated like royalty. (Mrs. Hilda Francis)

My first memory of arriving at The Cottage Farm was the lovely dining room and Mrs. Francis smiling – she took my hand and told me I would be living there. For the first time since leaving my family in Liverpool I felt safe. My brother Pat (four years older) joined me later after school. We settled in immediately. Mrs. Francis asked me could I sing,. I replied yes, but didn't want to at the moment. I liked her asking me that as I was used to my Dad playing the banjo and singing along with the family. We came from a large family.

Mr. and Mrs. Francis included us always, we dined with them, went visiting their families and had some lovely days out. After Pat went home I spent part of my summer holidays with the sister of Mrs. Francis – it was on a farm and there were other children and we splashed around in a river nearby. Somewhere I remember a tree house.

Getting back to life on the farm, it was lambing season and a fond memory for me aged 5 or 6 was holding an orphan lamb and feeding it with a bottle. I loved the cows with their big brown eyes. At milking time I was allowed to watch and sometimes take part in the different things that happen on a farm. I was never bored. Pat and I loved blackberry picking on the hill behind the house and occasionally we helped collect eggs from the hens. The delight I had in holding a new baby chick.

At one point there were Italian prisoners of war, they were always singing. In their spare time they would make jewellery from cut-off cable – in red, yellow, blue and green. They gave me a little bracelet.

One hot summer's day Pat said he had found a message, it was serious – the Germans were coming over the hill to capture Marton village and the farm, and to get help immediately. As Mr. Francis was out harvesting with the farmworkers we didn't have time to find them, so it was up to us: Pat, another boy Tom, and me, to protect the farm and village. Pat and Tom got twigs and cut points on the ends, then they left messages on the trees in the woods for help. My job was to keep watch, Pat gave me a whistle. I had to blow it three times if I saw a stranger. I soon got tired and fell asleep – goodness knows what happened then – I was woken up to go home for tea. I didn't realise it was a game.

During the summer holidays on Mondays we were taken along to market. We loved those days – we shopped, ate out in a lovely café and somewhere in my memory we went to an auction of farm animals. Of course we couldn't go during school time.

Mrs. Francis always brought back surprises – ribbons, slides, books, cardboard dolls with cut out clothes. A special present she brought back was a doll in a red velvet called Pam. I had it for many years after going home. How kind was that? I was encouraged to read – my favourite books were by Enid Blyton. Mrs. Francis allowed me to read a poem from her weekly magazine by Patience Strong. Each year I still receive a Christmas card containing a poem by Patience Strong.

Before I started school Mrs. Francis gave me a knowledge of the three Rs. She also taught me to knit and sew.

The evacuees used the village hall for lessons. Miss O'Connor and Miss Alexander were our teachers from Liverpool. It was a happy atmosphere. We were Catholics. Mrs. Hughes the Headmistress allowed a Catholic priest to use the school classroom each Saturday to say Mass. I received my first Holy Communion in that classroom which is an important occasion for Catholics. Miss Alexander presented me with a white prayer book and a medal to mark my special day. Playtime was spent in the main playground – the evacuees used to skip around singing:

Roll along little buses – roll along,
Take me back to Liverpool where we belong,
Marton village sure is fine but Liverpool is mine
Roll along little buses, roll along!

Sports day in the field was exciting – running was my favourite. Pat was good at sport and won more than I, even won a race to thread a needle with a girl who was staying at the Inn. He loved sport and grew up to be a swimming and gym instructor and games organiser on the liners that sailed to New York and Canada. He says those school sports days whet his appetite for his future career. During the war, sports activities in Liverpool inner city schools were not possible. Our school was bombed, the only thing that remained was the school bell.

As Pat and I walked to school I was intrigued by the Manor House in the village. He told me if you work hard and save up it is possible when you grow up to own a house like that. However we didn't reach a mansion but we did manage to own our own houses.

A girl from school invited me to see the new kittens where she lived down the lane next to the Inn. They named the kittens Spitfire, Hurricane, Bomber and other war related names. I asked why those names, and it was only then I realised something about the war.

Going home from school I used to walk zig zag along the road thinking I would get home quicker.

I loved the kitchen at the farm. There was a huge unit where I kept my toys – the longest table I had ever seen (even to this day) and the highest mantelpiece. On baking day Mrs. Francis allowed me to help (or hinder); it was nice. On a sunny afternoon we sometimes had afternoon tea laid out on the table in the garden. It was a beautiful garden; I remember an orange blossom bush and a little pear tree in front of the sitting room window. When it rained the brook at the back of the house used to rise. I used to put my wellingtons on and paddle (this was not allowed). I loved the rain. When there was a thunderstorm I enjoyed sitting on the window seat in the dining room and watching it. Eventually the evacuees went home. I was the only one who stayed. I was in Miss Turner's class. She helped me sew a soft blue ball for a baby. By then Mrs. Francis had a little son John and I gave it to him. I became very fond of him and it was sad leaving him behind.

I was given permission to go to church with Mrs. Francis. I enjoyed the atmosphere and the singing. Later I took part in the Sunday School. For some reason I was presented with a book entitled *The Golden Girl*. It was my first hardback. I felt so important. I was interested and enjoyed both religions – as a result I now believe in Ecumenism.

Eventually it was time to go back home to Liverpool. I had that much luggage Mrs. Francis sent it separate by rail. My mother was overwhelmed as the clothes and toys I had collected over the years were useful for my little sister. After I arrived home Mrs. Francis sent me parcels of fruit.

After many years I went back to visit with my family – my husband Bernard and five daughters aged 5-17 years. We had a wonderful time – lovely food and it was a perfect day retracing places where I once played. I felt sad the school wasn't used as a school any more. It was nice to meet John, Pam, Peter and Sue. Going back home that day was emotional. Part of me will always be there. My memories of Mr. and Mrs. Francis, their families and the farm and also Marton village, the school, the church and the people are happy and warm. God bless you all. With love. (Mrs. Tessa Howard, 2009)

In 1941, nine evacuees remained from St. Francis de Sales, who had been joined by further children from three Liverpool schools: 14 from Our Lady R.C. School, three from St. Albans R.C. School, and three from Arnot Street Council School, with a further 35 Shropshire children including two unofficial evacuees.[4]

The *Oswestry and Border Counties Advertiser* gave an account of some Liverpool parents' visit to the Shropshire homes of their children. The Women's Voluntary Service played a vital role in the organisation as they arrived at Shropshire train stations:

LIVERPOOL PARENTS' DAY OUT

VISIT CHILDREN IN SHROPSHIRE

Happy Reunions

MANY BRING TOKENS OF GRATITUDE

Several hundred fathers, mothers, sisters and brothers of evacuees from the Liverpool and Birkenhead district arrived in Shropshire on Sunday morning to visit their young relations, some for the very first time and most for the first time since they made an initial visit to see what sort of homes their children had been settled in on the eve of war.

There were two special trains, the first arriving shortly after 11am, and the second just before noon. On the first there were more than 500 passengers, and of these 30 detrained at Whitchurch, 20 at Wem, about 250 at Shrewsbury and the remainder at Craven Arms, Ludlow and Leominster. The second train, which had come via Gobowen, had 140 on board from Birkenhead, and contingents alighted at Gobowen, Oswestry and Baschurch, and the final party, of a few over 40, at Shrewsbury.

There were cheerful scenes on Shrewsbury station and on the station approach, where not only a considerable number of children awaited their parents, but also a large number of Shropshire members of the Women's Voluntary Services and friends with cars ready to take the visitors out to the country villages.

After the *Liverpool Echo* printed a letter in February 2009 asking any Marton evacuees to reply to our e-mail address, Mrs. Patricia Stephenson, née Hopley, responded and gave an account of her wartime experiences as an evacuee at The Sun Inn:

We arrived in Shrewsbury by train then were taken to the village hall in Marton by bus. There was me and my two sisters. I was the biggest and my mother warned me not to be separated from my sisters. We went to the Manor House where there was a dairy with a wonderful slab floor. We learnt singing and tap dancing at home and we used to practice dancing in the dairy but we weren't allowed. Then we went to stay with Mrs. White at The Sun Inn who was the District nurse. She had seven evacuees altogether. She was wonderful to us. The Sun had a granary, dairy and an orchard then. On Sundays Aunt Bella used to take us the seven miles to Welshpool in her Austin Seven to go to mass at the Roman Catholic Church. The Italian prisoners of war went there and sang the whole of the mass in Latin. We sang with them. It was lovely. The German prisoners of war used to come to Marton to work on the farms. They stopped at the Sun Inn for petrol. In those days the pump was on the forecourt. They taught us to speak German. There were two teachers at Marton School, Mrs. Hughes the headmistress and Miss Cousins from St. Francis de Sales. They were very good. My friend Mary Walker and I both passed the scholarship exam and wanted to go to Welshpool or Shrewsbury to school but the Shropshire Education authority wouldn't let us because we were from Liverpool. So Mary's mother said she could go home and go to school. Mary went back to Liverpool and was killed in an air raid, aged 11. My mother wouldn't let me go back.

We used to toboggan down the road to school in the winter and turn in at the school gate. Another good place for tobogganing was down the Banyard. When the boys played football in the field by the village hall I was always goalie.

Peter White from the Sun went to Oxford University. When the war started he left and joined the airforce. He became a flying officer and was shot down over France and injured. He was imprisoned in Stalag Luft III. At the end of the war he came home and there was a big party for him in Marton (see plate 25). He became a solicitor. I still have a photograph/postcard taken that day. (Mrs. Patricia Stephenson. 2009)

I remember Mrs. White was so pleased and proud of her son. He had been educated at the little village school in Marton and then gone on to Secondary school and University. She was always amazed at his achievements. (Mrs. Hilda Francis, 2009)

# Chapter 22

# Of Wakes, Horses' Heads and Celebrations

The country year has always had its celebrations or 'wakes' which often have roots in the past which are obscure, but these events were anticipated with eagerness by everyone and repeated year by year for centuries. In the busy demanding routine of agricultural life any such occasion would have a been an opportunity to meet and socialise not only with your immediate neighbours but also with those who were drawn in from a distance by the prospect of chat, dancing, music, feasting and making new friends. Marton can claim only one such recorded celebratory event as its own – The Beach Dingle wake – but the Halliwell Wakes at Rorrington would have attracted many from neighbouring villages including Marton.

Of the local ancient and defunct customs there are various written accounts, the most accurate of which are probably the details recorded by Sir Offley Wakeman and the Rev. Waldegrave Brewster. The former spent a large part of the summer at his Lodge at Rorrington and shared his interest in local history with the Rev. Waldegrave Brewster, Vicar of Middleton in the late 19th century.

The latter kept a 'Commonplace Book' in which he copied local tales, stories and superstitions told to him by the older people in the neighbourhood. This account of the Halliwell Wakes related by Samuel Roberts hints at a pre Christian origin to the celebration with druids and goddesses roaming the hills above Rorrington among the springs, wells and ancient stones:

> Statements and extracts given by Sam Roberts blacksmith of Marton age 81 in 1884 to Sir Offley Wakeman and me [Rev. Brewster]. Extract as to Halliwell from old book owned by his relations when he was young:
>
> In respect of these wells tradition says that the waters sprung from them long before the birth of Christ were of a poisonous nature. The Druids inhabiting the Rorrington and Middleton hills traces of which may be seen at the present day ... and the report goes on to say that one of their priests in wandering over these hills upon a very hot day discovering this spring of water kneeled down to drink [and] found the water bitter. When it is said that one of their goddesses named Halliwell and was possessed of healing powers (came and cured the water)? ... So a procession was formed at Mitchel's Fold headed by an image

167

*Beach Dingle Wake. his own account:*
*took place on △ Sunday. The beach con-*
*sisted of 4 small cottage. When on the*
*Sabbath 300 or 400 people of all ages & classes*
*assembled about 2 p.m. Then singular*
*to say there was a stone several tons*
*weight a short distance from the Beach*
*called the Shirl-stone. Sh. stood in the*
*middle of the brook & was said that every*
*time it heard the cock crow it turned*
*round (so it did) But on this Sunday*
*it turned Nether it heard the cock*
*crow or no.*
*Relystone. his acct I took.*

*The Rev. Waldegrave Brewster, a keen collector of folk-lore and customs, records in his Commonplace Book, Sam Roberts' account of the Wake which took place in Beach Dingle on Trinity Sunday. (Courtesy of Shropshire Archives)*

of this supposed deity carried by 4 of their priests to these wells when a healing ceremony took place and immediately the water became delicious and continues so to this day. This procession was continued for several 100 years.' It took place on Holy Thursday afterwards the procession ceased and it was kept up on the Sabbath day.[3]

Another written account details some of the customs developed at the wake:

Of the Halliwell Wakes at Rorrington I am able, thanks to the kindness of Sir Offley Wakeman to give a full account gleaned from the old folk of Rorrington and its neighbourhood who attended the wake in their youth.

It was celebrated on Ascension Day at the Halliwell or Holy well on the hillside at Rorrington Green. 'Are you going to the Halliwells on Thursday?' one neighbour would say to the other as time drew near. The well was adorned with a bower of boughs, rushes and flowers and a Maypole was set up. The people used to walk around the hill with fife, drum and fiddle, dancing and frolicking as they went, and then fell to feasting at the well side finishing the evening by dancing to the music of the fiddles. They threw pins into the well, an offering which an old man, a blacksmith at Hope, says was supposed to bring good luck to those who made it; and to preserve them from being bewitched; and they also drank some of the water. But the pure spring water was not the only, or chief material of the feast! Soon after the Chirbury Wakes (St. Michael's Day) a barrel of ale was always brewed on Rorrington Green which on the following Ascension Day was taken to the side of the Holy well and there tapped. Cakes of course were eaten with the ale. They were flat round buns from three to four inches across, sweetened, spiced and marked with a cross. They were supposed to bring good luck if kept.

The Wake is said to have been discontinued about the year 1832 or 1834 at the death of Thomas Cleeton who used to brew the drink.[1]

An injunction taken out by the vicar of Chirbury in 1860 to end the Halliwell Wakes finally stopped any lingering observance of the tradition.[2]

As for the well itself, in the early Middle Ages the Augustinian Canons at the Priory in Chirbury founded and consecrated a Chapel of Ease at its site that became known as the Chapel of St. Mary's Well. In 1534 it paid a tithe of 8s. to the priory. The well became a place of pilgrimage and celebration particularly on Ascension Day. The discovery of a matrix in the churchyard at Chirbury of Mary, the mother of Jesus carrying the infant Jesus, which could have produced numerous tokens for sale to pilgrims supports this conclusion. Following the dissolution of Chirbury Priory in 1535 the Chapel of Sanctae Mariae de Fonte seems to disappear from the records, to be replaced by the Chapel of Rorrington mentioned in an inventory of 1553. This noted that the parishioners of this chapel had sold three bells for 12s. 2d. and lent the money to Sir John Braye, cleric, for six years. The interest on the money was to be his payment for his duties connected with the chapel. But after the six years had expired Sir John had not returned the capital to them in spite of many requests to do so. At this time the chapel belonged to the Herefordshire Commandery of St. John of Jerusalem in Dinmore, an organisation dissolved by Henry VIII in 1540. The chapel was sold on rapidly to the Kerry family of Bin Weston who retained it until 1637. The site of the chapel of Rorrington is possibly marked by a cross shown on the Smith map of 1804 (plate 19) placed in the area of Wilmington/Rorrington. Though the Holy Well site on Stapely Hill has been identified, the whereabouts of the Chapel of Sanctae Mariae de Fonte is unknown.[4]

Trinity Sunday, when the Beach Dingle Wake was celebrated, is the first Sunday after Pentecost. This festival day was formally established in 1334 by the Roman Catholic church to celebrate the Trinity of the Father, Son and Holy Spirit, and during the late Middle Ages churches were decorated with green branches and it became an occasion for joyful celebration, a tradition which continued into the 18th century.[5] This explains the relevance of the day appropriated for the Beach Wake. Rev. Brewster's 'Commonplace Book' notes, again from Samuel Roberts' account:

The Beach consisted of four small cottages when on the Sabbath 300 or 400 people of all ages and classes assembled about 2pm when singular to say there was a stone several tons weight a short distance from the Beach called the

Whirlstone which stood in the middle of the brook. It was said that every time it heard the cock crow it turned round (so it did). But on this Sunday it turned whether it heard the cock crow or no.[6]

The addition of the Whirlstone and crowing cock appear to hark back to an inexplicable superstition from a distant past. By all accounts the Whirlstone is still in Beach Dingle lying in the Lowerfield brook a distance from the road. It's not so easily accessible these days as it was when the steep slopes of the Dingle were carefully managed by those who lived in the cottages by the brook.

This custom continued up to 1837.[7]

Unrelated to these traditions of the past is a curious find discovered at Gunley Hall near Stockton during the 1950s. The existing building is an elegant house constructed in 1810 with an extension in the same style added in 1906. Behind the present house was a far older building which was demolished in 1965, when a strange discovery was made. When the floor boards of the oak panelled room were removed beneath them were 24 skulls, some of cattle but for the most part of horses They lay between the joists, one to each square yard. They had been placed on flat split stones and the stones were laid on earth. One of these skulls was taken to Powysland Museum where it is still possible to view it.[8]

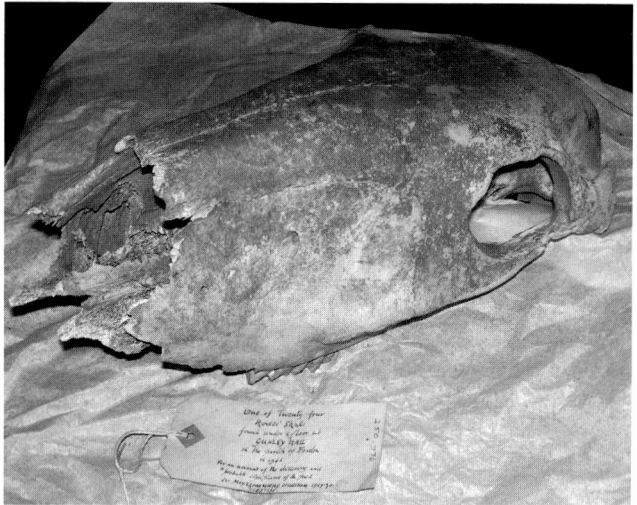

*One of 24 horses' skulls found during renovations under floorboards at Gunley Hall in 1965. (Courtesy of Powysland Museum, Welshpool)*

There have been other similar discoveries in Wales and England during old house and church renovations, the heads being deliberately placed under floorboards or in ceiling spaces, behind baking ovens or in a chimney breast. Two explanations have been given. The one suggests the heads have an acoustic function to improve the resonance of a room where music might be played, and the other maintains that it was an old custom to keep horses' skulls in houses to 'dispel the spirits.'[9]

When we knocked some of Gunley Hall down – the old library which was all oak panelled – they found horses' heads underneath the floorboards. That was something to do with keeping the witches away. One of them went to the museum in Welshpool. (Miss Peggy Pryce, 2007)

# Chapter 23

# Follow up, Follow up and Play The Game

By the early 20th century the village of Marton had a population which included independent tradesmen, schoolteachers, tenant farmers, farm owner occupiers, farm labourers, children and 'the ladies'; it had two churches with their respective incumbents and a school. The community at large seemed to have sufficient time and energy to organise and join in regular social events: for the schoolchildren; for particular organisations; to raise money for projects at home and afar; and purely for enjoyment. Functions connected to the school or the church were frequent and apparently supported enthusiastically according to the reports in *The Corndon Magazine* made by the vicar, the Rev. G.W. Hounsfield who on one occasion commented, 'Marton folk know how to make things go'.

Empire Day (24 May, Queen Victoria's birthday) was celebrated with a half day holiday for the schoolchildren. After morning lessons the children, all equipped with flags, marched past the flagstaff and saluted it. Later there was a tea in the schoolroom prepared by the ladies. They sang Empire songs and the National Anthem after tea and also had an address on the meaning of Empire Day given by the vicar.

A library of books were available for loan at the school house for a six-monthly subscription of 6d. Access to the library was for one hour on Friday afternoons.

One school concert in particular mentions the items the children staged for the amusement of their audience: Morris Dancing, *As You Like It*, and a Cranford Tea party (at which the children performed a scene from *Cranford* by Elizabeth Gaskell). At Christmas there was always the children's tea party, games and presents. In 1920 a visit from Father Christmas was an extra thrill for the 65 children present.

Church Harvest Festivals were attended by crowded congregations and abundant produce was sent in by parishioners. The church choir had an annual trip to Aberystwyth. A rummage sale at The Vicarage, at which the Longden brass band played, raised money for heating apparatus in the church, the local Scouts helping to set up the stalls. Bible classes were held for the older confirmed children on Sunday afternoons. Every year the Harvest Home tea and sports were followed by a social and dance. There were awards for regular school attendance presented to the children by Mrs. Mostyn Pryce. Dances were held in the schoolroom and Mr. Ellcock played the piano. At Christmas a Douglas fir donated by Mr. and Mrs. Mostyn Price was put up and decorated by the scouts. A children's flower service was held on Easter Sunday afternoon. A service of praise included recitations by the children and items by the choir led by Mr. Powell. A lantern lecture on the work of the Missionary Society given by Rev. S. Woodhouse was another function which was held in the schoolroom before the Congregational Church hall was built. There were regular Sunday School classes for different ages as well as the annual Sunday School party, prize giving, tea and games. On one occasion the Sunday School children were taken to the Wrekin for the day. The Mothers Union met and were invited to tea and a service at Brook House, Westbury. In 1920 the Church of England Men's Society held regular meetings in the schoolroom.

Baden Powell founded the Scout movement in 1907. The ideas contained within his *Scouting for Boys*, published in fortnightly instalments, generated huge interest at home and abroad and the movement spread rapidly. The first scout troop in England was the Staines and Egham Hythe corps formed in 1910 by Baden Powell in the south of England. Around the year 1913, Sam Gardner from Marton attended the scoutmasters' camp at Hythe and returned home determined to set up a second Scout patrol for Marton during the next winter, which presupposes that one local troop was already in existence. Wolf Cub rules were introduced to allow boys as young as ten to join the organisation and take part in activities which their older brothers enjoyed. The Scoutmaster was Rev. A.C. Higgins and the assistant scoutmasters were H. Butler, S. Gardner and Wm. Whettall. The members of the Scout troop were R. Williams, H. Evans, P. Woodhouse, J. Pinches, G. Evans, A. Maddox, E. Owen, E. Davies, E. Jarrett, E. Whittall, C. Jacks, W. Griffiths, A. Evans and W. Gittins.

Football passion ran strong and hot in Marton in the first quarter of the 20th century. The Marton team had an exciting match against local rivals Pontesbury. Hayward, playing for Pontesbury, charged the goalkeeper and broke his leg in the resulting mêlée. In 1922 Marton defeated Hope 2-0, and also Westbury, but lost against Berriew and Garthmyl. The second team defeated Middleton. Matches at home were followed by tea in the schoolroom. Dances were held to raise funds for the football club, on one occasion Miss Stoessiger played the piano, at another the Welshpool band provided the music. Mr. Wainwright was chairman of the football club. That year also saw a football club invitation supper for 20 people at The Sun followed by a social evening and dance.

> Marton had a good tug of war team, also a good football team, but in 1920 gave up football because someone stole the goalposts. Mr. Albert Woods was a goalkeeper at the time and he was the first person in Marton to have a car, a Ford. (Memoirs of Tom Butler)

> Marton used to play on one of Groton's flat fields having changed at The Sun (those who did change!). The great derby match was versus Snailbeach. Snailbeach was a tough outfit. Mr. White from The Sun and his brother Sam

who ran The Herbert Arms in Chirbury played full back for Marton. These two were considered to be outstanding players. (Mr. I.G. Griffiths)

After the First World War social and dancing classes restarted under the tuition of Mr. Jacks. The first whist drive was held and was such a success that it became a regular event. (It is still a monthly fixture in the village hall supported by 40 card enthusiasts from Marton and neighbouring villages). One of the features of the whist drive is the raffle. The usual prizes on offer these days are baskets of fruit, chocolates, flowers and plants. The first prize in 1919 was a black leghorn cockerel donated by Mr. Hughes from Marton Hall.

The Marton branch of the Druids Benefit Society, which is mentioned occasionally in *The Corndon Magazine*, appears to have been a group of individuals united by an interest in mutual assistance and benevolence. One of their aims was fund raising, hence an annual concert and dance. This type of function was often the means of raising money for local good causes such as the Royal Salop Infirmary, the Eye, Ear and Throat Hospital, the Chirbury Nursing Association or to provide for starving children. Sales of work in the schoolroom were organised by the ladies when there was a local need such as funds for the school porch. As the *Parish magazine* reported in 1935:

> The Druids Club walk, followed by the usual service, tea and sports, was attended by fewer this year; a large number of juniors were present. Canon Ball addressed us in the Church and speeches were made in the Clubroom afterwards. Benefit Societies such as this have suffered owing to the National Insurance. Still they have a real place in our village life and offer a real help in sickness and death.

Two classes of First Aid were held in the schoolroom during the winter for men and women. All the women who entered the St. John's Ambulance examination passed and received First Aid Certificates, two of the men failed.

The ladies of Marton were neither in the background nor anonymous. It's fair to say they were as industrious, organising and talented as any group of ladies anywhere and merit full credits. Mrs. Gardner, Misses May and Marjorie Oliver, Miss Lewis, Mrs. Colley, Mrs. J. Maddox, Mrs. Oliver, Mrs. Watkins, Mrs. Bebb, Mrs. Gwilt, Mrs. Jenkins, Mrs. Vaughan, Miss A. Jenkins were always in the frame.

The following extract by Rev. Hounsfield is from *The Corndon Magazine*:

> The Sunday School were invited to tea at The Vicarage on Saturday September 16th by Mrs. Hounsfield, who was able to be present and see the little ones, and welcome them to the house. An excellent tea was provided by Mr. Oliver, Upper Shop and some sweets and oranges by Miss Oliver, Post Office which were greatly enjoyed by the children. After tea various games were indulged in by the company; races and scrambling for sweets; Miss Hounsfield and her friend Miss Way kindly arranged the programme which was much appreciated and enjoyed by all present. A bran tub in charge of John Wynne took the place

of the usual prizes and afforded much amusement to all present. On going home some hymns were sung and God Save the King. Miss Gardner proposed a vote of thanks to Mrs. Hounsfield for the pleasant tea which they all had so much enjoyed.

Mr. and Mrs. Bally enjoyed their visit; they suggest that the attention of the Ladies be called to the brasses which need cleaning. Is this so?[1]

*Villagers present a cheque for £2,800 to the CT Scanner Fund, c.1988*

# Chapter 24

# Half a Century of WI and YFC

**Marton Women's Institute**

The founding meeting of Marton WI was held on 21 March 1951 when all Marton's ladies interested in setting up a branch of the organisation gathered in the Congregational church hall. There was a power cut during the meeting and Mrs. Alice Oliver volunteered to pop home and fetch candles; when she returned she found she had been elected President. Mrs. Jessie Beddoes became Secretary and Mrs. Joyce Forgham, Treasurer. There were 28 members and the subscription was 3s. 6d. Meetings were to take place on the third Tuesday of the month in the Congregational hall/village hall (the current venue). The monthly meetings followed the usual pattern of business first, followed by a talk or demonstration given by an invited speaker, and the evening ending with a 'social half hour' of games and songs. Outings were soon arranged and one of the first was to Stratford to a Shakespeare performance. Funds were low in those immediate post war days, but invited speakers usually made no charge. Their expertise ranged from 'repairing men's trousers', to supper dishes, household DIY, gardening and fabric printing. A 'plastics' demonstration (tupperware?) proved popular, and in 1956 the Midlands Electricity Board gave a talk on electrical repairs. Often a series of evening classes would be arranged to allow members to further their skills in a particular craft. This is still a feature of WI life, though the classes now are likely to be card-making or watercolour painting. Needless to say, every branch of cookery skills, gardening and flower arranging has been an enduring interest.

In 1975 Marton WI hit the press under the headline 'Game grannies try almost anything'. *The Shrewsbury Chronicle* published an article on their adventures which included pony trekking, car rallying and a gypsy camp in Betton Dingle 'which was so authentic that the area bailiff threatened to have them removed before he recognised them'. Rumour has it that Marton WI was the first WI to form a rounders team. In 1979/80 the team performed well, eventually losing to Snailbeach who were runners-up in the final. Fifteen members also took part in a 20-mile sponsored bike ride in drizzling rain over a very hilly course and raised £130 for to help maintain the county WI headquarters.

During the 50 plus years that Marton WI has existed, many fun events have had the underlying purpose that any funds raised would be donated to a charity. In 1986, the Marton WI darts team took part in the Montgomery and District Round Table darts contest and donated the £68 raised to Multiple Sclerosis research. In past years donations have been made to the Cancer Appeal fund, to the Shrewsbury Splint fund and towards the Bishop's Castle swimming pool fund. After a successful coffee morning in 1996, £200 was sent to the Meningitis Trust. Often money raised would be donated in response to a current crisis such as the Kosovo appeal for which £70 was sent for the relief of suffering. More recently the Hope House children's hospice received £180 after a speaker from Hope House explained the needs and provision of care in the hospice at an open evening in the village hall.

Marton WI has always taken part in county and national events. Delegates were sent to WI Council meetings and to the AGM at the Royal Albert Hall. This was always a special occasion, often combined with a shopping spree and a theatre visit. The most memorable occasion was in 1965, the National Federation of WIs Golden Jubilee year. The Corporation of London invited members to champagne cocktails at the Guild Hall where the gold plate was on display. It was all most impressive to the seven members from Shropshire who received invitations. There was also a garden party reception at Buckingham Palace and Marton's President, Mrs. Chris Burton,

*The WI Cake Stall at a craft fair held in Marton Village Hall, spring 2008:*
*Doreen Trow, Mona Thomas and Margaret Evans*

was one of the lucky ones chosen to attend. Under Mrs. Burton's presidency in 1968, a resolution was submitted to the council 'That Marton WI urges all local authorities when planning public buildings to eliminate steps and narrow entrances and where possible having lifts to upper floors thereby facilitating the aged and physically handicapped'. Whether or not this was adopted the proposal was a thoughtful move to support disabled access legislation in its early days.

> For several years the County Office used to hire a train in March to take Shropshire members to the Ideal Home exhibition. Can you imagine 500 WI ladies on Shrewsbury station leaving at 7.30am to arrive at Paddington at 10.30am? The return train would leave Paddington at 11pm arriving in Shrewsbury at 2.30am. If you were late and missed it the next train left at midnight, stopping at all stations to pick up and drop off milk churns and mailbags, arriving in Shrewsbury at 6.30am. Our farmers' wives would arrive home just as the men were going out to milk. (Mrs. Hilda Francis, a founder member, 2002)

On the home front, the WI has been thoroughly involved in village activities. In 1970, conservation year, members bought and planted flowering trees in the village and spring bulbs around the Marton sign. In the Millennium year an oak tree was planted by the chapel. Back in the fifties there was a children's sports day arranged by the WI with teas provided. Outings for local 'silver citizens' were a regular feature and as was an annual tea party with entertainment following (see plate 26). The Institute has taken part successfully in the WI section of Minsterley Show. In 1981 three ladies scored a hat-trick in the Madeira Cake competition. Marton's own mini show was last held in 2001. No WI is complete without its own recipe book; Marton's was published in 2001 and copies are still available for £3.50. Finally, after much form filling and head scratching, the WI applied to the National Lotteries charity board to claim a Millennium grant and were given £3,000 plus to buy chairs, tables, material for curtains and smart new crockery for WI use in the village hall.[1]

## London visits

### 1953

> We went by train to London with the WI. It was Coronation time. We went to the museum and we were supposed to meet the bus to take us to catch the train back. But the bus was late. The driver kept saying 'We'll get you there on time. We'll get you there.' When we got to the station a load of Welsh people were there. The porter wouldn't let us through. He thought we belonged to them. So we missed the train and had to catch the midnight one. My father and Bert were just going to work and we were just coming home. We had a packed lunch and kept a pork pie; we were enjoying this on the way back. The best of it was we travelled back first class because they'd made a mess of it. But we saw all the Coronation lights lit up because it was getting dark. (Miss Peggy Pryce, founder member)

Today D. and I have a mission and there is no time to dip into galleries and museums and shops ... we must go to the Royal Albert Hall where the WI are holding their AGM. We have a cup to collect. We must be on time. 14.22 precisely. I drew the short straw and will go on stage to receive the cup and am seated on Row 1. D. has a seat elsewhere – in the circle – where she, unlike me, is not under the stern gaze of the Board of Trustees and where, if she doesn't want to clap or stand for a standing ovation – (which, it transpires, are quite popular) she won't have to. On best behaviour then ....

We missed the morning session. The afternoon began with our presentations. The Lady Denman Cup was presented to a lovely lady from north Wales who had written a ghost story. She posed with her trophy – a large piece of silverware not dissimilar to the FA Cup. Now that is something to take home and show the gals. Big clap for her and cheers from the Clwyd and Denbighshire ladies in the far distance.

My turn next. My cup, The Elizabeth Bell Trophy, is about the size of the average champagne glass. Anyway, I blink in almost-disbelief. We've come all this way, rising at dawn, new frock, new hair, new shoes, blah-blah. For this? Ah well, it must be the thought that counts. A few inane grins for the camera – remembering to breathe in and present slenderest profile. Then down the steps and to my seat. The meeting continued.

The speakers were mostly entertaining. Eve Pollard, who made some particularly pertinent comments which the WI might like to heed; the man from Taylors Tea, Jonathan Wild, who hardly mentioned his products at all; and Richard Stilgoe who spoke and then performed with some apprentices from The Orpheus Centre.

Some 7 hours later we are back in Shropshire. The train trundled out of the city and we watched the ragged suburbs disappear in the gloaming and the sky

*Marton WI and the Elizabeth Bell Cup won in the national 'One Step Further'*
*Competition 2009. Standing left to right: Doreen Bowen, Lil Richards,*
*Margaret Evans, Margaret Hale, Christine Richards, Joanna Hepper, Lynn West.*
*Sitting: Doreen Trow, Rosemary Davies, Hilda Francis, Sarah Bromley,*
*Penny Kenward and Felicity Bevan*

turn dark through its windows. A rosy sunset bodes well for tomorrow. It's been a long day – not particularly tiring because a lot of it has been spent sitting down and indoors. Regretfully, we've not seen much of London. How tantalising it is to know there is so much to see and do left undone by us today.

It is nearly midnight as I drive back up the narrow lane to Trelystan. A few moths flutter in my headlights and a sole badger scuttles into the hedge as the pickup approaches. Half a moon is bright over my shoulder, a few clouds gib across its face. How still it is here. How quiet.

Footnote: The cup was awarded for our entry in the 'One Step Further' competition. This was part of an initiative to promote healthy living. Members were asked to devise a walk (walking = healthy!) and produce an A4 leaflet describing it. Marton's 'Stapeley Hill Leg Stretcher' won first prize and its production was very much a team effort, involving Rosemary Davies, Penny Kenward, Felicity Bevan and Doreen Bowen. It describes an 11-mile circular walk in Shropshire's 'Blue Remembered Hills' – which I'm ashamed to say I have not yet walked. I am very familiar with it on paper though, where it appears nice and flat and easy. I think the real hills will come as a big surprise. (Felicity Bevan, 2009)[2]

## Chirbury and Marton Young Farmers Club

In 2008 the young farmers celebrated their 50th anniversary with a dinner dance held in a marquee at Woodmoor Farm near Chirbury. More than 300 past and present members and friends enjoyed a very fine summer's evening in the marquee at the home of Mr. and Mrs. John Thomas. After the meal Mr. Edward Windsor spoke of their many achievements at county and national level during the preceding 50 years. The club had been begun in 1958 by Mr. J.A. Beavan of Winsbury who was the first president, with Mrs. A. Oliver of Marton and Mrs. Emrys Humphreys of Chirbury[3] as members of the founding executive committee. Mr. Windsor was the first chairman and the two other executive officers were Miss Susan Wainwright (secretary) and Georgina Pugh (treasurer).

The annual *YFC County Handbook* has been the means of disseminating information around the clubs in the county. Through the yearly reports sent in by club secretaries something of the changing nature of club life can be seen.

## Chirbury and Marton Y.F.C.(1964-65) club report

The club had another satisfactory year entering numerous competitions, many with considerable success. Members represented the county at the Royal Dairy Show, the Birmingham Fatstock show and the London Smithfield show. In the county events the junior public speaking team came second in the area rounds, the senior team reached the final and one member was chosen for the county team. This year the club entered both hockey and football competitions and eventually won the hockey and reached the semi final in the football. The programme included classes on civil defence, Ferguson machinery, a visit to a pantomime in Wolverhampton, classes in lampshade making, flower arranging, cake icing, hedging, two farm walks, dances and a car rally. Meetings are held once a fortnight on Monday evenings at 7.30pm alternately in Chirbury and Marton village halls.

President: Mr. T.A. Francis, Cottage Farm, Marton; Advisory Committee: Mr. J.A. Beavan, Mr. M. Holloway, Mr. P. Sheppard, Mrs. Dempsey, Mr. C. Poole, Mr. K. Venables, Mr. C. Jones; Club leaders: Miss Sue Wainwright, Mr. John Beavan; Chairman: Mr. James Brook; Vice-chairman: Mr. Robert Davies; Secretary: Miss Eirwen Chislett; Treasurer: Ann Oliver.[4]

## Club Report 1968-69

Probably all clubs have been in the doldrums during the last year suffering from Foot and Mouth pressures and we in Chirbury and Marton are no exception. An all out effort to recover started with a programme planning evening in February when all the members pooled their ideas in order to formulate a programme for the remainder of 1968. The summer months included two dances, stock judging evenings, talks and slides on farm safety, demonstrations for our girl members on flower arranging and cake icing, preparation for the West Midland show and County rally and a natter with Mrs. Quale about recruitment and how to keep meetings interesting. 1968/69 will be a testing time and with our programme printed the enthusiasm to carry ideas through and a spirit of pulling together we know this year will give us a lot of fun.

*YFC visit to Bibby's, Liverpool, 1959*
*Back row, left to right: John Wainwright, Emrys Humphreys, Martin Mills,*
*two of Bibby's staff*
*Next row: Roy Pritchard, Sylvanus Jones, Robert Jenkins, David Ware,*
*Roger Williams, Robert Davies, Neil Brook, John Beavan, James Brook,*
*David Wigley, John Mills, Coach Driver, Derek Marston, Islwyn Jones*
*Next row: Eileen Clifton (Jenkins), Mary Pryce (Beddoes), Doreen Mills*
*(Humphreys), Valerie Pye (Lewis), Valmai Owen (Jones), Edward Windsor,*
*Jean Windsor (Jones), Joan Richards (Williams), Pam Thompson (Francis),*
*Beth ? (Wigley), Susan Ware (Wainwright)*
*Front row: Lawrence Potter, David Poole, John Jenkins, John Francis,*
*John Humphreys*

President: Mr. J. Corfield, The Mount, Chirbury; Club leaders: Mrs. J. Windsor, PC Bryan, the Police Station, Chirbury; Chairman: Mr. John Francis; Secretary: Miss Josie Bishop; Treasurer: Mr. Brian Timmis.[5]

## Club Report 1974-75

Over the past year we've had a fair amount of achievements. Our annual poultry whist drive was the best one we've ever had, raising £192. Once again we were unable to go carol singing. Through the year we've had demonstrations on dried flower pictures and shell sculpture for the girls, and grass conservation and a talk by a vet for the boys. We held 11 dances. Once again we organised a summer ball and a clay pigeon shoot, both being well supported. In competitions we were runners up for both cups in the YFC section of the West Midland Show and at the Rally we won the junior and senior sections and, for the first time, the Home section cup. At County level once again our members represented Shropshire in a number of National competitions. To finish the year along with Alberbury YFC we organised a 24-hour sponsored ploughing marathon and Barn Dance and Barbecue in aid of charity. Between the four ploughmen they ploughed 116 acres and raised a great deal of money. We look forward to another eventful year and wish to thank everyone who helped us over the past year.

Club president: Mr. Edward Windsor, Heightly, Chirbury; Advisory Committee: Mr. and Mrs. J. Beavan (snr), Mr. and Mrs. F. Holloway, Mr. and Mrs. E. Windsor, Mr. and Mrs. J. Beavan (jnr), Mr. C. Jones, Mr. J.P. Jones, Mr. G. Holloway, Mrs. R. Oliver, Mr. and Mrs. T. Trow, Mr. P. Trow, Mr. E. Humphreys, Mr. A. Francis, Mr. J. Francis, Mrs. K. Humphreys, Mr. D. Tilsley, Mr. J.L.Thomas, Mr. H.K.Venables, Mr. B. Roberts, Mr. D. Pritchard, Mrs. S. Pugh, Mr. M. Holloway, Mr. D. Evans, Mr. J. Corfield, Mr. H. Evans, Mr. P. Sheppard; Club leaders: Mr. and Mrs. Bryan Challinor, Mr. H.K. Venables; Chairman: Mr. Mike Holloway; Secretary: Mrs. Margaret Williams; Treasurer: Mr. Winston Jones.[6]

## Club Report 2006

Last year started off well for Chirbury and Marton YFC. Three nights of carol singing went very well, except for the idea to use CB radios in the cars so everyone knew where to go. It was working well until Huw shouted 'left' when he really meant 'right'. Three cars and a landrover rammed down a tight cul de sac. It was fun getting back out.

On to the drama competition. We all set off for Whitchurch with two trucks and stock trailers full of costumes, props and scenery. We performed then packed up and left not being placed in the top three, but we had fun and definitely will be competing again this year. Then it's the show time of the year; a successful summertime and West Mid Show was had by all members, lots of very late nights float building in a shed surrounded by fertiliser, farm implements and a strict Mrs. Thomas keeping everything in order into the early hours.

Then September time comes around and it's time for Cruckton ploughing match. Six members competed with Huw Thomas coming first and Richard Breeze getting a third in his first match. The club also was awarded the cup for most points scored by a Shropshire YFC club. The raft race the day after was undertaken with our old vessel cruising in to take second place. Overall a busy year with a lot more events taken part in. I hope we can have just as good fun this year and you will be seeing us out and about in the country. Ian Millington, Club chairman 2005-2006.

President: Mr. M.J.Trow; Advisory Committee: Messrs. R. Lewis, C. Cookson, T. Sheppard, R. Bevan, G.Breeze, J. Corfield (jnr), J. Corfield, D. Trow, Mrs. K. Lewis, Mrs. C. Hudson, Mrs. R. Davies, Mrs. C. Jerman and Mrs. J. Jones; Club leaders: Huw Thomas, Carl David; Chairman: Ian Millington; Secretary: Daniel Powell; Treasurer: Richard Breeze.[7]

The chairman of Chirbury and Marton YFC in 2008 was Kelly Mellor from Forden. She now works as a veterinary nurse at Llansaintfraid after completing two years training at Rodbaston College.

> I also do relief milking at weekends usually on my grandparent's farm. We have 32 members of Chirbury and Marton YFC at the moment. They're all very active and range from 13 years to 25, boys and girls. This year we had a trip to Lindstrand hot air balloon centre and were shown how balloons were made. It was very impressive. The visit to the fire station in Shrewsbury was good. A few of the girls fancied the firemen but not the job. We've been to Dairy Dreams Ice Cream at Churchstoke. That's right on our doorstep. It was encouraging. They started out with an idea and it has grown into a thriving business. (Kelly Mellor, 2009)

The current chairman is Kathryn Lewis, Becky Jones is secretary, and Matthew Roberts, treasurer. After a year as vice-chairman of the Shropshire Federation of Young Farmers, Huw Thomas from Woodmoor took over the role of County Chairman in 2009. A full social calendar of county events including the Annual Dinner and Ball, and the County Rally will demand his attention (see plate 27).

> It's a great thing, the more you put in, the more you will get out. The clubs give young people tremendous opportunities to develop not only practical but social skills. I've taken part in all aspects of club life from stock judging and fencing to acting in the annual drama competition. Many of our events are dual purpose – fun and fund raising. We cycled to Blackpool on one occasion and walked to the Royal Welsh Show at Builth Wells another year to raise money for charity.

This year Huw's county chairman's project will be an ambitious and imaginative scheme – with a group of a dozen or so young farmers from around Shropshire he plans to build a greenhouse on the roof of the world. The valley of Spiti in the Himalayas is cut off for part of the year and the villagers cannot get fresh vegetables. The finished greenhouse will enable the local people to grow their own fresh vegetables all the year round.

# Chapter 25

# Pantomime

All villages seem to have a speciality, something they have made their own; it might be a Giant Gooseberry Competition, a Sweet Pea Show or even be known as the place where one buys the best ice cream in the county.

Marton was renowned for its annual pantomimes. Entertainment in the early days was largely what you made for yourselves, there was no television and the cinemas in the local towns were an unfeasible journey away for a community with few cars. Each year would see a sumptuous production, opening on Boxing Day and playing to packed houses, staged not only in the village hall, but also in the halls of other local villages.

No one seems quite sure of the date of the first pantomime, but the cover of the programme for 1962's *Puss in Boots* announces that this was the 30th production by the Marton Players. A quick calculation indicates that they therefore first took to the stage in 1932 and continued annually into the 1960s when it lapsed. A revival came in the '70s, and the annual production continued until 1996. That the tradition continued for so long is no mean achievement for a village of about 200 inhabitants.

> Mrs. Oliver from The Villa, used to produce the pantomime every year. Most of the village used to appear in it and it was the end of year event. Mr. [Dick] Oliver and Mr. Sam Gardner were the two comedians. Everyone used to put on the show at quite a lot of the surrounding villages. (Glenys Broxton)

*A rare photograph of Mrs. Alice Oliver, the driving force behind Marton's pantomimes and an active member of the community*

*The jubilee production of* Cinderella *in 1957*
*Standing, left to right: Sally Pugh, Eddie Roberts, Eileen Jenkins, Tom Trow,*
*Yvonne Watts, Dick Oliver, Sue Wainwright, Mr Hatton*
*Kneeling: Bill Jenkins, John Jenkins, Robert Davies, Roy Pritchard*

Over the years The Marton Players have presented all the old favourites – many of them more than once. The Jubilee production of *Cinderella* in 1957 was the third time it had been staged. The driving force behind the players was the producer, Mrs. Alice Oliver, who also wrote the scripts. She was a force to be reckoned with and is remembered by all as 'firm but fair'. She remained the producer of the pantomime until she was in her 80s. When she died, the local newspaper, *The County Times*, printed the following obituary:

Mrs. Alice Gertrude Oliver, The Villa, Marton, Near Welshpool who died at her home on December 10th, had taken a very active part in the life of the local community.

Mrs. Oliver was born in Leighton in 1900, and was the only daughter of the late Mr. and Mrs. J.D. Bennett. She was educated at Leighton and Castle Caereinion Primary Schools from which she obtained a scholarship to Welshpool County High School.

From there she trained as a teacher at Barry Teachers Training College, South Wales and later taught at Aston-on-Clun and Berriew Council Schools, before she married Mr. Dick Oliver in 1935. After her marriage she ceased teaching to help her husband in his business in Marton.

Mrs. Oliver was a founder member of the WI; the producer of the village pantomime for its first 30 years; a member of both District and Parish Councils; governor of Bishop's Castle High School; a Sunday School teacher in Marton and a voluntary Education coach of pre secondary school children.

With the Pantomime chosen and the cast selected, rehearsals could begin, usually in the early autumn, reading through the script until everyone was word-perfect. Rehearsals held at the shop are remembered:

> There was a bread oven at the back of the house. That's where we used to start our Pantomime practices. We used to think it was lovely to go in the bakehouse than to go down to the old hall in the cold. There was always heating in the bakehouse. The man that lived here [The Villa Stockton], did all the hand-painted scenery at the Pantomime. (Peggy Pryce, 2008)

The warm bake-house is remembered by one villager, who also recalls two of the Players biggest assets:

> After practice one time I remember staying at Dick Oliver's old shop (That was Jill's grandad). He made his own bread. He had a big trough in the kitchen. When I came down in the morning the bread was rising in this trough. He was one of the stars, and Sammy Gardner the blacksmith. One was tall and one was small. (Lil Richards, 2008)

In the early days the audience could look forward to the comic genius of Sam Gardner and Dick Oliver, by day blacksmith and shopkeeper respectively. On stage their natural talent was guaranteed to 'bring the house down' and they are both remembered by all with great enthusiasm.

> Do you know, Sam Gardner and Dick Oliver were better than anything on the telly today. He was a great tall man and Sam was only about that high. They were marvellous in the Pantomimes. Mrs. Oliver that kept the shop, she was very good. (Ruby Bourne, 2007)

As well as all the principal roles there was always a chorus of youngsters. Evacuee Tessa Howard, who was placed for the duration with Mrs. Francis at The Cottage, remembers:

> The annual Pantomime was always exciting – my first part was a fairy. Mrs. Francis made me a lovely dress in lavender taffeta. As I got older I went into the chorus. Mrs. Oliver stands out in memory as having something to do with the pantomime. I remember she made lots of cakes. She allowed me at one time to choose first.

A big cast on stage was supplemented by a hardworking backstage team who made costumes, scenery and props – much of which is still stored carefully in attics and cupboards in Marton; the beautifully detailed backdrops painted by Mr. Davies – known as 'Swank' – are now a little faded but still can transform the stage at the village hall into an upside-down house, woodland scene or a village street as they did 50 years ago.

The 1970s revival saw a new group of villagers taking to the stage with enthusiasm – and taking their production further afield than Marton too. The little stage of Marton Village Hall remained their home though. It's hard to believe that such a small space could accommodate the ambitiously large cast and scenery each production needed. Indeed an extension was needed as the cast might exceed 30 people who would need to gather for the Grand Finale.

*Dick Oliver, Sam Gardner and Sam Williams in* Alice in Wonderland

Backdrops – those same cloths painted many years previously – were hung on bamboo poles and raised and lowered using forked props. A lick of paint here and there brightened up the duller patches and a bit of tape was judiciously applied to mend minor tears. Dick Oliver also turned his capable hands to scenery and staging. Members of the cast often made their own costumes – although the skilled workmanship of Jackie Clare (née Trow) along with that of her mother, Mary Trow was responsible for many more, including pantomime horses, cows, chickens, geese and even an emu – which featured in *Beauty and the Beast*.

Perhaps it would be invidious to single out any cast members in particular – this was after all team work at its best. Some people did, though, make certain roles their own: Maureen Jenkins made a particularly entertaining Dame, and Liz Tuffin

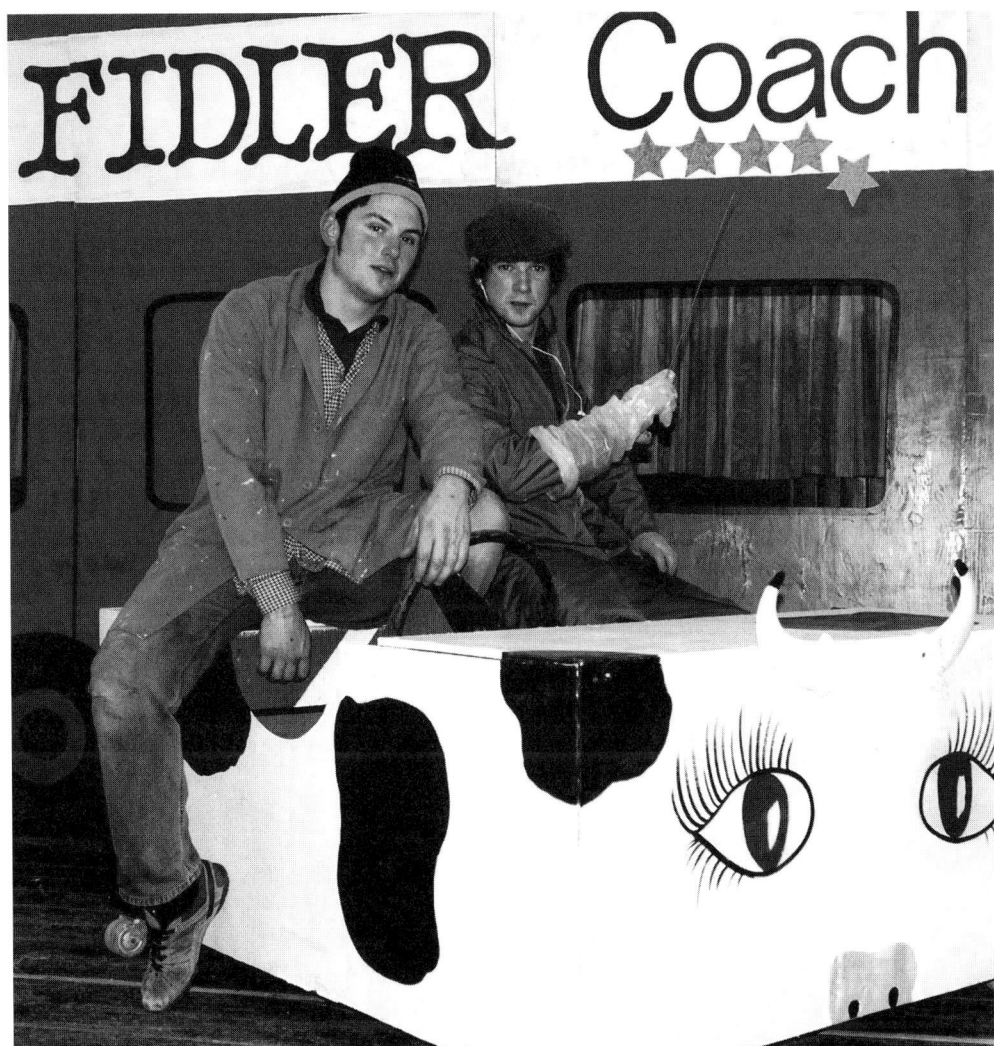

*Huw Thomas and Ian Millington come to the rescue of a broken down bus in their 2008 entry in the YFC Shropshire drama competition*

a fetching and melodious Principal Boy to Christine Richard's (née Trow) Principal Girl. There was no shortage of cast members to continue the comic tradition either, and the audience were sure to be well entertained. Marton is a village that knows how to have fun (see plate 29).

The curtains closed on the Marton Players for the last time in 1996, the final pantomime being *Hansel and Gretel*.

In recent years, however, the tradition shows signs of a revival now that Chirbury and Marton Young Farmers club have got the acting bug. Their production of *The Magic Tractor*, originally staged by the Marton Players in 1984 was very well received in the YFC Drama Competition staged at Church Stretton in 2006. Subsequent entries in the competition, including 2008's *The Cow with the Golden Milk*, continue to please Marton's audiences (see plate 28). It appears there is life in the pantomime tradition yet.

The new village hall promises to be an excellent venue and hopefully an annual production will feature in the village calendar once again.

# Chapter 26

# The New Hall,
# Present Day Clubs And Organisations

An interesting twist in the story of the old village hall arose in 1949. The original donors of the site of the hall in 1926, Messrs. Hughes of Marton Hall, then living in Newport, Shropshire were asked to re donate the land, which was then the site of the village hall, to the Shropshire Congregational Union as Trustees. Perhaps the original Deed of gift was lost or there was a problem with its legality. Whatever the reason, Messrs. Hughes were traced and agreed to co-operate in the making of the new Deeds. In 1979 all the property owned by the church (Marton Congregational Chapel and Trust properties, already a charity) was transferred under a Charity Commission scheme to the Congregational Federation Ltd as Trustees.

In 2004 the Village Hall Committee purchased the building and the adjacent car park from the Federation with two options in mind, either its restoration or its replacement. After 83 years of regular use, wear and tear from the elements, not to mention the lack of modern facilities required by current law, the conclusion was reached that the old hall was worn out and beyond repair; a new building was needed. Plans were drawn up siting the new hall away from the roadside on an extension to the site provided by landowners Mr. and Mrs. Eddie Davies from Marton Hall Farm. A Village Hall Steering Group, an offshoot of the Hall Committee, was set up to pursue the project, its members comprising: Mr. Graham Sheen (Chairman), Mrs. Maureen Jenkins (Secretary), Mrs. Pat Blakemore (Treasurer), Mr. David Yapp, Mr. John Parry, Mr. Hilaire Pugh and Mrs. Christine Richards. They had to make a sustained and determined effort to successfully negotiate the requirements of the Lottery Fund in the run up to obtaining an award of £350,000.

The village gathered for a celebratory evening on 28 March 2009 to hear the news officially that the application for a Lottery grant had been successful and that all the funding for the new Village Hall was in place (see plate 30). The total budget for the project was to come from a number of sources: Marton Village Hall Committee (in effect the people of the village and surrounding area), £26,000; South Shropshire District Council Opportunity Fund, £6,000; South Shropshire District Council

Available Resources, £50,000; Shropshire County Council, £35,000; and The Big Lottery Community Buildings Fund, £350,000. The total estimated cost of the project is £467,000. Other costs incurred in the run up to the project have been met by the money raising efforts of local people (£22,861.99) and the remainder by grants from Bishop's Castle Partnership and Big Lottery Development Grant. Local company, S.J. Roberts Construction Ltd., was selected to build the hall from a number of tenders.

There will be no let up in the need to raise funds for the new hall, demanding hard work and innovative ideas from the Fund Raising Committee which comprises Mrs. Maureen Jenkins (Booking officer), Mrs. Sally Pugh, Mrs. Laura Yapp, Mrs. Lynn West, Mrs. Christine Richards (Events recorder) Mrs. Nicky Trow, Mrs Felicity Bevan (Secretary), Mrs. Pat Blakemore (Treasurer), Mrs. Heather Thomas, Mrs. Liz Tuffin, and Mrs. Sue Colley. Those clubs and organisations using the hall will find the new building an exciting venue for their meetings, but equally the wider range of facilities offered by the hall will open up new possibilities for other ventures.

One of the most well supported groups already meeting once a week on Thursday mornings during term time, is the Extend Exercise class. This is facilitated by the Community Council's Care Development Team, but organised locally by a committee comprising Mrs. Lynn West (Chairman), Mrs. Jenny Parry (Secretary), Mr. John West (Treasurer) and led by a qualified Extend teacher. It's very popular with a wide range of older people aged 60 and above. Not the least enjoyable part is the tea and chat which follows on, often until lunchtime.

One of the joint organisations with Chirbury is the Marton and Chirbury Luncheon Club for retired people which meets once a month at a local hostelry, currently the Herbert Arms, for a meal. There are 39 members and an average of 30 at each lunch. The club has been running about 15 years under the auspices of Age Concern. Recently the club Chairman and Secretary, Mr. and Mrs. John Parry, retired after many years in the driving seat. The new Chairman is Mr. John West (from Marton), the Booking secretary is Mrs. Jill Hughes (from Chirbury), and Mrs. Hazel Highley, also from Chirbury, is the Treasurer.

In September 2009 the Marton Youth Club reached its 30 years milestone. The children meet on Fridays evenings at the hall to enjoy games, crafts, cooking and much besides under the supervision of Mr. and Mrs. R. Evans, club leaders, with the assistance of an organised rota of willing parents. There are never less than six adults at a session.

The Youth Club began in 1979 in response to a perceived need in the village identified by Mrs. Maureen Jenkins, Mrs. Rosemary Davies and Mr. Graham Evans who set up the club in its early days. At that time Marton School was still functioning with 22 children on the register forming a nucleus of youngsters who happily supported the club's activities and encouraged others from surrounding villages to join them. The number of children attending the club has varied over the years; at its maximum there were 50 youngsters regularly attending, currently between 7 and 20 children turn up on Friday evenings drawn from the Marton and Chirbury areas.

We encourage all the children to do everything for themselves, under supervision of course, but the end result of their activities is entirely their own work, whether it's a pizza or a home-made birthday card. We can hire some craft making tools from Shrewsbury and Atcham Borough Council for an evening of badge making or pyrography, but we were able to increase our own collection of equipment and musical instruments considerably by a Lottery grant of £3,000. Outdoor activities include canoeing, camping, rounders and a summer barbecue.

The club survived the school closure but our own children are now grown up and it's hard to keep in contact with parents of younger children who might support the Youth Club. I do believe the Youth Club is an asset to the village. If the local children are familiar with the village hall and use it regularly it seems to me they're more likely to continue to support functions there when they're adults. We hope to continue running the club but we need a sound group of committed volunteers, grandparents, neighbours, anyone with a little bit of time to spare if it's only to raise money. At the moment we pay £10 per session, that is £40 a month to the village hall for the hire of the building less cancelled sessions or outside activities. Parents pay a term fee of £10 per child. The finance can be a worry sometimes though we do appreciate donations we receive from such as Harry Tuffins and Chirbury Show committee. Fortunately under the umbrella of the Shropshire Youth Service, the club pays a reduced insurance. An annual grant of £600 would cover the hall, insurance and administration costs. (Mrs. Yvonne Evans, 2009)

In Autumn the village continues to celebrate the end of the harvest season with a thanksgiving service held alternately in the Anglican church and the Congregational church which in turn are lavishly decorated with flowers, fruit and vegetables donated by local families. The harvest supper in the village hall is a social occasion enjoyed by residents, their families and friends. This is followed immediately by an auction of all the produce which was decorating the church – and more. Extraordinary prices have been paid for jars of pickled onions and piccalilli, coffee sponge cakes, beetroot and marrows in the heat of the competition to secure the more delectable items. In recent years the auctioneer has been Mr. Carl Thomas and the proceeds are usually divided between the two churches in the village.

Another event teetering on the verge of becoming an annual occasion is the Burns Supper evening held in January near the date of the poet's birthday. The enthusiasm for this Scottish celebration owes a little to the Scottish influence in the Village Hall Committee who aim to roll out the event in authentic style. All the traditions of the evening, from piping in the haggis to poetry readings and a toast to the ladies, have been adopted and, for those claiming Scottish ancestry, it's a grand opportunity for full kilt and sporran regalia.

The hall is used regularly for a chiropody clinic with appointments made in advance through the village hall secretary. 'Flicks in the Sticks' is a popular event in the winter months. Bingo sessions, whist drives, table top sales and a waste paper collection regularly help to swell the hall finances.

The new hall with its spacious accommodation and catering facilities offers many opportunities for future users and undoubtedly this wonderful new building will make a major contribution to village life.

# Chapter 27

# A Different Landscape

Two schemes which, had they materialised, would have changed the landscape around Marton forever, have been long forgotten by most residents and are but ghosts from the past. The first was for a railway between Minsterley and Chirbury passing through the Rea Valley, the other, proposed in 1972, was to flood the valley and create a reservoir.[1]

The 9½ mile railway line from Shrewsbury through Cruckton which terminated in Minsterley, closed in 1967. It had been built as a joint enterprise by the GWR and the LNWR in 1862 to transport milk from the large creamery at Minsterley and lead ore from the Snailbeach mines to their respective markets. This branch line was a successful example of the railway mania of the time which carried along many other schemes which, with hindsight, seemed doomed to fail. The good burgesses of Bishop's Castle were equally determined to connect their town with the wider rail network and take advantage of better connections, faster travel, and possibly, the increased prosperity that the railway would bring. Their immediate plan to bring the rail link to Bishop's Castle from Craven Arms was completed, despite financial setbacks, in 1865. This line was part of a larger scheme to connect Bishop's Castle to Montgomery and the Oswestry to Newtown line via Chirbury, and to Minsterley along the Rea Valley through Marton. The Act of Parliament which sanctioned the Minsterley to Chirbury branch line was passed in 1865 with the understanding that the link would be completed soon after. However the unforeseen failure of the Overend and Gurney bank in 1866 spread financial panic through the country and railway mania hit the buffers. The Bishop's Castle Railway Company was forced to abandon its plans for the Chirbury / Minsterley extension and deal with its own imminent bankruptcy.

But this was not the end of the railway dream for the Rea Valley. Another set of proposals was formally put forward in 1897 by Chirbury Rural District Council and other promoters. Among these were L.J. Lee of The Rectory, Worthen; Charles S. Pryce of Montgomery; Bernard Whitaker of Hampton Hall; and engineers H. Croom Johnson and Algernon E. Johnson. The plans aimed to connect the Minsterley line, which was jointly controlled by the LNWR and the GWR companies, to the village of Chirbury through Worthen, Marton and Wotherton. The Wotherton No 2 barytes mine was in full flow between 1873 and 1911, producing a yearly average of 3,000 tons of good quality barytes. This output was transported by road using steam tractors and traction engines to the mill at Hanwood. It would have been a slow tedious journey causing much damage to the roads along the way. The proposed rail link to Minsterley, where the branch line to Shrewsbury and Hanwood connected, may have seemed the obvious solution to the logistics problems both to the landowners, the Wakeman estate, to the mining company and perhaps to the Rural District Council (RDC). However a Wotherton station was not mentioned in the proposals, even though the line would have run through the mining company's land.

One of the primary duties of the RDC was to look after roads, bridges and footways. Much time and expense was allocated to inspections, surveyors' reports, provision of stone and to roadmen in the execution of their responsibilities. Particular users like the Wotherton Mining company was constantly blamed for the condition of roads by the RDC. 'Complaint to Mr. Timmis the contractor, that the driver of the engine is in the habit of steering in the same course thereby causing unnecessary damage to the road' was followed by a 'request to the man to vary the track as much as possible'. In response Mr. Timmis, the owner of the traction engine, said that the driver had been changed.

A further complaint insisted that the Wotherton traction engine had now caused serious damage to the road and threatened that the council would take legal action. Mr. Timmis responded with an offer of a payment for damages of £67 10s. 6d., which the council accepted. In 1896 the council received a letter from the solicitors for the Shropshire Hauling company stating that the Wotherton Mining company was satisfied that damage done to the roads was not done by the traction engine but by farmers hauling heavy loads in narrow wheeled vehicles.

In 1897 a special meeting of the RDC to discuss the question of a Rea Valley Light Railway was convened and Mr. Whitaker proposed to apply for authority to allow a light railway from Minsterley to Chirbury. The proposal was carried unanimously

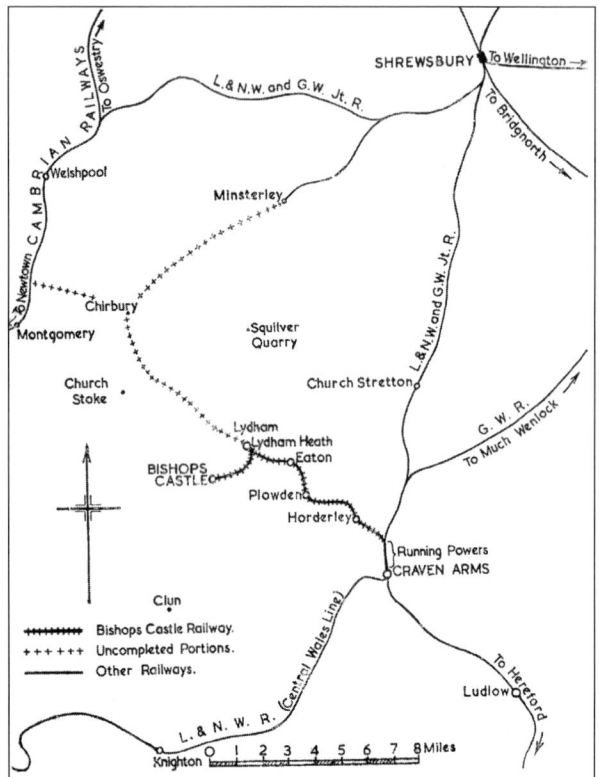

*Rail network in the Bishop's Castle area, including the proposed track between Minsterley and Chirbury (1865 proposals)*

and the council agreed to fund a quarter of the total the cost of the railway. The Rea Valley Light Railway plans which were subsequently advertised in the local papers proposed that the line would run for 8 miles, 6 furlongs and 7.5 chains using 30 acres and 2 rods of land in Minsterley, Worthen and Chirbury parishes.

A capital loan of £32,000 was to be raised to finance the venture with shares sold at £1 each. Provision for raising extra capital was included in the proposals. The full plans could be seen at the offices of Morris Marshall and Poole in Chirbury and any objections could be addressed to the Secretary, The Light Railway Commission, written on one side of a sheet of foolscap paper. There were to be four stations constructed – at Minsterley, Worthen, Marton and Chirbury. In the parishes of Chirbury and Marton the track ran across the land of three landowners – Lord Bridgeman, Sir Offley Wakeman and the Earl of Powis – affecting 15 of their tenants. It would have crossed several roads by means of level crossings with the engineers lowering or raising the ground level as was necessary. Two roads in Chirbury parish required bridges – the Walkmill and Heightley private roads. The Camlad bridge was to have a span of 55ft, with a height of 14ft 6ins.

However the council's initial enthusiasm took a severe blow when the bills for some preliminary expenses arrived, one of which was from the solicitor in the amount of £170. The railway proposals very quickly became a source of contention and concern within the council, who wrote to Sir Offley Wakeman explaining the situation. The reply from Sir Offley in 1899 reveals how the expenses of the railway scheme had been overwhelming:

> The joint railways had given no definite reply to the application by the Rea Valley Light Railway promoters and I think it would be unfair that the ratepayer of the Chirbury district at large should be expected to remain any longer out of pocket by the considerable sums they have advanced in respect of the scheme. I now therefore for myself and others interested in it enclose a cheque as repayment of the moneys advanced by the Rural council as set out in your letter to me.

The money was given subject to certain conditions relating to the success or otherwise of the scheme. The cheque for £308 10d. was accepted and the debts relating to the railway repaid, councillors further proposing that the council incur no further preliminary expenses concerning the railway scheme. The lack of interest by the joint companies cast doubt on the future of the railway, that and the expense were a reality check heeded by the majority in the council. There were some enthusiastic individuals who nevertheless continued to pursue the dream, but it proved to be in its final dying stages. The scheme had been promoted late in the century, well after the railway mania of the 1850s when investors happily sank their money in prospective railway companies in the expectation of good returns. In this instance, the financial problems encountered by local Bishop's Castle Railway Company may have been a warning to investors. The company failed to make any money on the Bishop's Castle line and was in receivership by 1867. The line survived for another 69 years but its inability to make good returns would have completely undermined investment security in the proposed Chirbury line.

It was probably inevitable that the proposals for the Minsterley Chirbury Light Railway line failed to attract enough willing speculators and the plans had to be dropped.

The problems caused by the traction engines on the roads therefore continued to be a regular matter of concern for the council and had their own heading in the council minute book: 'Extraordinary traffic'. In 1904 the council wrote to Mr. Taye, who had taken over the haulage of the Wotherton Spar, suggesting that an arrangement be made for the use of the road at so much an engine between 1 April and 1 October. The road should not be used between October and April. In reply the secretary of the mining company said that since the last claim had been made the company had only hauled in summer and had caused no road damage and that was the future intention of the company.

The Marton Rea Valley basin, its waterways and marshes have been much reduced over the centuries by the determined efforts of landowners to create useful farmland from the wetlands. So successful were these draining projects that many valuable acres have been added to the local farms.[3] When rumours of a scheme to flood the valley surfaced in 1972 it was the local farmers whose land was affected who rose up in protest. The plan, put forward by the officials of the Water Resources Board, was to form a mile-long storage reservoir with a stone and earth dam at each end to hold water pumped over the Long Mountain from the River Severn. The reservoir would have flooded more than 1,000 acres between Marton and Brockton, affecting 11 properties of which six farms would have lost all their land.

A meeting was arranged by the local NFU in Marton Pool Hotel (The Lowfield) to form an action committee. The licensee at the time, Mr. Allen King, was also opposed to the scheme as he considered his living would be at risk under the shadow of a 100ft-high dam. The chairman of the committee, Mr. William Croft, declared at the meeting 'We have some of the best corn producing land in Shropshire in this valley.' Local farmers Messrs. Stan and Percy Jones, Mrs. Jones and Joyce who had lived in the valley all their lives joined the protest group, as did Mr. Jim Dale who stood to lose 500 acres of land if the scheme went ahead. Yet another protester was Mr. Colin Passant who farmed tenanted land on Lord Bridgeman's estate. Thirty people attended the first meeting and all but a few opposed the scheme. One of those who did not object was Mrs. Yardley from the bungalow near Marton Pool, 'If it is for a good cause and there is no other site I don't see any use in fighting it', she said. 'There's nothing here of historical value. Of course it's good farmland but I think some of the farmers know I'm right. They are making all this fuss just to hold on'.

In spite of the opposition, the Water Resources Board continued with their exploration into the potential of the valley as the location of the new reservoir. Borings and site tests took place to establish the exact underlying geological strata with the eventual conclusion reached that the valley was unsuitable for the project so the scheme for Marton/Rea Valley was abandoned.[4] There were two other potential sites for a reservoir under consideration at the time, but the only one listed on the Severn Trent website that was constructed in that period is the 230-acre Foremark/Dove reservoir opened in the 1970s in south Derbyshire.

# Chapter 28

# Marton Pool, Modern Meremen

In the tranquil surroundings of Marton Pool, among the trees and neatly mown lawns are 75 privately owned caravans providing holiday accommodation for people from near and afar. The furthest afield was perhaps the owner who comes from Canada and the nearest probably one who hails from neighbouring Worthen. Many also come up from the Midlands or over the border from Wales, attracted by the fishing, the peaceful rural environment and a change of scenery (see plate 31).

From various vantage points on the hills around Marton the site is almost impossible to see with the naked eye. The caravans are well screened by indigenous trees and by trees and shrubs planted in the landscaped site.

The site was developed in the first instance by the Yardley family from Marton Pool Hotel (later to be named The Lowfield) when it was a smallholding called Northcote Farm. Initially a few caravans were let out at weekends and holidays, mainly to fishermen. Planning permission to extend and develop the site had already been granted when it was sold by Mr. John Lloyd to the current owners in 1980.

> We wanted a well designed site which blended in with the surrounding countryside but with some of the facilities required by holiday makers [such as a] swimming pool, tennis court and a bowling green. (Karl and Richard Eaves)

In the last eight years the nature of the pool has changed noticeably. The water level has dropped and many more reeds have sprung up around the water's margins. A sonar measurement has put an end to all the 'bottomless pool myths' by revealing that the northern end of the pool is the deepest at 25ft, the rest being about 15ft deep. A deep layer of silt lies on the pool bottom. An approximate measurement of the area shows the pool now to cover about 25 acres. Karl and Richard Eaves, the present owners, believe the pool is fed from underwater springs as well as by the Lowerfield Brook and another tributary flowing down from the Long Mountain. But it is noticeable that the Rea Brook leaving the pool appears to drain a larger volume of water than actually enters the pool. In 2008 the pool was completely frozen over, something which is becoming increasingly rare.

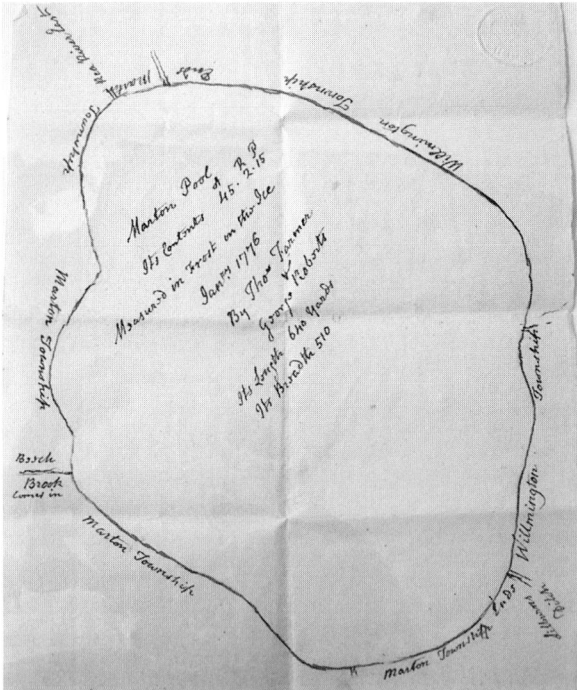

*A measurement of the frozen pool in 1776 shows Marton Pool to be a little over 45 acres, considerably larger than today's dimensions of approximately 25 acres*

The stream which flows into the pool in the south-western corner has been reduced to an intermittent trickle of water in a deep cut. In 1815 it was known as Leifers Ditch and those tenants whose land it ran through were responsible for maintaining it. The first bridge on the Groton Farm lane below the new housing development marks the watershed. All the watercourses on the west of the bridge flow into the Aylesford brook and then into the Camlad. The main tributary to the Camlad now is the Rorrington Brook flowing from the highlands south of the pool through the lands of Groton Farm into the Aylesford which then joins the Camlad south of Stockton. Drainage cuts in the meadowlands also add to the volume of water.

In the late 1980s, Marton Pool was designated a site of special scientific interest by English Nature. There are resident swans, herons, duck, grebes and reed warblers whilst kingfishers find a secure habitat on the lakeside. On a warm day damsel and dragonflies flit about the water's edge. In the deepest recesses of the pool lurk the pike that gave Marton a modicum of fame in fishing circles in the late 20th century. The largest known specimen of pike caught recently is a 28½lb fish landed by a local fisherman which has been preserved in a wall mounted display. Other coarse fish in the pool are roach, rudd, tench, bream and eel. These latter are thought to come up from the Severn via the Rea. There are also fresh water molluscs (swan mussels) in their pearly shells.

It's a fine place for bird watching; every variety of garden bird can be spotted and the less common – goldfinches, tree creepers and nuthatches. Last winter 18 different species of bird were observed and counted at one time. In the winter it's a favourite fishing spot for cormorants. Their appetite for fish is phenomenal but they appear to prefer eel and flat fish. In June 2009 a white bird with a black head appeared and flew around the pool circling the water several times. When it eventually landed the bird appeared unafraid of humans. It was subsequently identified as an arctic tern.

Otters have returned to the more remote parts of the lakeside in recent years, but only the lucky and patient observer can catch a glimpse of them diving amongst the low-lying branches on the poolside or under the jetty. It's a little easier to find the remains of their breakfast on the poolside. That unwanted import, American Signal Crayfish, has a presence in Marton Pool, not yet huge but in sufficient numbers to provide another food source for the otters.[1]

> We were fencing down by the old course of the River Rea where it used to meander through the valley before the canal was put in. That was in the 1980s. There was an old fence post which we removed. All the water came bubbling up. It felt like you were pulling the plug out of Marton Pool. It was an old test borehole that wasn't capped properly. When I was a youngster I was keen on shooting and the old folk told me that when the valley flooded it would be covered with wildfowl.
>
> There is a linear water meadow down the field on our ground where they used to dam the brook to flood the meadow. Up at the farm there was a sluice gate to dam the stream so that the cattleyards would flood. The muck would all float into the brook after the gates were raised. Then it all floated down to the meadow and was left on the ground when the water was released. I think they did that in the 1700s. (Mr. Glyn Jones, 2009)

The story of Marton ends where it began with the ever-present Marton Pool. In some respects it's a story of losses; the loss of wetlands around the pool through centuries of drainage operations; common land taken out of use; loss of the school; two churches, but no resident man of the cloth; loss of several now deserted settlements and a medieval hamlet; the loss of local indigenous pear trees and a breed of cattle cross-bred to extinction. From this perspective the past seems to offer a richer tapestry of life.

*An early post card view of Marton Pool*

199

What we have today are more acres of productive farmland and a protected haven for wildlife in and around a Marton Pool much reduced in size. Those deserted settlements have their own ambience for anyone to appreciate. Nature quickly covers over the efforts of man to tame the land; trees and hedges grow wild and buildings fall into ruin. Traces of human activity in the past still linger to provoke curiosity in the walker along these neglected byways however.

Whatever the pros and cons of modern farming methods, the fields and meadows continue to be cultivated, new and old breeds of livestock are kept, hedges trimmed, new ones planted, fences repaired, waterways cleared, sheds of steel and concrete go up alongside the old barns, woods are replanted and crops produced in the timeless seasonal rhythm of good agricultural practice.

The past was forged by people and their decisions and occasionally by events beyond their control. Our heroes in Marton might be Mr. William Jones, the Commissioner who looked after the interest of the landless cottagers, or Dr Thomas Bray who energised a demoralised church. We should remember Mr. Nevett and the Rev. Wilding for responding in practical ways to the spiritual needs of the village, George Lloyd for his charitable endowment and the Rev. G. Griffiths for taking action to provide a hall for the use of the village. There are the soldiers of two world wars, each remembered by family and friends. The independent village tradesmen whose commitment to the community kept families clothed, shod and supplied with groceries. Ladies like Mrs. Oliver and Mrs. Jenkins who fought for the right to keep the village school also deserve to have their names on the honours board.

But what of the modern day heroes who take Marton into the 21st century? They are still in the making, yet to be recognised, as yet unsung – but rest assured that that robust spirit which forged a small Shropshire village is alive and well in this most beautiful part of England. Marton folk, as the Reverend Hounsfield observed, still 'know how to make things go'.

# References

**Abbreviations used**

| | |
|---|---|
| DCPCBR | Documents Concerning the Parishes of Chirbury, Brompton and Rhiston (one of a series of books produced by Shropshire Archives and available through the library system and in the Archives) |
| Mont. Coll. | Montgomeryshire Collections |
| SA | Shropshire Archives |
| *TSAS* | *Transactions of the Shropshire Archaeological Society* |

## Chapter 1  In the beginning
1. Margaret Weale, *Through the Highlands of Shropshire on horseback.*
2. Miss L.F. Chitty, 'Dug-out canoes from Shropshire; *TSAS*, Vol.XI, 4th Series, 1927-28.
3. *TSAS.*
4. SA 1488/37, Marton Pool measurement 1776, Goolden Collection.
5. Beth McCormack, *Prehistoric sites of Montgomeryshire*, Logaston Press.
6. Rev. Charles Hartshorne, *Antiqua Salopia*, (1841).
7. www.discovershropshire.org.uk, Sites and Monuments Record, SMRN 001732; also www.answers.com/cumbrianclub.
8. 'A new Centre of Stone Axe dispersal', F.W. Shotton, L.F. Chitty, W.A. Seaby, Miss Chitty Collection 6004/3763.

General reading
    Oliver Rackham, *The History of the Countryside.*
    Mrs. G. Broxton, 'Memoirs of Tom Butler', (family diary).

## Chapter 2  Stockton Wood Iron Age Fort
1. M. Gelling, *Placenames in the English landscape.*
2. Foxall, *Shropshire Field Names.*
3. DCPCBR, Ordnance Survey Archaeological sites.
4. *The Gale of Life; Essays in the History and Archaeology of South-West Shropshire*, South West Shropshire Historical Society & Logaston Press.
5. www.discovershropshire.org.uk, SMRNO 01420.

## Chapter 3  A Roman Road through Marton
1. *The Gale of Life; Essays in the History and Archaeology of South-West Shropshire*, South West Shropshire Historical Society & Logaston Press, chapter 4.
2. W.G. Putnam, *Archaeology in Wales*, Newsletter of C.B.A. GP.2, No.4, 1964. Also Mont. Coll. Vol.61, W.G. Putnam, *The Roman Road from Forden Gaer to Westbury.*
3. Marton Enclosure Map and Schedule, 1815, (private collection).
4. *Victoria County History of Shropshire*, Vol.9.

## Chapter 4  Marton, Name and Identity
1. M. Gelling. *Placenames in the English landscape.*
2. Foxall, *Shropshire field names.*
3. Oliver Rackham, *The History of the Countryside.*
4. Marton Enclosure Map and Schedule, 1815, (private collection).

5. SA Marton Tithe Apport. Map, 1843.
6. Domesday Book, Shropshire.
7. Mont. Coll., Vol.29, p.218; www.omacle.org/Anglo
8. Foxall, *Shropshire Field Names*.
9. Sarah and John Zaluckyj, *The Celtic Christian Sites of the Central and Southern Marches*, Logaston Press
10. Mont. Coll., Vol.29, p.220.

General reading
  Emma Mason, *The House of Godwine*.
  Michael Wood, *In search of the Dark Ages*.
  Domesday Book, Shropshire.

## Chapter 5 Trelystan ... Christianity survives
1. www.saintchads.org.uk.
2. Sarah and John Zaluckyj, *The Celtic Christian sites of the central and southern Welsh Marches*, Logaston Press.
3. Robert Bevan Jones, *Ancient Yew Trees*, p.18.
4. DCPCBR, Shropshire Lay Subsidy Rolls 1327.

## Chapter 6 An Englishman's Home is his Castle
1. Domesday Book of Shropshire
2. Drs A. and J. Welton, *The Story of Montgomery*, Logaston Press.
3. 'Subsidiary Castle Sites West of Shrewsbury', *TSAS,* L111, (1949), pp.86-90.
4. D.J. Cathcart King and C.J. Spurgeon, 'Mottes in the Vale of Montgomery', *Archaeologia Cambriensis*, CX1V (1965) pp.69-86.
5. www.discovershropshire.org.uk; SMRN 000109.
6. DCPCBR, Shropshire Lay Subsidy Roll 1327.
7. *Ibid.*
8. D.J. Cathcart King and C.J. Spurgeon, 'Mottes in the Vale of Montgomery', *Archaeologia Cambriensis*, CX1V (1965) pp.69-86.
9. SA Haywards Map, 1788, CM/2/9.
10. SA Charles Smith Map, 1806, CM/2/31.
11. Marton Enclosure Map, 1815, (private collection).

## Chapter 7 Marton Juxta Hathewildeford
1. Eyton, *Antiquities of Shropshire*, Vols. 11-12.
2. P.S. Page, *Deserted Villages in Shropshire*, Oxford University, (March 1977).
3. DCPCBR; Eyton, *Antiquities of Shropshire*, Vols. 11-12.
4. *Ibid.*
5. *Ibid.*
6. Roll of the Shropshire Eyre edited by Alan Harding for the Seldon Society.

## Chapter 8 Conflict over the Manor of Marton
1. British History on line, Staffordshire Plea Rolls No. 53 1241.
2. Eyton, *Antiquities of Shropshire*, Vols. 11-12, also Hereford Cathedral and Diocese England, Festival booklet 1976 by A.L. Moir.

3. Eyton, *Antiquities of Shropshire*, Vols. 11-12. Suit de audienda electione brought by Thomas Corbet of Caus against those named, in 1263.
4. VCH *Shrops.*, Vol.9, p.81.
5. SA D365VB/1/5/309/3 Anecdote.
6. Mont. Coll. Vol. 6, Sheriffs of Shropshire, p.115.
7. *The Gale of Life; Essays in the History and Archaeology of South-West Shropshire*, South West Shropshire Historical Society & Logaston Press, chapter 12.
8. National Archives website SC 8/127/6350.
9. *The Gale of Life; Essays in the History and Archaeology of South-West Shropshire*, South West Shropshire Historical Society & Logaston Press, chapter 12.

## Chapter 9   Civil War 1642-1646
1. J.D.K. Lloyd, *Montgomery Castle*, Dept.of the Environment Official Guide book, 1973.
2. DCPCBR; Manuscripts and miscellaneous items.
3. Terry Bracher and Roger Emmett, *Shropshire in the Civil War*.
4. Mont. Coll. Vol.9.
5. Mont. Coll. Vol.6, Sheriffs of Montgomeryshire, pp.132-134.
6. SA; Frances Stackhouse Acton, *Garrisons of the Civil War, 1642-48*, (1867).
7. Michael Siochru, *God's Executioner*.
8. South West Shropshire Historical Society lecture by Terry Bracher and Roger Emmett, 2009.
9. Peter Roberts, The Roberts family history.
10. SA P62/6/1/1, Chirbury churchwarden accounts.

## Chapter 10   Thomas Bray 1658-1730
1. SA Chirbury parish registers.
2. *Ibid.*
3. Mont. Coll. Vol.6, *Sheriffs of Montgomery*, p.113.
4. DCPCBR.
5. SA 1488/35 Marriage agreement, 1688, Goolden Collection.
6. SA 1488/36 Covenant to levy a fine, 1694, Goolden Collection.
7. DCPCBR.
8. www.oswestryschool.org.uk.
9. National Library of Wales website, Welsh Biography on Line.
10. Archivist U.S.P.G. London.
11. familysearch.org.
12. www.uspg.org.uk.

General reading
   Thomas Bray Tercentenary Booklet. (Marton memorial service).
   H.P. Thompson, *Life of Thomas Bray*.

## Chapter 11   The Lloyd Family of Stockton and Marton
1. DCPCBR; Leach, *County Seats of Shropshire*.
2. *Ibid.*
3. Mont. Coll. Vol.6, Sheriffs of Montgomeryshire, p.122.
4. Mont. Coll. Vol.16, Sheriffs of Montgomeryshire, p.12.

5. Mont. Coll. Vol.21 Early Montgomeryshire wills at Somerset House, p.154.
6. Mont. Coll. Vol.16 Sheriffs of Montgomeryshire, p.15.
7. Mont. Coll. Vol.16 Sheriffs of Montgomeryshire, p.16
8. Mont. Coll. Vol.6 Sheriffs of Montgomeryshire, p.120.
9. Mont. Coll. Vol.26 Early Mont wills at Somerset House, p.181.(footnote)
10. Mont. Coll. Vol 6 Sheriffs of Montgomeryshire, p.135.
11. SA 1488/35 Marriage agreement, 1688, Goolden Collection; Mont. Coll. Vol.17 Parish of Forden, p.82n.
12. Mont. Coll. Vol.26, Early Montgomeryshire Wills at Somerset House, p.183n.
13. *Ibid.*
14. Mont. Coll. Vol.17 Parish of Forden, pp.82-83.
15. Mont. Coll. Vol.6 Sheriffs of Montgomeryshire, p.134.
16. Mont. Coll. Vol.26 Early Montgomeryshire wills at Somerset House, pp.184-185.
17. Mont. Coll. Vol.26 Early Montgomeryshire wills at Somerset House, p.181.
18. Mont. Coll. Vol.16 Sheriffs of Montgomeryshire, pp.18-19.
19. Mont. Coll. Vol.6 Sheriffs of Montgomeryshire, p.138.
20. *Ibid.*
21. Mont. Coll. Vol.6 Sheriffs of Montgomeryshire, pp.138-139.
22. Mont. Coll. Vol.6, Sheriffs of Montgomeryshire, p.113.
23. SA1488/35, Marriage agreements, Goolden Collection.
24. SA 1488/45-6, Marriage Settlement, Goolden Collection.
25. SA Lease 1791 1488/47, Goolden Collection.
26. SA 1488/51-3 Estate Survey, Goolden Collection.

**Chapter 12  The Lords, Ladies and Freeholders of Marton**

1. SA Enclosure Map and Schedule, 1815, transcribed by Mrs. Marion Roberts.
2. *Ibid.*
3. Quarterings are the method of joining several different coats of arms together on one shield by dividing the shield into equal parts and placing different coats of arms in each division or quarter.

**Chapter 13  The Enclosure Award**

1. SA *Eddowes Journal*, 4 March 1812.
2. SA1488/71, Goolden Collection.
3. *Ibid.*
4. SA 1488/65, Goolden Collection.
5. SA 1488/69/3/1, Goolden Collection.
6. SA 1488/69/3/1, Goolden Collection.
8. SA 1488/71, Goolden Collection.
9. SA 1488/69/4/1, Goolden Collection.
10. SA 1488/65, Goolden Collection.
11. SA 1488/66, Goolden Collection.
12. SA 1488/63, Goolden Collection.
13. SA 1488/67, Goolden Collection.
14. SA 1488/74, Goolden Collection.
15. SA Marton Enclosure Map and schedule transcribed by the late Mrs. Marion Roberts.
16. SA 1488/63, Goolden Collection.

**Chapter 14  From Tithes to Rent or Cash replaces Corn**
1. SA Marton Tithe Apport. Map and Schedule.
2. *Ibid.*
3. *Ibid.*
4. Ancestry.co.uk Census 1841 Marton.
5. *Ibid.*
6. SA 1860 D 365/B/51/7/1/5. Estate sale details.
7. SA 1862 SC/5/73, also DCPCBR. Marton Estate sale 1862.
8. www.nationalarchives.gov.uk. Archives. Network. Wales. Glanyrafon Estate records, GB 0210 GLAFON.
9. DCPCBR Marton Estate sale
10. ancestry.co.uk Marton census 1841.
11. Estate Sale map 1879, Mr. Kevin Pugh.
12. Ancestry.co.uk Marton census 1841.
13. Foxall, *Shropshire Field Names*.
14. Ancestry.co.uk Marton census 1841.
15. Family history. Mr. Tipton
16. Marton Censuses.
17. Michael Shaw, *The Lead, Copper and Barytes Mines of Shropshire*, Logaston Press (2009)
18. Adrian Pearce (ed.), *Mining in Shropshire*, p.175.
19. John Burnett, *Social History of Housing 1815-1970*.
20. SA Marton Tithe Apport. Map and schedule.
21. *Ibid.*
22. Details Mr. R. Kenward.
23. SA Marton Tithe Apportionment Map and schedule.
24. *Ibid.*

**Chapter 15  Just another Farming Village in Shropshire**
1. ancestry.co.uk Marton census.
2. *Ibid.*
3. Paul Stamper, *The Farmer Feeds us All*.
4. Mont. Coll. Vol. 19, Smoky-faced Montgomeryshire cattle. Also Morris and Marshall sale details 1885 Mr. E. Owen, Lydbury North.
5. www.westmidshow.co.uk.
6. www.herefordcattle.org
7. ancestry.co.uk Marton census.
8. George Ewart Evans, *The Farm and the village*.
9. John Burnett, *Social History of Housing 1815-1970*.
10. Martin Watts, *Working Oxen*, Shire publications.
11. DCPCBR Marton sale 1862.
12. SA 1488/38 Lease 1776.
13. Ken Kilby, *Coopers and coopering*, Shire Publications.
14. DCPCBR Marton sale 1862.
15. Notes from Dr. T.G. Hill.
16. ancestry.co.uk 1961 Marton census.
17. www.worldwidewords.org.

18. Letters. 1886 -1900 Mrs. Sally Pugh.
19. SA ED 1604/6 Marton School log book
20. Northwood records Churchstoke village tailor.
21. Diana Jacks. *Growing up on a Shropshire Farm*, Logaston Press (2008).

## Chapter 16 Highways
1. SA 1768 Act Bishop's Castle Turnpike Trust, qs 41.2.4455/1.
2. SA Marton Tithe apportionment map and details, 1843.
3. Mont. Coll. Vol. 57.
4. SA 1801 Act Bishop's Castle Turnpike Trust 552/6/1.
5. SA Bishop's Castle Turnpike Trust 552/6/7.
6. Richard Moore-Colyer, *Roads and Trackways of Wales*.
7. www.postalheritage.org.uk
8. Richard Moore-Colyer, *Roads and Trackways of Wales*.

## Chapter 17 The Village Inns
1. Alan Rose, *Shropshire Inn Signs*.
2. Documents re Sun Inn, Mr. and Mrs. Gartell and family.
3. Census 1861.
4. SA 1862 Marton Sale details.
5. SA Returns of Licensed Houses.

General reading
   SA John S. Clarke, 'Toll Houses and Turnpikes', *SWS Historical and Archaeological Journal*.

## Chapter 18 Changing Times, From the 19th Century to the Present Day
1. Shropshire NFU 1908-2008, *One County, One Century, One Chronicle*.
2. Gunley Estate sale catalogue (private collection).
3. Marton Hall Estate sale catalogue (private collection).
4. Marton Manor Estate sale catalogue (private collection).
5. Edmunds/ Howel Evans Mont. Coll. Vol. 19, p.230
6. Mr. Bob Jenkins.
7. Gwilt family descendents.
8. Mr. John Francis.
9. VCH *Shropshire* Vol. 4 Agriculture.
10. Mrs. Pat Davies.
11. Gwilt family descendants.
12. Powys Family History Magazine. David Roberts, Headmaster of Cantal school Radnor, 1909.

## Chapter 19 Gathered Together – Two Churches and a Hall
1. SA Shropshire Religious Census 1851.
2. www.congregational.org.uk
3. Congregational Church deeds, transcribed by the late Mrs. Marion Roberts; Mrs. H. Thomas.
4. Congregational Church deeds, transcribed by the late Mrs. Marion Roberts.

5. *Ibid.*
6. SA Religious census 1851.
7. Tea Invitation, Mrs. H. Thomas.
8. Congregational Church deeds transcribed by the late Mrs. Marion Roberts; Mrs. H. Thomas
9. SA ED 2699/41/7 Managers' returns under Education Act 1902.
10. Congregational Church Hall minute book; Mrs. H. Thomas.
11. Concert leaflet, copy held by Doreen Bowen.
12. 1927 Recipe book, Mrs. G. Evans.
13. Appeals leaflet, copy held by Doreen Bowen.
14. Papers of the late Betty Mulroy, held by Doreen Bowen.
15. *Ibid.*
16. Betty Mulroy, *Profile of Marton and its Church.*
17. *Ibid.*

General reading
    Elliot Ernest, *A History of Congregationalism in Shropshire*, (1898).

## Chapter 20  Schooldays and a Rebellion

1. ancestry.co.uk Census 1841.
2. *Corndon Magazine*, Mrs. Kinsey, Churchstoke.
3. Note in the Betty Mulroy papers.
4. SA ED 2699/41/7, Managers returns under the Education Act 1902.
5. SA ED 1604/6, Marton School Log Book 1909-1935.
6. SA ED 1604/6, H.M.I. Report 1910, Mr. Pawle.
7. SA ED 1604/6, Marton School Log Book.
8. SA ED 1604/6, H.M.I. Report 1913 Marton School Log Book.
9. SA ED 1604/6, H.M.I. Report 1926 Marton School Log Book.
10. *Corndon Magazine*, Mrs. Kinsey Churchstoke.
11. SA ED 1604/6, H.M.I. Report 1934 Marton School Log Book.
12. SA ED 1034/2 ,Marton School Log Book.
13. SA ED 1034/2, Diocesan Inspection 1939.
14. Extract from the County Council minute book for 11 October 1947.
15. Newspaper cuttings re Marton Rebel School, Mrs. F. Francis.

General reading
    HMI report 1951, photographs, newspapers cuttings Rebel school, Mrs. Muriel Taylor,
    Mrs. Judith Goodman.

## Chapter 21  Lest we Forget ... Two World Wars

1. A Private Perspective of the Great War; The Diaries of Harrison Richard Powell. At war
    during 1917 and 1918, transcribed and edited by his daughter, Mary E. Powell.
2. Shropshire NFU 1908-2008. One County, One Century, One Chronicle.
3. SA ED 1034/2, Marton School Log Book.
4. *Ibid.*

## Chapter 22  Of Wakes, Horses' Heads and Celebrations

1. DCPCBR, Robert Charles Hope, *The Legendary Lore of the Holy Wells of England*, (1893).
2. Steven Harding, 'The Holy Well Rorrington', *Shropshire Unfolded*, Feb. 97.
3. SA Rev. W. Brewster's Commonplace Book.
4. DCPCBR.
5. Catholiccultue.org Feast of the Holy Trinity.
6. SA Rev. W. Brewster's Commonplace book.
7. Charlotte S. Burne, *Shropshire Folk Lore*, (1883-6)
8. Powysland Museum Welshpool.
9. Mont. Coll. Vol. 61, pp.133-135. J.D.K. Lloyd.

## Chapter 23  Follow up, Follow up and Play The Game

1. Corndon Magazines 1896-1950 courtesy Mrs. J. Windsor; Corndon Magazines 1909-1935 courtesy Mrs. B. Kinsey.

## Chapter 24  Half a Century of WI and YFC

1. Marton WI history produced for Shropshire Federation WI, 2004.
2. mountainear.blogspot.com
3. *County Times* report, July 2008.
4. Shropshire YFC County handbook, 1964-5.
5. Shropshire YFC County handbook, 1968-69.
6. Shropshire YFC County handbook, 1974-75.
7. Shropshire YFC County handbook, 2006. (Extracts with permission of YFC County HQ).

## Chapter 27  A Different Landscape

1. SA DP521.
2. www.bcrailway.co.uk
3. *County Times and Express*, Feb. 1971.
4. www.stwater.co.uk

General reading:
   Edward Griffith, *The Bishop's Castle Railway 1865-1935*, (1969).

## Chapter 28  Marton Pool, Modern Meremen

1. Wildlife observations by Graham Cox, 2009

# Index of Contributors

# Index of Historic Names

Where a number of given names are listed under a surname this is because we have
established they are related in some way: husband and wife or mother and son etc.
Other persons sharing the same surname are not necessarily related and are listed separately.

# General Index